MARK WARREN'S
ATLAS OF AUSTRALIAN
Surfing

ANGUS & ROBERTSON PUBLISHERS

Unit 4, Eden Park, 31 Waterloo Road,
North Ryde, NSW, Australia 2113;
94 Newton Road, Auckland 1,
New Zealand; and
16 Golden Square, London W1R 4BN,
United Kingdom

First published in Australia
by Angus & Robertson Publishers in 1988
First published in New Zealand
by Angus and Robertson NZ Ltd in 1988
First published in the United Kingdom
by Angus & Robertson (UK) in 1988

Published by arrangement with
Dolphin Publications Pty Ltd,
44 Cowan Drive, Cottage Point,
NSW, Australia 2084

National Library of Australia
Cataloguing-in-publication data.

Warren, Mark.
  Mark Warren's atlas of Australian surfing.
  Includes index.
  ISBN 0 207 15681 6.

  1. Surfing — Australia — Guide-books.
  2. Australia — Description and travel —
  1976-   — Guide-books. I. Title.
  II. Title: Atlas of Australian surfing.
797.3'2'0994

Editor and designer: David Stewart
Associate editors: Andrew Witton , Lisa Foulis and Daphne Rawling
Design consultants: Tony Gordon and Margret Mulray
Illustrations: Matt Perry
Cartography: Margret Mulray and Marlo Campbell
Indexer: Diane Regtop
Project manager: Peter McGill

This book was developed and designed
on Apple MacIntosh Computers.
Bromides were printed on Linotronic
by Walter de Blaere.
Printed in Hong Kong

MARK WARREN'S
ATLAS OF AUSTRALIAN
Surfing

ANGUS
& ROBERTSON
PUBLISHERS

CONTENTS

SEAN DAVEY

F O R E

As an active and committed surfer for most of my life, I've always sought to understand why a particular wave broke the way it did, why it worked one day and not the next, and why each wave had its own quirks and characteristics — some forgiving, some less so. Surfing all over the world has given me the chance to better understand the factors governing breaking waves, though finding them remains as difficult as ever. Especially when you're trying to write a book.

I have been lucky enough to see surfing come of age as an international sport. Professional surfers are now widely respected for their skill and dedication, and Australia's pre-eminent position in the sport is ensured by the strength, adventurousness and daring of the new generation of young surfers — the grommets.

Australia is the largest island on a watery planet and offers the local surfing population a panorama of surfing challenges. Our waves come in all shapes and sizes. From the distant

coral reef breaks off Queensland's north coast to the cold, powerful swells which pound the exposed coasts of Australia's southern regions; from the idyllic point breaks of northern New South Wales to the challenging waves of Australia's remote north-west coast; from the clean and empty beach breaks of rural Australia to the crowded and polluted city waves. Fat waves and hollow waves; gnarly, dangerous breaks and soft, lazy mushburgers; protected corners for the beginners and wild ocean reefs for the brave.

This book has been written to inform, advise and entertain. While at times the text may appear light-hearted about the hazards — particularly sharks — these warnings should not be taken lightly. Australia is a vast and often unforgiving environment, where isolation can turn dreams into nightmares in a matter of moments.

You'll notice in the glossary of terms at the back of the book that a 'local' is 'anyone who's been there a day longer than you'. This attitude has prevailed in surfing for many years, creating territorial reactions towards 'outside' surfers. I would suggest that such an attitude is restrictive. There will always be cocky young grommets paddling inside you, but that's just the way it ought to be. All surfers like to get variety in their surf spot diet and it's only fair to expect others to want a wave at your break, just as you would want one at theirs. A little respect goes a long way. The reality is that the surfing population is expanding all the time, placing greater demands on popular breaks. Everyone likes to travel and surf other places when they get the chance, so we all need to be a little tolerant.

All of Australia's best known surf spots are covered in this book, though some lesser-known breaks have been left out, mainly because of

W O R D

inaccessibility, but also for reasons of personal safety. Mine.

While we have taken the trouble to create new maps for vast areas of Australia's coast, they are simplified and only meant as a rough guide. If you are travelling I suggest you pick up current detailed maps of the area you are planning to surf.

I'm hopeful that in the future, as surfers become more aware of the environmental threat to our beaches posed by pollution, attitudes can be changed towards the value placed on our coastal environment. Short-sighted policies towards waste disposal already threaten many fragile coastal ecosystems and the future will see an ongoing struggle to preserve them.

Outside the urban stretches of Australia's coast you can still discover true surfing adventure. The inhospitable sections of wild coastal areas in distant parts of the continent continue to hold many unnamed and perhaps unsurfed waves. For anyone willing to gear-up and prepare for the harsh outdoors the rewards are there, but for the majority of the world's surfers, that adventure remains a dream.

This book would not have been possible without the photographers who constantly put it all on the line to capture that very moment which expresses the unique challenge and thrill of surfing. Surf photographers are a rare breed. Unlike many sports, where one needs little more than a powerful lens, surfing creates a unique challenge for photographers, who have to place themselves in positions of considerable jeopardy to get the truly great photos.

This book represents a photographic showcase for the great Australian surf breaks, which have never been seen in one book like this before. So I want to offer a special thanks for the help and support of guys like Peter Crawford,

Peter Simons, Dick Hoole, Marty Tullemans, Jeff Hornbaker and Tony Nolan, who have been photographing surfers and surfing so well for so many years. A thanks also to the new breed of photographers, like Steve Triance, Ted Grambeau, Sean Davey, Mark Sutton, Clive Slater and Dave Kelly.

The photographic contributions are great... they have only been enhanced by the work put in by this book's tireless production team. To document Australia's surf spots and create our first atlas sounded like a good idea, but to actually assemble all the information in a cohesive package was a daunting task. The team that gave impetus to this project was handled by the dolphin, David Stewart, who has been known to slip into the odd wave himself. He hunted out and gathered together the right people to assist in the production. Andrew Witton was a discovery in himself, a dedicated water-man from southern climes who proved invaluable in researching more isolated coastal regions and followed through as an important member of the production team. James and Matthew Dayton gave us invaluable assistance on Tasmania and Matt Perry created original art work for our diagrams. Margie Mulray and Marlo magically mapped away on the Mac, while Peter McGill and Geoff pitched in too. Thanks also to Helen for her magic fingers, and her help with the book, and a special thank you to Peter Wilson and the Quiksilver crew. To the many other people who contributed to the book in lots of ways, I trust you are happy with the finished product.

Mark Warren

INTRODUCTION

The Australian surfing environment is unique. Around the coast of the planet's biggest island there is a broad variety of climactic and geographic regions each supporting its own type of surfing locations. To understand the surf, and its patterns on a particular stretch of Australia, it's helpful to know basics about its climate, tides and other natural influences to maximise your surfing experiences.

STEVE TRIANCE

In the beginning

The known history of surfing in Australia is a relatively short story, almost half as long as the story of European settlement on this, the planet's greatest island. Scientists believe that human occupation of the continent stretches back some 50 000 years and while we know that the original Australians tended to follow the coastline and rivers, there is no evidence that they surfed. At the time of the first arrival of the original Australians, the water level was some 100 metres below current levels. This meant that it was possible to walk from New Guinea to Tasmania, although there was always at least 50 kilometres of open water between this continent and Asia. Scientists also know that Australia was once a part of Antarctica and has been drifting north since it broke away million of years ago. We are, in fact, *still* drifting north, at the rate of around 5 centimetres a year.

If we imagine the continent 50 000 years ago, with water levels 100 metres below those of today, the coastline would have looked very different indeed. All the famous Australian breaks of today, such as Burleigh, Lennox, Angourie, North Narrabeen, Bells and Margaret River were many kilometres inland, with waves breaking against what is now the continental shelf. On the east coast, this meant a difference of 15 kilometres, but in other areas vast tracts of land were covered by the rising of the waters at the end of the last Ice Age, some 15 000 years ago.

The rising waters, which established the coastline as we know it today, also left some areas isolated. Tasmania, where the original Australians had already been in occupation for 10 000 years, became totally isolated from the mainland. On Kangaroo Island (off the South Australian coast) and in the Dampier Archipelago (north-west coast) clear evidence remains of the Aborigines who once lived there, prior to isolation caused by rising waters.

So, while there is no evidence that the original Australians learnt to surf (as did the Hawaiians), the question cannot be clearly answered because the coastline of that time is under 100 metres of ocean. We do know that they enjoyed living close to the ocean, as do modern Australians. In fact three-quarters of the current Australian population live within an hour's drive of the ocean and if one imagines a 50 kilometre strip of land stretching around the coastline from Perth to Cairns, it would hold 90 per cent of current Australians.

All the indications point to that being the pattern of life on this continent for many thousands of years, as the Aborigines chose all the same areas to live that were selected by European settlers when they arrived at the end of the 18th century. Modern centres of population, such as Melbourne, Sydney, the Gold Coast, Brisbane and the Sunshine Coast were all major areas of Aboriginal culture. At the time of the arrival of the First Fleet in 1788, the coastal strip from Perth to Cairns held a similar appeal for the black population as it does today for white Australians.

One of the few areas of that coast where Aborigines have direct access to the ocean is at Wreck Bay on the New South Wales south coast. Just south of Jervis Bay, an Aboriginal settlement has developed a talented and committed team of young surfers who regularly rip the waves apart there. There's no argument with these guys as to who is the local.

Waves have been surfed on boards in Australia since early this century and surfing is one of our youngest sports. Remember that public 'bathing' was not allowed on Australia's beaches until the turn of the century (it's still banned by law in many states), and even then changes in attitudes came very slowly. Body surfing became immediately popular (having been introduced by a Polynesian visitor) and in 1915 one of the world's most affable sporting champions visited Australia. Duke Kahanamoku was invited to Australia by the New South Wales Swimming Association, having won the Olympic gold medal (representing the USA) for the 100 yards freestyle at the 1912 Stockholm Games. As Australia was a nation proficient in swimming talent, the Duke was known here and his clashes with the great Australian swimmer Boy Charlton were legendary. But it was on 15 January 1915 at Freshwater Beach, just north of Sydney, that the Duke attracted one of his biggest crowds, as thousands watched him catch wave after wave on a surfboard. Interest in surfing has been growing in Australia ever since that day. In fact it was on that very day that the first Australian stood on a surfboard, when the Duke invited a young girl called Isabel Latham to join him for a tandem demonstration. They caught several waves together and Isabel so became the first Australian to ride a surfboard. A woman, no less.

After World War I, the solid wooden boards of the Duke's era gave way to hollow boards, a development hastened by the invention of waterproof glues and plywood. The Surf Living Saving Association served as a breeding ground for all those interested in the surf, and board-riding developed within that framework.

It was the post-World War II development of plastics that changed the face of surfboards and surfing forever. The late 50s and early 60s saw a massive explosion in the numbers of kids wanting to surf. The smaller, lighter boards (they were *only* about 3 metres long and 15 kilograms in weight) offered by

Duke Kahanamoku on the beach in Sydney during his visit to Australia in 1915

synthetic materials gave more people the chance to surf. As numbers exploded so did designs and manufacturing techniques and before long length and weight had been radically reduced, with performance and verticality of movement becoming the benchmarks, as surfers looked to do things that had never been done before.

The birth of the continents

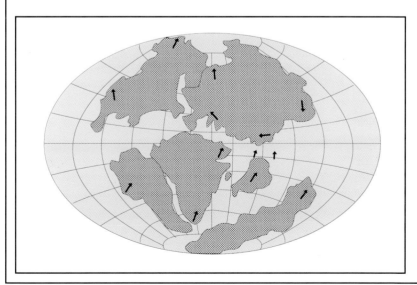

Scientists have determined that the different continents on the planet today once made up one single continent, called Pangaea, with two major land masses which have been called Laurasia and Gondwanaland. These land masses (Gondwanaland was made up from Antarctica, Australia, Africa, South America and peninsular India) were almost separated by a shallow sea, known as Tethys. The remaining surface of the earth was a single vast ocean, Panthalassa, which has evolved into today's Pacific Ocean. It is thought that the process whereby the continents broke up began around 190 to 136 million years ago; most of today's continental forms have been established for at least 6 million years, although the drift continues to this day.

Our changing coastline

Despite popular notions, coastlines are not permanent lines on the map. They represent a constant battleground between the elements, where the kinetic energy of the ocean meets stationary land masses, day after day, year after year, millenium after millenium. This causes a never-ending process of change, as the barrier coastlines are weathered and eroded by constant water action.

The ocean levels have risen and fallen many times with the Ice Ages, and the twisting and turning of the continents in their development has created interesting variation to this pattern. Around Mount Gambier, in South Australia, the coastline has risen over the last few thousand years, whereas the area around the Murray River mouth, less than 500 kilometres away, has sunk. This twisting has slowed and Australia today is a relatively stable continent. The coastlines, however, are constantly changing as the pattern of erosion moves sand and rocks and eats away at the ocean's major barriers.

Scientists have endless classifications for types of coastline, but let's keep it down to four main varieties:

• **rocky coasts,** with high cliffs and few, if any beaches
• **beach coasts,** dominated by sandy beaches scalloped between rocky headlands
• **tidal plain coasts,** dominated by mangroves and swamp flats
• **protected stillwater coasts,** where offshore reefs dilute all wave action and allow gentle waters to lap at the shoreline

We get all these varieties of coast around Australia. The coastline created where the Nullarbor Plain meets the Great Australian Bight is definitely a great example of the rocky, inaccessible (no waves) coastline. The east and west coasts are classic beach coasts, with sections of inaccessible cliff but also beaches which stretch so far they've been named by their length. Tidal plain coasts are found in both north Queensland and Western Australia, and around the gulfs of Adelaide. The Great Barrier Reef, which stretches more than 2000 kilometres from Torres Strait to Rockhampton, shields a vast section of the Queensland coast from any wave action at all.

It's in the south of the continent that we find excessive wave action, with coastlines exposed to the powerful south swells. The centrepoints of the east and west coasts have good access to more northerly swells, which often come with cyclones. The southern coastline also tends to have a narrower continental shelf, permitting more wave energy to be carried into the swell.

Scientists have recently confirmed the existence of a hole in the ozone layer over Antarctica and a thinning of the protective ozone layer in many areas, including Australia. A rise in the ocean levels is now being widely predicted as the earth's atmosphere warms. In the future, suburbs currently well away from the coast could end up as prime real estate.

Below *The delicate coastal environment is easily upset and the pattern of sand distribution changed.* **Right** *The photogenic Shark Island barrel*

DICK HOOLE

How long is our coastline?

Measuring the length of any given stretch of coastline is not as easy as you may think. If you trace the outline of the continent and measure the line, the coast seems to be about 15 000 kilometres long. But if you measure all the twists and turns in the coast created by headlands, inlets and beaches the effective length is much greater, perhaps as much as 50 000 kilometres. And that's more than the circumference of the earth.

ANDREW WITTON

DAVE SHAW

The pattern of shifting sands

Australia's east coast has numerous river mouths which contribute to silt and sand build up along the adjacent beaches. When strong summer nor'-easters blow day after day, the sand along the beachfront tracks south, building up in sandbanks off the southern points up and down the coast. These banks will often prove perfect for a south swell, turning on southern point breaks up and down the coast. During winter, prevailing southerly winds move the sand northwards, often over many hundreds of kilometres. Sand from the central New South Wales coast has been shown to move as far north as Fraser Island, off the central Queensland coast. While all surfers love to find perfect waves, an awareness of the seasonal pattern of sand movement may be of considerable help in finding the sandbank going off in any given set of conditions.

Weather and waves

The ocean has always represented a challenging and hazardous environment for humankind, from the earliest tribal people who ventured across the oceans in bamboo and balsa boats, to the age of the modern explorers who overcame their fears and sailed over what they believed to be the edge of the world.

Only recently has the scientific community come to accept the close interrelationship of the oceans and the atmosphere, though from the earliest times it was clear that the ocean responded directly to weather and wind patterns. Even the slightest breeze will ripple the ocean surface and strong winds can quickly change a placid ocean into a raging torrent of swell and spray.

Winds are generated by the movement of atmospheric air created by high and low pressure systems which circulate the planet. High pressure areas tend to be large and slow moving and are usually associated with good weather and light winds; low pressure systems tend to be smaller, faster moving and are associated with strong winds and poor weather. In the oceans there are similar patterns of circulating movement, created partly by wind but mostly from convection forces within the water. Surface currents tend to be wind-driven, but deepwater movement is generated by density differences between water masses.

The oceans are influenced by a number of natural forces. All the major oceanic basins feel the gravitational pull of the sun and moon, which create tidal undulations. Underwater seismic activity causes so-called tidal waves (more accurately, *tsunamis*) and the influence of wind across the waters causes wind waves. Residual wind waves which no longer act under the influence of their generating influences are called swells. Such waves contain massive amounts of energy and generate 40 kW per metre of coastline, causing a constant process of change and movement to the ocean foreshores.

Wave size is influenced by three wind factors: the speed of the wind which has generated the wave, the length of time the wind has been blowing, and the distance over which the wind has been blowing. Because winds rarely maintain precisely the same direction and strength for long periods, many wind swells tend to be confused and choppy. They form individual peaks and have varying intervals between the waves. Over a distance these bumps tend to even out, making the waves more consistent and the swell line straighter. Hawaii is a classic example of this phenomenon.

Waves are also influenced by tides, currents and other waves and the interaction can cause hazards and havoc. When a large swell is opposed by tidal or current forces near a continental shelf, freak (or, more accurately, episodic) waves can be generated. Such waves have been documented in the logs of early mariners, but were doubted by oceanographers until relatively recent times when several instances of such waves forced a new understanding of the complexity of the ocean's natural forces.

In 1933, the *USS Rampoo*, a 146 metre tanker travelling from Manila to San Diego, was overtaken by waves up to 34 metres high travelling at 55 knots through open ocean. These are the highest reliably measured waves ever recorded in the open sea.

PETER CRAWFORD

Waves at sea rarely exceed 25 metres in height: if they reach a height more than one seventh of their length, the surface tension in the wave breaks down and the wave disintegrates in spray.

Ocean waves arriving on the coast can create the impression that the sea is travelling with them, whereas in open ocean, apart from the influence of currents, it seldom moves.

Above *Violent storms from the south occur regularly along the east coast during summer. Here, the Sydney skyline is lit up by a typical southerly buster.* **Below** *A perfect barrel at Cronulla, one of the first places in Sydney to catch a new south swell.* **Left** *Wild Tasman Ocean power, at Sydney's Dee Why Point*

Understanding the ocean

It seems a strange paradox that a planet called Earth is actually more than 70 per cent ocean. The world ocean is a living, moving form with a total area of some 1370 million square kilometres that stretches right across the globe and distinguishes our planet from all others in the solar system.

The areas of ocean are concentrated in the southern half of the planet: the northern hemisphere is dominated by its huge continents. The oceanic southern half of the planet has its origins in the break-up of the land masses from a single continent and the drift of the continents into their present positions, a process which has taken millions of years.

Scientists define two types of ocean floor: the deep ocean basins and the shallow continental margins adjacent to land masses, many of which were above water during the periodic Ice Ages when water was locked up in massive icebergs and glaciers, resulting in water levels considerably lower than those of today.

Like land masses above water, the ocean floor is comprised of deep trenches and mountain peaks, which often reach the water surface forming islands and atolls. These oceanic islands are mostly of volcanic origin, and appear more frequently in the Pacific than in the Atlantic or Indian Oceans. Between the latitudes of 30 degrees north and 30 degrees south, most oceanic islands are surrounded by reefs, some encircling the island and others extending over long distances up to 100 kilometres from the shoreline.

Top *Jim Banks shows his understanding of Shark Island.* **Below** *A Duranbah barrel*

Making sense of the weather to get more waves

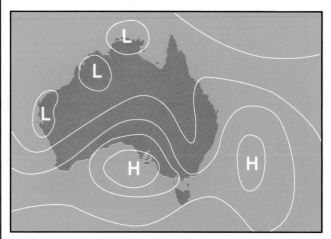

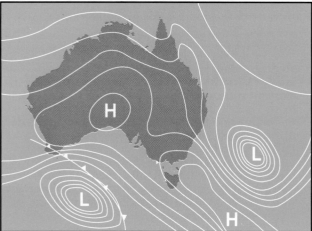

Dedicated surfers make a point of being able to interpret the evening weather report. Only that way can they forecast when and even where the best waves will be found. Sailors, fishermen, skiers and wave sailors all closely watch the weather, which forms such an important part in the life of outdoors minded Australians.

The Australian continent's climate is one third tropical and two thirds temperate, the north receiving its annual rainfall in one big wet during summer, the south from a series of cold fronts, mainly during winter. Tropical cyclones generate good swells in the north during summer and in winter cold frontal depressions, born in the Antarctic, sweep into all exposed regions in the southern half of the continent.

The two diagrams at left show typical weather patterns in summer and winter. In the top diagram, a broad band of low pressure cells — typical of summer — dominate the top half of the continent. Intense tropical cyclones are most likely from December through to April. The southern parts of the continent are dominated by a large high pressure system which usually brings settled weather and light winds.

The lower map shows a typical winter pattern, with low pressure fronts circling the planet further north of their Antarctic regions than in summer, bringing strong southern ocean swells to southern regions. In these conditions Victoria's west coast (as well as all the exposed coasts of South Australia, Tasmania, Western Australia and much of New South Wales) will be off its tits and Thredbo will be top to bottom. Winter paradise.

What are tidal waves?

Over the years, the term tidal waves has been commonly used to define those waves generated at sea by seismic action. These waves, in fact, have nothing to do with tides and are more accurately called *tsunamis* (from the Japanese words *tsu* and *nami* meaning port and wave respectively). These waves are quite different to wind waves, travelling at speeds of up to 650 kilometres per hour over widths of hundreds of kilometres.

The incredible speed of these waves through open ocean, when they are often only a metre in height, means they can arrive at a coastline within hours of being generated perhaps hundreds, even thousands, of kilometres away. As the wave passes over the continental shelf and into coastal waters it slows in speed but jacks up radically as it approaches the shoreline. There have been accounts of tsunamis in the Pacific islands which sucked all the water off the reefs prior to their arrival then rushed ashore in a massive surge, destroying everything in their path. As the rush of the wave is dissipated by rising ground, it then rushes back to the ocean, wreaking further devastation. The Pacific Ocean is generally regarded as the home of the tsunami: a 'ring of fire', surrounded by the volcanic and earthquake activity which generate these extraordinary waves. The most famous tsunami was generated on 22 May 1960, after a severe earthquake off the coast of southern Chile. The damage caused on land by the earthquake was severe, but slight compared to that created within minutes by the tsunami which struck the Chilean coastline. From its epicentre off the coast the wave also radiated across the Pacific, building in size and speed, striking the Hawaiian Islands only 15 hours after the earthquake and then the coast of Japan — where it caused massive damage to the coasts of Hokkaido and Honshu — only 24 hours after the originating earthquake and more than 16 000 kilometres away on the other side of the Pacific.

So, put simply, you can forget about riding tidal waves: the ferocity of so much water would guarantee that the first wave would be your last.

When cyclones arrive

Australians have good cause to fear the destructive power of tropical cyclones. These highly mobile depressions feed from the moisture of warm oceans during summer and can be totally unpredictable, moving south in erratic patterns until they die out over colder water. These systems also bring with them the kind of waves surfers talk about for years.

Tropical cyclones were once only named after women, a practice started during World War II. Now they are given male and female names alternately.

News of a cyclone brings concern to communities in its path, but always gives surfers itchy feet. The best cyclones for waves are those which track wide of the coastline in open ocean, so the swell travels further before reaching the coast, making the swell lines straighter and more uniform. When such conditions coincide with offshore winds dream waves are usually the result.

Below is the satellite photo and related isobar charts for two cyclones, Anne and Agi, which dominated Australia's northern weather in early January 1988, creating great swell all the way from Noosa to Sydney.

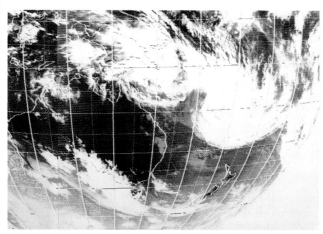

Top *Swains Reef, some 300 kilometres north-east of Rockhampton, is exposed to considerable cyclone swell action.* **Above** *When cylone-generated swells hit Noosa, the waves get as crowded as the car park.* **Below** *South Maroubra Point on a big day*

JODY PERRY

MARTIN TULLEMANS

GLENN DUFFUS

Tides

Much of the change and variation we see on our coastal regions is caused by the undulations of sea level. These tidal movements, which occur in varying heights and frequency in all seas and oceans, are a result of the gravitational influence exerted on our planet by the sun and the moon. These forces have the effect of drawing the planet's waters towards that point of the surface which is closest to them. Such movements occur as currents and periodic oscillations of the water level, and they vary from day to day and place to place.

Due to its proximity, the influence of the moon is twice as significant as that of the sun, and it is because the interval between consecutive meridian passages of the moon is 24 hours and 50 minutes that the tidal highs and lows advance by 50 minutes each day. At some places like Tahiti, where the solar influences are dominant, tides occur at the same time each day.

On gently sloping beaches the most noticeable feature of tidal movement is the horizontal movement of the water line, whereas on steep coastal areas the verticality of the tidal movement is its most dominant feature. Currents associated with tidal movement are imperceptible at sea, but strong in coastal rivers and estuaries.

These days, a tide chart can readily predict tidal times and levels, although a complete understanding of the complex behaviours of tides is yet to be reached. Nevertheless, tidal charts — which are based on astronomical information backed by local experience — offer a practical guide for the travelling surfer, with inaccuracies too subtle to be of any significance.

On some parts of the Australian coast there are two high tides a day on other areas only one. The two high and low tides, when they occur, can vary greatly, as does the height of the tide. On the north-west coast the water level can rise and fall as much as 12 metres, whereas in other areas — for example, the section of coast south of Perth — there is negligible tidal movement at certain times. This variation is created in part by the various oceans and seas surrounding Australia; each are subjected to independent forces and varying tidal pattern. In some areas tidal forces combine, in others they cancel each other out.

The tidal range tends to be broader in areas of wide continental shelf or broad-mouth bays, where inner shores confine the tide and amplify the rise and fall. In an area such as Port Phillip Bay, with its wide bay and narrow mouth, the restricted flow of

How tides work

Both the moon and the sun exert sufficient gravitational force on the planet to cause a bulging of seas and oceans towards that point closest to the force of influence. When the moon is new or full, the earth, sun and moon are in line and the gravitational forces, and the tides with them, are greater. At these times the gravitational pull of the sun and moon are combined and the result is higher-than-average tidal movement, the so-called spring tides (which have nothing to do with the season). When the sun and moon are at right angles, in relation to the earth, they tend to counteract each other in terms of gravitational pull and tidal movement is reduced. These reduced tidal movements are called neap tides. At any given point on the surface of the earth, the point of greatest gravitational pull from the moon is reached every 24 hours and 50 minutes, which advances the point of high or low tide at that point by 50 minutes a day. The sun also influences these high and low points, as does the moon's tilted plane of orbit in relation to the earth's axis of rotation. At the equator, where the sun's maximum influence comes when it is overhead, peak tides occur at the equinoxes, in March and September. In most areas of Australia, particularly south of the Tropic of Capricorn, the peak tides come at Christmas.

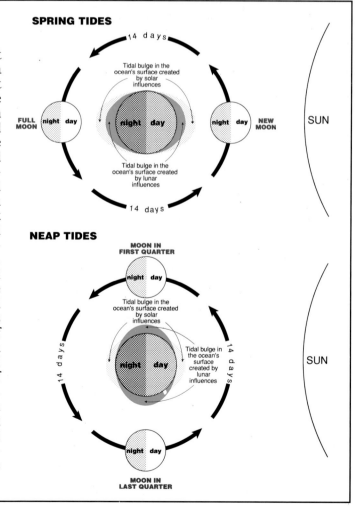

water results in reduced tidal movement. In some areas, for example the corners of the Gulf of Carpentaria or the Western Australian coast south of Geraldton, only one tide a day reaches the shore.

For any surfer, particularly a travelling surfer, it's important to have a good understanding of tides and how they affect local breaks. It can be disappointing to travel great distances to a spot only to find everything right except the tide ('You shoulda been here this morning...'). It's easy to pick up tide charts from a local surf or fishing shop and schedule your arrival for the favourable tides.

Above *Waves breaking over reefs or rock shelves are totally dependent on the depth of water over the reef and are usually at their best for only a few hours each day. Little Avalon, on Sydney's northern peninsula is a perfect example and is best at higher tides.* **Below** *Tidal flats in Tasmania*

Australian waves

The era of modern surfing was born in the Hawaiian Islands, where the waves are still considered to be the most challenging in the world. While there can be little argument that Hawaii offers the biggest waves, the Australian coastline has many waves which, on their day, can match anything in the world. There are also several spots, particularly in Victoria and Western Australia, which regularly turn on giant swells.

There is, however, a distinct difference in the character of Australian and Hawaiian waves, which is a result of the different coastal profiles. Each of the Hawaiian Islands is the peak of a volcanic outcrop, reaching up sharply from the deep ocean floor below and surrounded by lava reefs. As swells move in from open ocean and deep water they suddenly 'feel bottom' on the lava reef and jack up, creating the fast-breaking, bonecrunching monsters for which the islands are renowned.

Most of Australia is surrounded by a continental shelf varying in width from 50 to 100 kilometres. This allows the waves to feel bottom much further from shore, effectively slowing them well before they reach the point of breaking. This diminishes their size, speed and strength, relative to the same swell size in Hawaii, though on a big day at Bells Beach or Margaret River the point is somewhat moot.

What our waves may lack in raw power they make up for with variety. This comes from the different bottom conditions over which waves break around the coastline: sandy beaches and rivermouths, reefs of rocky boulders or flat, limestone platforms. Australia boasts some of the best point breaks to be found anywhere in the world, and names like Kirra, Burleigh, Noosa, Byron, Lennox, Crescent and Sandon are known and respected worldwide for their quality and consistency.

The sand build-up at the mouths of many rivers are responsible for another set of famous breaks, including those of Currumbin, North Narrabeen and Merimbula.

Australia is not without coral reefs: the Great Barrier Reef is some 2000 kilometres long and blocks the Pacific Ocean swells from the Queensland coast all the way from Rockhampton to Torres Strait. At several points along the length of the world's largest reef, perfect (and secretly guarded) waves can be found, some 30 to 50 kilometres offshore.

While Australian surfers travel constantly to Hawaii to surf the lava reef breaks and to Indonesia for the lacerating coral reef waves, international surfers are coming here to experience classic point break perfection. Kirra Point has to be one of the classics. Huge rock boulders surround the point, which attract a covering of fine sand that is swept up and down the coast by constant ocean currents. When it turns on, Kirra is a wave of rare perfection, as its spinning barrel and thick, sandy lip work down the line with machine-like precision.

There's also the regular occurrence of tropical cyclones in the South Pacific or Tasman seas, which sends lines of perfect swell in to Australia's east coast. At these times all the point breaks can ignite, with swells stretching corduroy-like to the horizon. Perhaps only four or five other point breaks anywhere in the world could match Kirra's perfection.

Australia's coastline, particularly on the east coast, features sandy beaches punctuated by rocky headlands which create many fine reef breaks, though all are highly dependent on wind and swell directions. In Victoria and Western Australia, the reef breaks tend to be over wide rock shelves and further offshore than the east coast.

Australian conditions can be very fickle. At times you'll find the wind and swell direction perfect for a certain spot, but the sandbanks or tides prevent the wave from performing as it should. While you wait for the right tide, the sea breeze arrives and everything

Below *Shark Island, one of the roundest barrels you'll find anywhere*

PETER CRAWFORD

How waves break

Australia

Hawaii

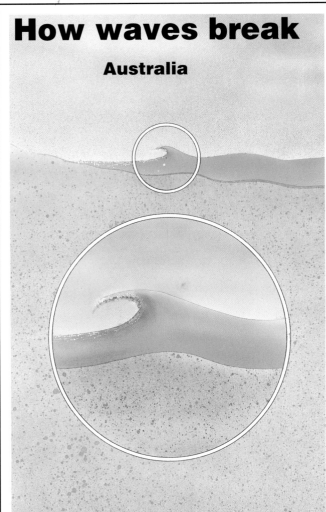

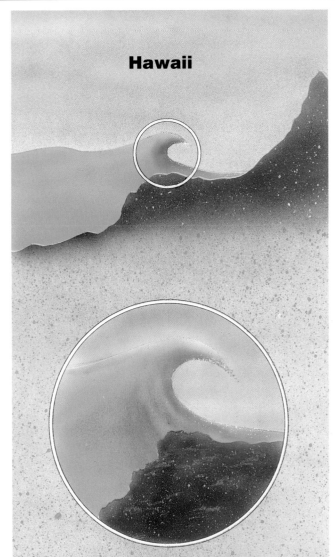

Australia is an old continent and the continental shelf is relatively wide, slowing and weakening our ocean swells. In some areas the shelf is narrower and the ocean bottom contour more dramatic, creating stronger waves, but generally Australian swells are 'feeling' bottom for kilometres before they reach the coast to become breaking waves. In the diagram above showing a typical Australian beach break the ocean bottom is gently sloping and the wave profile is thin, producing a more gentle wave than the reef-break on the right.

The Hawaiian Islands are renowned for their powerful waves. Swells travel unhindered through the Pacific Ocean until they reach the lava reefs around the Islands. The swells 'jack-up' out of extremely deep water and break over shallow lava. A few spots in Australia have similar wave power but rarely the size of Hawaiian waves.

MARTIN TULLEMANS

Getting deeper inside

Getting deep is something Rabbit Bartholomew is very good at, particularly on his home breaks on Queensland's Gold Coast. Controlled barrel riding is a skill Rabbit learned over many years of surfing all over the world. In this quite famous photo, Rabbit is reaping the benefit of his surfing experience. The average surfer would be lucky to ever get this deep inside, even at Kirra. And even then the chances of making it back out again are remote. Only after years of dedicated surfing can you expect to ride hollow waves with any real authority.

blows out. Many international surfers find this constant change extremely frustrating. Every single day there are perfect waves to be found somewhere in Australia, but few of us have the Lear jet necessary to take advantage of this.

If you've ever tried paddling into a jacking, suckey reef break — like Shark Island, Little Avalon, Express Point, Jervis Bay Pipeline or Kalbarri — on a longer, malibu-style board, it doesn't take long to realise why those waves were never surfed in the longboard era. These fast, hollow waves were simply not suited to the limitations of a slower, longer board, no matter how good the surfer. The developments in design over the past twenty years created shorter, lighter boards, with an accent on performance and manoeuvrability. These boards have opened up a whole series of breaks which were rarely surfed in that era.

Little Avalon, on Sydney's northern peninsula, is a prime example. It was a famous spot for body surfing in the 1960s (the boards were all up at the other end of the beach at North Avalon) and it was only in the 1970s that the 'boardies' — as the body-surfers called them — were on boards capable of negotiating the critically steep take-off. In Queensland, beaches like Greenmount and Currumbin were far more popular in the malibu era than Kirra and Burleigh, which came into their own during the early 1970s.

The shorter boards had their disadvantages too, especially being far harder to paddle, but they meant you could make the drop on a steep wave. A malibu board would be pearling (nose-diving) severely on every take-off as the jacking wave pitched you in headfirst, straight down to China. And these waves are often associated with hard, unforgiving and shallow bottoms, which tended to add to the pain and punishment. On a short board, however, you could jump to your feet quickly and stomp on the tail, angling down the steep face with far more success. It wasn't just the change of length that made the difference. Contemporary boards — and

Barton Lynch with a full quiver of boards. Until recently quivers were only used for Hawaii, but are now more common in Australia, where varying conditions require optimum board selection.

current designs, which had their origins in the 1970s — have far narrower tails than earlier boards and 'edgier' rails. Then came the fin development, which went from one fin to two, three and even four. This gave added traction to hold the board in the face of a steep wave and drive up high on the wall as it pitched, tucking higher and deeper in the barrel of the wave. Performance became the key and the accent changed to those waves which broke 'round'. In the 1980s they've started surfing the waves which break 'square' (that's rounder than round).

It was Simon Anderson's *Thruster* that became the most accepted development in this multi-fin era. One of the sport's great all-time surfer/designers, the 'gentle giant' helped establish North Narrabeen's reputation worldwide as a training ground for red-hot surfers and won contests all over the world. Whenever the swell was big, Simon was the one to beat; he was the first surfer to really attack big waves, ripping them apart in a style followed by Mark Richards, Tom Carroll and Gary Elkerton.

Simon's Thruster stemmed from experiments in the early 1970s, by Reno Abellira in Hawaii. This design was based on a large central fin and two small side fins, but Simon revolutionised the design of modern surfboards with three fins that were all the same size. Today, despite Mark Richard's four world titles (on two fins) and Cheyne Horan's success on one, most surfers ride boards with three fins, a tribute to Simon Anderson's design foresight.

No wonder then that surfers went crazy in the 1950s and 1960s over the long point breaks of the east coast like Noosa, Currumbin, Byron Bay, Crescent Head and Green Island. In those days, as long as you could negotiate the take-off, the board generated plenty of speed across the face of long walls, guaranteeing enough speed to negotiate the fast, crumbling sections. Momentum was the key and it could get you through.

Today surfers are striving for more and more radical changes in direction and verticality (up *and* down). In the 1960s and 1970s, if a surfer got his hair wet it was a tube ride, or at least a cover-up; today, as surfers ride deeper and longer inside the barrels (even the word changed) of a ferocious wave, they are placed under far greater demands. In these

PETER CRAWFORD

What about metrication?

The Australian coastline, in many areas, stretches on forever as it scallops the coast in strips of golden sand. In many places they simply ran out of names for beaches and resorted to names based on their length. So we have One, Seven, Nine and Twelve Mile Beaches in New South Wales, Seven and Twenty Mile Beaches in Tasmania, Seventy Five Mile Beach in Queensland, One, Two and Eighty Mile Beaches in Western Australia and Two Mile Bay and Ninety Mile Beach in Victoria. These names defy the onslaught of metrication. In fact the whole surfing industry has managed to ignore metrication with all surfboards ordered and bought in feet and inches. Even fifteen year olds, who have grown up in a totally metric world, know whether they want a *five eight* or a *six two*. One suspects it will still be like that at the turn of the century.

How surf breaks get named

Australians have long been known for their rather bizarre approach to nicknames and this eccentricity includes many of the names of beaches, headlands and breaks around the Australian coastline.

There are those which are obvious, like Grassy Head, Sandy Head, Boulder Beach and First Point. Surfers seem to prefer to choose names which pay credit to the power and ferocity of certain breaks, like Pipeline, Cylinders, Supertubes, Crackneck, Grunters, Backdoors, Express, Banzai and Boiling Pot. And judging from the number of different spots around the country named Guillotines, Gallows, Trapdoors and Hangmans, surfers have a true affinity with the neck-breaking action of waves and that particular form of execution. And then there are places like Massacres and Boneyards.

Other names are influenced by Aboriginal words, like Yallingup, Indjinup and Cowaramup (up means water), or Coogee (from koojah meaning 'bad smell' though the Eora people who lived at Coogee prior to the arrival of the Europeans would never

have imagined that the Sydney sewerage system would give new meaning to the word). Duranbah is named after a local Aboriginal leader and Barrenjoey, Mudjimba, Noosa, Narrabeen, Maroubra and Bondi all derive from Aboriginal names or expressions.

Marine creatures, especially sharks, contribute to some names, such as Shark Alley, Shark Bay, Shark Island, Shark Beach and Shark Point; other spots are simply called Spooks, Spookies or Sharkies. Some names, like Crazies, define the kind of person who would surf there. Other names, for example Headbutts, describe the kind of road you have to drive on to get there and the contact between you and the roof of the car along the way. Mufflers was named after its impact on cars which tackled the gnarly access road.

Some names — like Winda Woppa, Ghosties, Butterbox, Other Side of the Moon, Voodoo, Cyrils, Dum-Dums, The Three Bears and Vera Lynn — simply defy explanation.

waves, the surfer disappears completely behind the guillotine-like crashing curtain — and is expected to make it out the other end in one piece. This requires constant control to trim, deep inside the barrel, as the surfer drives higher for speed (and to avoid being decapitated by the lip), reaching for that sweet spot in one of nature's true wonders: the perfect barrel.

In the early 1980s, another development took the surfer even deeper inside the barrel. Central coast surfer and shaper Geoff McCoy pioneered the *no-nose* design, which squeezed area out of the forward sections of the board and substantially increased the tail area. Many people in the industry knocked the 'Laser-Zap' design, as McCoy called it, but Cheyne Horan piloted them to considerable success. Later, McCoy's original concept was modified many times, but the principle remained the same. His concept was to see surfers riding parts of the wave not previously utilised, especially that part of the wave higher and deeper inside the barrel.

Another of the sport's most influential individuals has been George Greenough, without doubt the most fondly regarded figure from American surfing in Australia, where he spends much of his time. A remarkable, ingenious individual, George saw new designs where others saw more of the same: in the early 1960s he was riding his famous 'spoon', a clear glass dish on which he pulled off carving turns that left other surfers speechless. He was the first to really question the traditional 'skeg' design for fins in the 1960s and he turned to the yellowfin tuna for his inspiration, modelling long, fine fins based on the ocean's number one speed machine.

In the future it's unlikely boards will get shorter, but new materials may reduce wetted surface area, weight and drag, enabling even more radical surfing. Modern materials have so reduced the weight of boards that they damage and snap easily.

A typical Australian reef break

GUY FINLAY

Safety in the surf

Despite what some people may say surfing is a relatively safe sport with relatively few injuries, though care needs to be taken at all times particularly when surfing at remote or unpatrolled beaches.

The Australian coastline has innumerable beaches which feature the scalloping action of swells breaking on shallow sand banks. As wave after wave crashes on the bank, sand and water are propelled towards the beach. The water has to return from the shore and forms channels between the banks as it retreats. These channels can have a strong current running out, which is useful for paddling out but needs to be treated with care.

When swells strike beaches on an oblique angle, water is pushed down the beach in side currents. When these currents reach the rocks at the end of the beach, they create a powerful rip running back out in the very corner. Sydney beaches like Whale Beach, Narrabeen, Dee Why and Manly are good examples of this kind of rip.

Some beaches are more vulnerable to rips, usually because of their narrow but direct access to swell, with limited means of retreat for the water. Powerful rips can be created when strong swells hit narrow beaches. Sydney's Tamarama Beach is an example of this kind of rip action. On Queensland's Sunshine Coast, Alexandria Bay — a favourite nudist spot — lies between two prominent headlands which create a funnelling effect on waters moving between them and dangerous rips can result.

In order to minimise risks, several basic principles should be followed:

1. Take the time to watch the surf carefully before you enter the water, utilising the time to do stretching and loosening exercises.

2. If you think you might not be able to handle the swim back in without your board (leg-ropes break all the time, especially in big swells), don't go out.

3. If you do get caught in a rip without your board, don't try to swim directly against the current (unless you are a very strong swimmer); swim across the main direction and then circle the area of current and make your way back to the beach. Terror can become a key factor here.

4. It's almost a cliché to say, 'Don't panic', but the fact remains that when you realise you're in trouble you need a clear head. Excessive movement and desperate breathing will drain your strength quickly, and remember that all the rip really does is drag you out the back — as long as you stay cool you can get back to the beach. The part which worries people is swimming back into the impact zone, but remember that this water is heading for the beach so get right in the middle of the sandbank and *not* on the edge of the channel, where you may end up going back out again.

Too many surfers rely totally on their umbilical cord, the leg-rope, so keep your swimming act together — it might just save your life.

Top right The never forgotten fear of being caught inside, southern Victoria. **Centre right** Stray boards can become lethal weapons, so hang on to yours. **Below** The crowd waits a set

Understanding rips

This illustration shows the pattern of water movement on a typical Australian beach. Sandbanks, punctured by channels, scallop the beach profile, sometimes for many miles. The shallower water over the sandbanks causes the waves to break there first, peeling both ways across into the channel where the water funnels back out to sea. Experienced surfers use these rips constantly, to minimise the paddle back out by riding in the natural outflowing current. But the inexperienced beachgoer is often drawn to the green unbroken water between the sandbanks, where a quick dip can turn into tragedy. If you are caught in a rip, swim out and across the back of the current; don't try and swim directly against it. Even a very strong swimmer will swim out of a rip by tracking across the flow, to get out of the main current before heading directly back to the beach.

STEVE TRIANCE

1

PETER CRAWFORD

2

PETER CRAWFORD

The invisible hazard

MARTIN TULLEMANS

It seems strange to have to include the sun as a health hazard, but there is no escaping the reality that Australia is the skin cancer capital of the world. If you want to spend a lot of time in the sun and you don't want to become a statistic, then you had better find out all there is to know about skin cancer and learn to cover up, particularly during the 'burn hours' of 10 am and 3 pm. Use zinc cream *and* sunscreens *and* hats *and* keep out of the midday sun whenever you can. There's also the problem of the shrinking ozone layer, or should I say the *apparently* shrinking ozone layer. At last count, the ozone layer over Australia appeared depleted by 3 to 5 per cent on levels of only a few years ago, and while the scientists are cautious about conclusions (especially ones with the impli- cations for the whole world of a shrinking ozone layer), it's not a time to be ignoring the warnings. There's no way around the fact that surfers are heavily at risk, and it's never too soon to get smart about the sun.

Sharks and other hazards

Surfing remains one of the very few activities left where you could be eaten by a wild animal while pursuing your favourite pastime.

Without exception, surfers' greatest fear is sharks. For the committed surfer, who spends anywhere between 20 and 40 hours a week in the water, they are just something to live with; though many would adjust comfortably to life without them.

In fact, since 1901 when records of attacks have been kept there have been 250 attacks on humans in Australian waters, with about 100 of those fatal. While this might seem like a lot, more Australians die on the roads each *month*. Yet sharks are constantly on a surfer's mind, particularly when surfing in dangerous waters, like South Australia, Victoria, parts of New South Wales, Queensland, Western Australia and Tasmania.

The white pointer or great white shark, *Carcharodon carcharias,* is the species most feared, not so much for the frequency of attacks on humans but more for the sheer size of the animals and the ferocity of their attacks. The most famous incidents generally involve 'whites' although the tiger shark (particularly in northern waters) and whalers have an equally aggressive record.

Shark attacks are less common in water below 21° C, which gives some indication of the likely time of danger; in summer, attacks are far more common, when more of the coastline has waters above this temperature. Although colder waters are statistically safer, they are also the habitat of whites, and although attacks are less common, they are almost invariably fatal.

In recent years, attitudes towards sharks have varied widely. Some authorities have promoted the view that sharks are essentially harmless, the victims of a prejudiced press. Many of these experts have, in their filming of shark encounters, used blood and berley to drive the sharks into a frenzy, as well as wetsuits filled with blood and blubber to measure methods of attack and the power of their bite. Other authorities point to this research and filming as an encouragement to these sharks to look on the human shape as a new food source.

The 1970s and 1980s have brought a new awareness that sharks have their part to play in ocean management and the natural food chain. They probably even contribute to the saving of human life; after all, how many more people would drown if the possibility of shark attack was removed?

Sharks are prehistoric predators, who have remained virtually unchanged over millions of years. Victims rarely see the shark that attacks them and recent research has established that sharks tend to attack from below and behind their prey.

While many surfers are happy to live with sharks, very few (especially me) want any personal involvement in their food chain. So when surfing outside meshed areas, particularly areas where attacks and sightings are regular, be aware that the danger is real. There are some general rules, though it needs to be remembered that sharks are extremely unpredictable creatures who rarely conform to behaviour patterns.

The view every surfer worries about

Sharks are known to be territorial creatures, regularly patrolling certain areas; at Summercloud Bay, on the New South Wales south coast, local Aboriginal surfers and fishermen have nicknamed a local shark 'saucer-eyes' after his habit of cruising by, with eyes rolled up, checking the 'two-legged surface fish'.

If you're the kind who loves to surf remote and desolate stretches of coastline, then you're probably

Suggested guidelines for avoiding shark attack

1. Avoid surfing river mouths (unless it's perfect).
2. Avoid being the first out in the morning or the last in at night, as these are known feeding times.
3. If there are large schools of baitfish around, get out of the water as sharks are known to move through these schools (even in broken water), chomping indiscriminately as they go.
4. If a shark is spotted, get out fast.

not bothering to read this, but Californian surfer George Greenough once offered me a piece of advice I've never forgotten: just by having another surfer in the water reduces your chances of attack by at least 50 per cent.

Should you find yourself in a close encounter with a shark, try not to panic (which, of course, is easy to say). Remember that sharks feel the vibrations of panic long before they establish eye contact and underwatertheir eyesight is at least 30 to 40 per cent better than yours. Keeping calm is the tricky part. I know surfers, divers and fishermen who have stressed the importance of remaining calm when close to sharks only to panic instantly when they found themselves in that situation. Never forget, keeping cool and calm just may make the difference.

Some cases have been documented where an attack has been fended off by aggressive behaviour towards the shark, such as punching it on the nose or gouging its eyes. These actions are, however, very much a last resort.

In the event of an attack (assuming it's not you) try to get the victim to medical help as soon as possible. It's important when tending a victim to understand that shock is worsened by rushing the patient senselessly to medical care. Sharks tend to maul flesh badly, making treatment difficult. Lay the patient down, apply bandages (and tourniquets) tightly to stem the bleeding and use blankets to keep the patient warm. Elevate the wound, if possible, and comfort the person, as a positive outlook on recovery is vital to the process of treatment. If possible get medical assistance to the scene, as this will minimise shock which is the biggest killer of those who survive the initial attack. In isolated areas, get the victim to a doctor or hospital immediately.

Stingers in the surf

GUY FINLAY

Around the continent of Australia there are a number of marine organisms, some deadly, which can prove hazardous to surfers. Generally, the warmer northern waters breed most of the deadly stingers, and they only affect offshore breaks in the Great Barrier Reef and Western Australia (and only in summer).

The rest of the stingers found around Australia are not deadly, though many are capable of inflicting a very painful sting to which some people suffer an extreme reaction. In Queensland, jellyfish are often a problem, sometimes getting so thick in the water they simply cannot be avoided. Itching tends to be more of a hassle than the sting, though some tropical breeds of jellyfish can leave a potent message.

The real hassle are bluebottles (also known as Portuguese man-o'-war, or *Physalia utriculus*). These quite unique organisms are composed of a gas-filled blue 'bubble' from which hang a series of tentacles up to 10 metres long, each dotted with poisonous barbs so tiny you can hardly see them. Each summer on the east coast, the onshore winds (particularly easterlies) not only ruin the surf but bring hordes of bluebottles in to the shoreline where they harass surfers, often wrapping around body or limb with excruciating pain being inflicted by numerous barbs, and in some people causing nausea, dizziness and an effect on the central nervous system. While single stings are rarely more than painful, multiple stings can cause severe reactions, and deaths have been recorded.

Where possible, attempt to remove the barbs with your fingers and (this is the hard part) *don't lift the arm or leg out of the water until you have peeled off the thread from the bluebottle*. An old wives' tale, once popular on the beaches, was that the best treatment was to rub the area with wet sand, but from my experience this simply aggravates the problem. Small sacs of poison are attached to each of the tiny barbs and rubbing the area seems to push more of the poison into the skin. The best treatment I have found is to scratch the barbs out with your fingernails and then, as quickly as possible, treat the area with vinegar. There's also a product available in chemists called 'Stingose' which is effective and well worth adding to the travelling surf kit, as quick treatment of a sting will make all the difference to the level of discomfort.

Unfortunately, bluebottles are something surfers simply have to live with. On many occasions I've seen perfect surf with almost no one out because of the 'blueys'. Some try full-length wetsuits, but they are uncomfortably hot in summer. Others try pantyhose, but you'd have to be keen!

There's another small jellyfish found along the east coast, affectionately known as 'purple people eaters', which occur regularly in waters about 19° C. These guys have small, round, purple heads and tentacles to about 10 centimetres in length. The sting isn't as nasty as a bluebottle but they can can prove itchy and irritating, especially in a good surfing session.

Caring for our coastline

Attitudes towards care and responsibility of the coastline have improved considerably in the past twenty years. Whereas a developer or pastoralist could once purchase or lease large tracts of coastal land, demand for public access to coastlines, both urban and rural, has forced many attitudes to be reconsidered.

Surfers have been caring for their cherished environment for many years; they were among the first to realise that responsibility for the environment begins at home and they have been at the forefront of many struggles to save sections of the coastline under threat. The travelling surfer should think constantly about any environment impact: whether that be driving a four-wheel drive through fragile sand dunes or simply leaving rubbish behind at a campsite.

Ocean beaches are Crown property and are generally accessible to the public, though entry may be restricted to paying visitors in areas where facilities such as camping areas or boat ramps have been established. If public access to the beach is blocked by development, the public generally has a right of passage.

The declaration of national parks has created permanent areas of conserved environments, where visitors get the chance to experience some of the original Australian flora and fauna. These parks are less concerned with servicing recreational needs than they once were, turning their priorities towards preservation of indigenous species of flora and fauna and their habitat.

In many areas it has been the surfers who have been the first to ring alarm bells about development or pollution. Sydney is a classic example of this. For many years the beaches have been getting badly polluted, particularly in certain conditions, but authorities have denied it. Every time I surfed at Manly I got sick, so I stopped surfing there and said so publicly which resulted in a howl of protest from Manly interests, concerned that potential visitors might go elsewhere if they knew Manly was polluted.

These pollution levels are now measured (by the Water Board's Surfline) and when levels are up, councils are advised to close affected beaches. But they rarely do. During the 1986/87 summer, the bacterial level at Sydney's Malabar Beach infringed safe levels on 18% of the occasions it was tested. Other beaches identified as being regularly polluted were Maroubra, Clovelly and Coogee on the southern side, and Manly and Freshwater on the north. The Water Board promised that the pollution problems will be fixed by 1992, when the new outfalls are in operation, but there remains a considerable question mark on the perception of authorities regarding the importance of maintaining our unique environment.

Surfers have been at the forefront of the struggle for the environment for several decades now. They travelled the country looking for surf in the 1960s and 1970s, frequently finding it and settling down in the area. They were often the first to see the unique environment at risk. One target in this campaign was the sandmining companies, which had for years cleared virgin coastal forests to sift through the valuable mineral-rich sands. They would then revegetate, destroying coastal dunes. Following the raising of the question by surfers, the public reacted and sandmining leases were reviewed. Thankfully much of the coast has been saved, and at least now Australians are beginning to appreciate that the true wealth of their country lies in the preservation of unique bush areas. Tourism is already Australia's biggest industry and our future may well rely on the unique flora and fauna being maintained at all costs.

The Myall Lakes area is a prime example. Just 200 kilometres north of Sydney, it is a unique stretch of wetland supporting a myriad of native birds, fish and animal life. The lakes are separated from the ocean by huge forest-covered sand dunes which the sandmining companies planned to mine. Persistent action by environmentalists (led by surfer Bernie Morgan) has seen a section of this coast set aside as a national park so it remains for all to enjoy.

Below left *Australia's only surfing reserve at Bells Beach, which followed years of negotiation between local surfers and government.* **Below** *Stuart Cadden inside a North Narrabeen barrel, now under threat from proposed development.* **Right** *Express Point on Phillip Island*

PETER WILSON

BILL McCAUSLAND

TED GRAMBEAU

An introduction to surf talk

If you're a 'surf nazi', or an 'off-the-richter' grommet, then you can ignore these comments. If, however, you have no idea what these terms even mean, then this is for you.

This book is written as an 'in-the-barrel' experience: that is in the real words used by surfers all over the world. This terminology has been employed throughout the book to describe recognisable characteristics of the waves. So a 'suckey' wave is quite different to a 'wedgey' wave, 'stubbies' are not gangs of surfing dwarfs, and 'spaghetti arms' is a condition which occurs before you get to the restaurant.

Changes in terminology have evolved over the years: a pipeline (1950s) became a tube (1960s) became a barrel (1970s and now); a gremmie became a grommet; baggies became boardies; and an egg became a kook (or a rubber-neck).

The terminology has also had to adjust to describe manoeuvres as developments in surfboard design enabled surfers to execute moves never previously attempted, let alone named. So the hot manoeuvres of the 1950s and 1960s were 'drop-knee cutbacks', 'quasimotos', 'hanging five (or ten)', 'cover-ups', 'head-dips' and 'soul arches'. In the 1970s, along with radically shorter boards, came 'roundhouses', 're-entries', 'backdoors', 'off-the-lips' and 'snap-backs'.

Now we're dealing with floaters, aerials and slashes. Meanwhile, the most sought-after waves have gone from steep to hollow to square and from rolling to tubing to dredging. Some things, however, never change: a local is always a local (that's someone who's been there a day longer than you). A full glossary of terms is included at the back of the book for reference.

New moves

Surfing is one of the world's fastest moving contemporary sports. The rate of progression, in terms of performance, is pushed along at a mind-boggling pace by younger surfers who constantly strive for more radical methods of utilising wave power. Development in surfboard design has obviously helped and will continue to do so. There are few craftsmen as committed to their trade as the hard-core surfer-shapers around the Australian coastline. The nature of surfing has changed from recreational to competitive, which many of Australia's original surfers saw as a decline. However, it's difficult not to be infected by the raw enthusiasm of our young surfers — they rip! The latest series of hot new moves tracks over parts of the wave previously untouched. Slashbacks are executed in steep critical wave faces, floaters allow surfers to utilise the outside of a falling curtain of water and aerials represent future moves where the sky really is the limit.

Right *Barton Lynch displays a near vertical attack.*
Below *Tommy Carroll's slash typifies modern power surfing*

Left *This surfer knows which way he's going.*
Below *Brett Warner pushing the limits at Queenscliff*

PETER CRAWFORD

Above *Gary Elkerton, renowned for power surfing, finds some here at Shark Island.* **Below** *Damien Hardman, already planning his next move.* **Right** *In sequence, Mr X, Glen Winton attempts an optimistic floater*

CHRIS ELFES

PETER CRAWFORD

PETER CRAWFORD

Top left *Mike Stewart, American boogie man, gets innovative in big surf.* **Above** *Getting airborne is one thing, maintaining control of the landing is another.* **Left** *Barton Lynch demonstrates his version of the floater.* **Below** *Rob Bain, power and precision*

2

1

TONY NOLAN

Above *Mark Occhilupo in sequence at the Coke Classic, showing his aggressive approach.*
Right *Martin Potter off the top.*
Below *Rob Bain explodes out of the white water*

TONY NOLAN

PETER SIMONS

CHAPTER 1

QUEENSLAND

Queensland has a surf season that lasts all year round, although many of the best remembered sessions occur during the cyclone season (December to March). What are known in other parts of the world as hurricanes are called cyclones in Australia and they can be equally destructive. While the majority of coastal people dread cyclones and the havoc they can cause, surfers wait impatiently for any sign of these intense low pressure systems off the coast and the huge swells they can generate. The best Queensland swells come from cyclones centred well away from the coast, so the swell travels further, becoming clean and straight prior to its arrival on the shoreline. Ideally, these cyclones travel away from the coast, minimising damage but bringing those classic days about which surfers constantly talk and dream.

During winter months, intense low depressions off the coast of south-east Australia (born in Antarctic regions) can generate strong S to E swells but these winter storms generally lack the swell action and ferocity of their tropically-born summer sisters.

Most Queensland waves break over sand, the quality being dependent on sandbank conditions which are themselves dependent on coastal ocean currents and prevailing wind and swell conditions. Few of these spots work in NE wind and swell, though these conditions help build the sandbanks for the southern points, which form the right-hand breaks for which the region is famous. In fact sand is the secret of Queensland's surf, as the slowly drifting sands (from as far south as the central New South Wales coast) seem to find their way onto the Queensland coast, forming the classic sand points of the Gold Coast and the islands of sand which stretch from South Stradbroke Island to Fraser Island, some 300 kilometres to the north.

'Butto' (Jason Buttenshaw) pulls into a classic
barrel at Kirra, one of his backyard breaks

Human intervention has influenced some sections of the Queensland coast, particularly the Surfers Paradise area, where rivermouths, estuaries and beaches have been moulded by man-made rock, concrete and landfill groynes to control the ocean's natural forces. The central part of Surfers Paradise was once a swampy, marshy area which has been filled, reclaimed and heavily developed. The developed coast which surrounds Surfers is sensitive, being regularly subjected to some serious cyclonic storms, though it's the development rather than the storms which cause the destabilisation of beaches and shorelines.

Even now, Kirra is under threat. This classic Australian wave has already survived major man-made cosmetics when the Coolangatta Groyne extension made Kirra too deep for all but the largest swells to break. Admittedly Kirra has made a comeback, but plans for another marina could eliminate this classic break from our next edition.

Much of the Queensland coast (all points north from Fraser Island) is denied surf by the Great Barrier Reef, which breaks down all swell action well out to sea. Though several spots in the outer reef are surfable, they are dangerous, exposed and sharkey locations, best surfed only by locals. The northernmost places where the swell gets in (at the southern end of the reef) are Fraser Island and Double Island Point.

Left *Barton Lynch, perfect backhand at Cylinders, on Stradbroke Island.* **Above** *Future Gold Coast mayor, Wayne 'Rabbit' Bartholomew exits a too-fast Surfers Paradise pipe*

NORTH FROM NOOSA

Surfers in New South Wales wondering what happened to all the sand to build their point breaks should take a good look at Queensland, particularly **Fraser Island**, which has been acting as a repository for this sand for millions of years. Subsequently, Fraser Island has ended up as the biggest sand island in the world: 120 km long and 22 km wide at its widest point, with sand piled up to 200 metres above sea level and 60 metres below it to the ocean floor. The island has rich, dense forests, from which soft and hardwoods were logged between 1865 and 1923, when the remaining forests were reserved by the state. Today around two thirds of the island is state forest.

Being a sand island, there's plenty of beach breaks along the vast expanse of beaches on the east side of the island. The sandbanks, however, tend be very straight and uniform, which limit surfing opportunities. About halfway up Seventy Five Mile Beach is the wreck of the **Maheno**, which can produce lefts and rights depending on the build-up of sand around its hull.

Some 50 kilometres further north is **Indian Head**, which can turn on a quality right-hander and is best in light S to SW winds. Further north is **Waddy Point**, one of the few rock outcrops found on the island. On its protected northern side there's a sandy point which can turn on long rights peeling down the point and into the beach beyond, but the quality is dependent on sand buildup and thus the break tends to be fickle.

Access to Fraser Island is via ferry from Inskip Point and you'll need a good four-wheel drive vehicle and some experience in driving on soft sand. Nevertheless, Fraser Island attracts more than 50 000 tourists a year to its environment. If you are planning a surf trip to Fraser Island, for best results steer clear of holiday periods as the beach highway and surf traffic can be a hassle. It's a long way to go for waves as crowded as your home break.

If the swell is working at Noosa, then it's often worth the trip north to **Double Island Point**. That's if you have a well-equipped, four-wheel drive vehicle but be warned; there are many wrecks of over-confident adventurers buried on the long beach that stretches from Noosa to Double Island Point. Along the way up this 80 kilometre beach you may find some beach breaks, but the sand build-up tends to be uniform and the waves closeouts. Inland is the vast and varied forests of the Cooloola National Park. Fishing is very popular along this coastline and marine life is abundant, including sharks, and while surfing at the

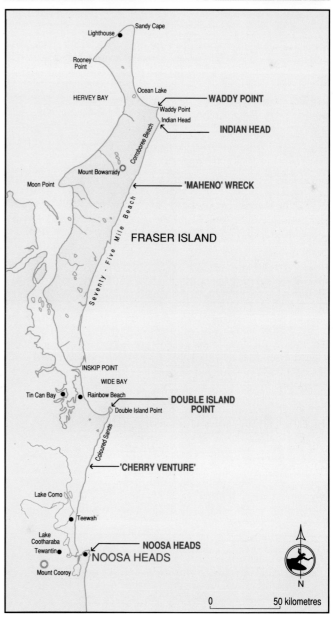

BEDE / BROBES

point your chances of a close encounter are almost as good as in South Australia. So take heed.

The Double Island Point set-up features a beautiful, long, sandy point with a mechanically perfect right, peeling so far into Wide Bay that your legs will ache. The paddle back to the point can be equally exhausting and most people walk back to avoid 'spaghetti arms' and minimise the 'human-lure' sensation. This break favours SE to E swells to 1.5 metres, but can hold 2 metres; it is best in south winds.

IAN SUBIACO

Top left *Fraser Island solitude.* **Top** *Robbie Sherwell carves at Double Island Point.* **Right** *Cherry Misadventure.* **Below** *Peak hour on the Fraser Island highway.* **Below right** *Fraser Island can turn on some real size*

DICK HOOLE

MARTIN TULLEMANS

THE SUNSHINE COAST

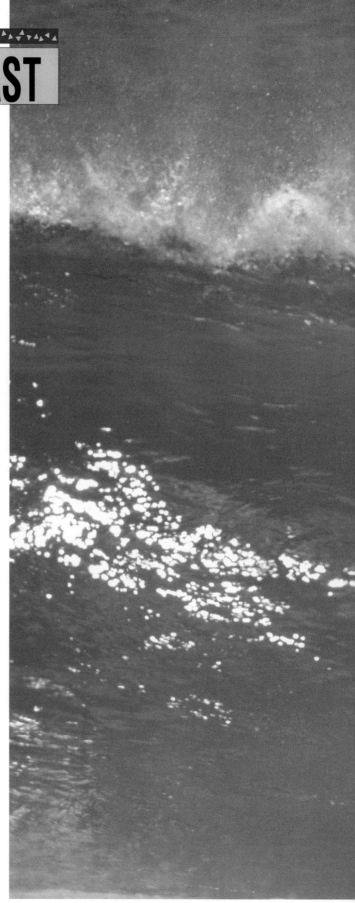

This sun-baked stretch of Queensland coast, extending from Noosa south to Caloundra, has found itself a part of Australia's tourist industry — which is understandable as it offers some of the best sun and surf conditions found anywhere in the country. The warm, clear and crystal blue water is appealing even without surf, which is fortunate because the surf here tends to be very inconsistent, dependent mostly on cyclonic depressions off the coastline to generate any real swell action.

Noosa Heads is the centre of a series of linking bays and beaches which can offer great surfing conditions. The area has become the centre of extensive tourist development over recent years, particularly during winter when hordes of frozen southerners flock to this stretch of coastline for some sun and (hopefully) surf. Many people have been critical of the development of this area but it was inevitable that any area as beautiful as Noosa had to be attractive to the tourist industry, as the holiday vibe is easy to feel in this small piece of sub-tropical paradise. They could have done worse.

Prior to white settlement of Noosa the area lay in the lands of the Undanbi people and the word Noosa is derived from an Undanbi word meaning 'ghost' or 'shade'.

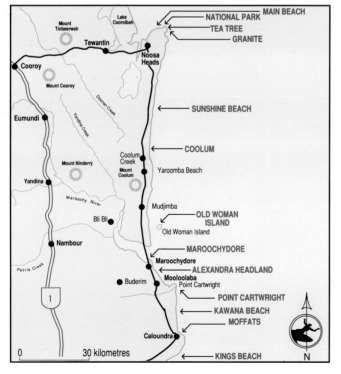

Boiling Pot, National Park, Noosa Heads

The original name for the headland at Noosa was *Wantima*, meaning 'rising' or 'climbing up', which is what the locals spend half the year praying the surf will do.

Perhaps Noosa should have been called 'Surfers' Paradise' or more precisely 'Natural-foot (Surfers') Paradise'. The area offers one of the world's best clusters of right-hand point breaks, but they can be fickle: they are consistent only for their inconsistency. However, when the swell and wind are right (if you catch it all happening) you will never forget the experience.

Noosa consists of a series of bays formed by weathered, roundish rocky points (built up with eroded boulders) and some low tide sand beaches. The bottom is urchin infested in places but the only real hazard is the odd shark. The crowds can be totally insane, especially when fed by the suburbs of Brisbane during holiday breaks.

Main Beach and **First Point** are the closest breaks to the town and the first sight of the mostly untouched Noosa National Park, which covers an area of some 382 hectares and offers great from-the-board native scenery between the sets. Main Beach is the best of all the Noosa breaks for beginners. First Point can get really good, but needs a humungous SE swell or huge E to NE swells. It's an easy point break with a rock bottom; best at low tide, as it tends to be very slow at higher tides. The swell is rarely over 1.5 metres but if you catch it above waist-high it's a real score!

Johnsons is the second bay and point into the park and can have easy point waves (at higher tides), which tend to be a fraction faster than First Point. When a solid 1.5 metre or bigger swell is on, there's an excellent outside section at Johnsons Point which can link from the next spot up the line (National Park). It is sometimes worth sitting on at lower tides, as outside surfers often fail to make the fast section and you can pick off the bigger waves of the set and ride right through Johnsons.

National Park, as the name implies, is the border of the Noosa National Park and a beautiful spot to be when the swell is up to 2 metres. The outside take-off can start 500 metres up the point at a swirling and often hairy area know as The Boiling Pot. National Park holds large swells which peel down the line over a sand and rock bottom through various sections to Johnsons, but be warned: if your leg-rope breaks in a large swell your board will be worked over on the rocks. The length of the wave and the depth of the bay produce a wave which tapers off quickly in size from the outside break, giving surfers the chance to choose that section of the wave which suits their various levels of skill and experience. Hotties can take off way up on The Boiling Pot and make it all the way through to Johnsons, but drop-ins on crowded days are, unfortunately, too common. When it's up to 2 metres on the outside take-off, the wave could be half that size at the midpoint of the ride, depending on the swell direction.

All Noosa points work mainly during the cyclone season (December to March), which generate E to NE swells. Sometimes, during winter, swells are generated by low depressions in the south and make it round the heads, but these south swells have to be bigger and tend to taper more quickly. Noosa's National Park can really max out at 3 metres and works best in W to SE winds.

When the word gets out that Noosa is going off, which takes a few hours at most, surfers appear from everywhere, almost out of the trees

BEDE/BROBES

Tea Tree Bay, the fourth of Noosa's points, is a scenic 25 minute walk from National Park (or, if you're hot to get out there, a 15 minute toe-stubbing sprint). The point at the eastern headland of this bay creates excellent waves, although the overall quality depends on the sandbars in the middle of the bay which connect the wave at the outside point all the way down to the centre of a pebbly beach. Depending on the tide, Tea Tree can get very hollow and sea urchins litter the bottom in some areas. The view of the park from the water remains as it was when first surfed, some 30 years ago. The outside take-off is a treat: when all the elements come together the swell line bulges and pitches beautifully, testing your skill right from take-off. Goofy-footers tend to perform better at this spot than at National Park, but it is a demanding wave, particularly on low tides. Tea Tree breaks mostly over sand with some sections of patchy reef and is best when the swell is NE to E (up to 2 and 3 metres) and the winds E to SE. On higher tides, girls love to boogie-board at this spot. It's a magic place, a great experience to slide across an exotic bay.

Within the Noosa National Park there are two other surf spots further east, accessible only after an even longer walk than that to Tea Tree. **Granite** is the next bay and the swell generally gets a little bigger as you continue out on Noosa's points. Best at 1 to 2.5 metres, Granite lacks the perfection and consistency of the inside bays and points although its seclusion makes it attractive, especially when the crowds are up. When the swells are big the inside points of National and TeaTree tend to be better value.

At the southern extremities of the National Park, just before Sunshine Beach, lies **Alexandria Bay**. There are two ways to get there: a long walk from Noosa car park, or from the northern end of Sunshine Beach. Alexandria Bay often has quality waves when the rest of the Sunshine Coast is flat, due to its open access to the SE swells. Excellent peaky lefts and rights abound here, over a sandy bottom. Speaking of sandy bottoms, this is a nudist beach, which may or may not be an added attraction according to your viewpoint. Best in small swells (to 1.5 metres) and NE to SW winds.

Above *The Glasshouse Mountains.* **Below** *Perhaps one of the few drop-ins this surfer could forgive, as Lisa Neil boogies into the action at Noosa*

MARTIN TULLEMANS

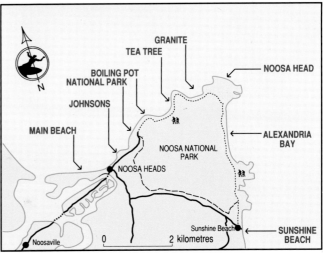

43

BEDE/BROBES

Sunshine Beach is a long stretch of sand which picks up all available swell and can produce solid, powerful waves. The selection varies from rip breaks to heavy peaks, peeling right and left. The best break is often right up in the northern corner, which is protected from the summer nor'-easters. It can hold swell to 2 metres or more and is best inNW to SW winds.

Over the stretch of coast from Sunshine Beach to **Coolum** there are numerous excellent beach breaks, which work in similiar conditions to Sunshine Beach. The pick of these is often **Pita Street** (situated at Peregian Beach at the end of Pita Street), which can turn on some great rights and lefts. Although this is a beach break the wave actually pitches over a rock bottom, which adds a little more punch than the average beach break. It holds waves to 2 metres and is best in offshore, NW to SW winds.

Coolum actually comprises two bays which face northeast and require swells of at least 2 metres to penetrate. Both bays can turn on snappy, clean waves to 1.5 metres. South winds blow offshore here. Coolum is worth a check in big SE to E swells, when the winds are SW to SE.

Just south of Coolum is **Yaroomba Beach**, which has an extremely powerful beach break with short, sucking, thumping peaks. This beach holds swells up to 2.5 metres and is offshore in NW to SW winds.

Around **Mudjimba** there are beach breaks right along the coast, which can be worthwhile at times. But when there is a real swell the majority of surfers head for one of the point or reef breaks which proliferate on this lazy stretch of verdant coast, set against the powerful Glasshouse Mountains.

Local Aboriginal legends explain the creation of this landscape in great Dreamtime sagas. According to these traditions, Mudjimba Island was formed when a local warrior, Coolum, was killed in a fierce encounter with

Above *Kelly Tindall tucks under a rare Sunshine Coast left.*
Below *Mudjimba Island*

MARTIN TULLEMANS

another man, Ninderry, who had kidnapped Coolum's betrothed, Maroochy. Ninderry used his club to knock Coolum's head right off his shoulders. It rolled across the land and into the sea to become **Mudjimba Island**. Today the island is leased by Peter Troy, who is possibly the most travelled surfer in the world. Peter has been one of the driving forces behind the establishment of the Surfworld Museum, now operating on the other side of the continent at Torquay Beach in Victoria.

There are two reef breaks here: one on either side of the island. The left, on the southern side, has real deepwater power and a treacherous bottom. On the north side, the right is fast and fearfully powerful. The left is offshore and best in light W to NW winds while the right is best in S to SW winds. It is possible to paddle to the island from the beach but it's a good 30 minutes, one way; as hairy a paddle as you'll find anywhere, especially on the way back when it seems far longer. If you surf this spot be humble and be able to surf — well. It's an awesome wave.

Heading south from Mudjimba the road veers inland just past Coolum Beach (and the Maroochydore airport) before swinging back to the south-east. It follows the banks of the Maroochy River to the thriving coastal towns of Maroochydore, Alexandra Headland and Mooloolaba which have almost merged over the years.

There are good beach breaks to be found off **Maroochydore Beach** on smaller SE swells and SW to NE winds. Down the beach there are good waves, sand over reef, all the way to **Alexandra Headland**, with the reef off the southern end of the beach producing a somewhat soft right-hander. Further south you can sometimes find an exceptional left, across the entrance of the Mooloolaba

River. South of Mooloolaba, the turn-off towards Kawana Beach and **Point Cartwright** and a walk down a narrow, potholed track (it's better to walk) leads you to a breakwall and a powerful right-hand reef break. The wave starts with a sucky take-off, followed by long walls and hollow sections before smashing into the boulders of the break-wall, which have an insatiable appetite for foam, fibreglass and flesh. For the most experienced surfers there's another right-hander called **Platforms** further out around the rocks towards the lighthouse. This is a heavy-duty, thick and hollow wave; a short intense ride with a closeout onto shallow rocks at the end, and a ride guaranteed to get your adrenalin pumping as long as you kick out in time. Like Point Cartwright, Platforms works on NE to SE swells to 2 and 3 metres, and is best in SW to SE winds.

When other spots are crowded or you are feeling like getting away from everyone, **Kawana Beach** (just south of Point Cartwright) can offer a great escape, with crisp, clean left and right peaks all the way up the beach. It holds swell to 1.5 metres and is best in offshore, NW to W winds. South of Kawana is **Wurtulla**, which faces more towards the south so the beach breaks tend to be more powerful than those at Maroochydore and Mooloolaba. The beach is obscured from the road by bushland which runs the full length of the beach and helps to keep crowd sizes down. There's a variety of peaky beach breaks, which are best at around 1.5 metres in westerly winds.

The reef at **Caloundra** is the most 'guts-up' spot in the region although it can be fickle, as are most good Australian reef breaks. It's a long paddle to this reef, north

Below *Gary Elkerton on home territory at Maroochydore*

of Moffats Headland where, on classic days, you can see right through the barrel as the peak pitches. The left is like Pipeline on its day, but the swell must be big — 2.5 up to 4 metres from the SE to E — for it to be 'real-reef' and your board will need to be big too. Board lengths of 6' 10" to 7' 6" might feel silly on the paddle out, but they are essential for the take-off. This wave stands up straight and fast, lurching forward with an unforgiving pitch which turns the wave inside out, usually finishing with spitting violence. You'll need experience in all fields of surfing horror for this one and have a strong leash. To take it on you want a clean SE to E swell, light westerly winds and a spare board.

Moffats has been described rather patronisingly as 'a great wave for malibus', but it can be very good. The headland provides shelter from prevailing S to SE winds and the right-peeling waves run down the point over a rocky platform bottom. At times, Moffats can be an unforgiving wave with long unmakeable sections falling way in front of you; it breaks in S to SE swells and is best around 2 metres.

Ann Street produces a gutsy peak with lefts and rights. The left offers the bigger and usually better rides, but occasionally the shorter rights, which peel off the peak, are hot too. It can get absolutely flawless in winter months and in summer the more frequent NE swells can give you a reasonable ride left down the beach and a real paddle back up to the peak. It's best in a westerly wind with SE to E swell around 2 metres.

Kings Beach can turn on a fun summer beach break, which handles NE swells. Best in swells to 1.5 metres and offshore in NE winds which, in this area, can reduce the number of surfable spots from scores to just a few.

Right *Les Abberly at Kings Beach.* **Below** *Ann Street*

Above *Deceptively beautiful, the reef at Caloundra*

Above *Sunshine Coast beach break*

Above *Robert Wolfe at Ann Street, Caloundra*

Newcastle's Nicky Wood on an early trip to Stradbroke Island, found Cylinders' walls very much to his liking

THE ISLANDS

South of Caloundra (as far as the Gold Coast), the swell hitting the coastline is blocked offshore by a series of sand islands: Bribie, Moreton and North and South Stradbroke. All these islands receive substantial sand buildups from the northerly drift of coastal sands and these banks can turn on some excellent, uncrowded waves.

The smallest of these islands, **Bribie Island** is sheltered from most of the south swell action by the other islands and usually only has small beach breaks. Up at the northern tip of the island there's a reasonably consistent sandbank, which can also be reached by a long paddle from Bulcock Beach in Caloundra. Access to Bribie is via the tollbridge, 20 kilometres from Caboolture.

Moreton Island is a real surf adventure, requiring camping equipment, food and water supplies, and can be reached by ferry from either Scarborough or from Bulimba

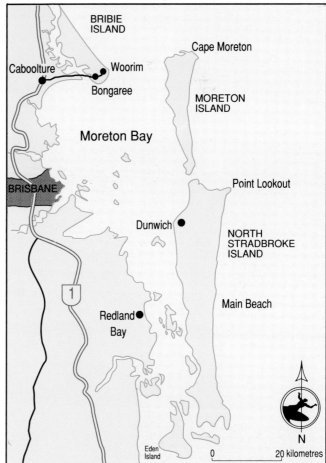

BEDE/BROBES

49

Wharf on Stradbroke Island. There are excellent rights, most of which are on the northern side of the island, offshore in south winds. There are also a variety of mixed beach breaks. In huge S to SE swells, at the very northern point of the island, rights peel over sand for hundreds of metres. Sharks in this area are an absolute reality and if you choose to venture here you could be on your own. So keep your eyes peeled and your feet up and don't even think of surfing too early or around sunset . . . that's feeding time.

North Stradbroke Island has much to offer surfers. This whole Moreton Bay area, which is fed by the Brisbane River, is a beautiful place which at one time supported a large Aboriginal population. Stradbroke forms Moreton Bay's major barrier to the Pacific Ocean, so the eastern and north-eastern shores of the island catch all available swell action. Often, when the Queensland coast north and south is tiny, 'Straddie' can be firing. Marine life is abundant and you can't forget that, in these waters, many a surfing contest/carnival has been held up by shark sightings. Manta rays are also relatively common. The fishing is excellent and whales are being spotted more often since the killing of them was stopped. Dolphins are common and this is one of the few spots in Australia where the dolphins actually assisted the Aborigines to catch fish, driving the schools into their spears and nets and then sharing the catch. The islands are rich in Aboriginal heritage sites and if the surf gets blown out, there's some Aboriginal sites that are well worth seeing.

Rabbit Bartholomew has told me about the great surfing contests on Straddie. As in traditional times when

Above *Moreton Island's shark stories keep crowds to a minimum, even on days like this at Blue Lagoon.*
Below *Sean Riley squeezes into a Stradbroke beach break*

Aborigines hunted and gathered throughout the area, the place is popular for people to congregate, hunt down a good time and gather valued APSA points. Access is via the ferry at Redland Bay or Cleveland.

North Straddie's best wave is **Cylinders.** The name may seem a cliché but the description is spot on: a long, barrelling right which breaks some distance from shore, grinding and punching through several heavy sections. The take-off is at an area called Deadmans and the break runs down to Windows, where sharks are seen — often — and caution should be employed at all times. Late surfs on cloudy, sultry summer days (December to February) should be avoided. The elusive great white is a known predator patrolling this area. Local shark fisherman Vic Hislop made his name as a big shark man in these waters and attacks on surfers have been recorded here. If you're still interested, Cylinders works best when the swell size is at least 2.5 metres, from the S to SE.

Another break, called **Fishermans** is often the saviour of North Straddie surfers as it is a spot which always has some sort of reliable wave, even when the swell size is down. Swell comes from the NE to SE and is protected from SE to E winds by the high cliffs. **Main Beach** is situated on the northern side of Stradbroke and stretches for many kilometres: here, a surfer with strong legs can discover their own perfect break. Hollow, gutsy peaks are found on scalloped sandbars the length of the beach. In more northerly swells, longer lefts peel off outside banks and hold a solid size swell. Best in offshore, NW to W winds and most swell conditions, up to 2 metres.

South Stradbroke is little more than a narrow sandspit with no ready access, so you'll need a boat and luck to find waves there.

Above *Point Lookout.* **Below** *Shaun Munro at Cylinders.* **Bottom** *Guy Ormerod, Point Lookout*

Surfers Paradise

THE GOLD COAST

Undoubtedly the most famous stretch of coastline in Australia, this 40 kilometres of coast from Southport to Tweed Heads, attracts some two million visitors every year, increasingly from America and Japan, who come to lap up the sunshine and (for those with surfboards) the chance to enjoy some of the best point breaks in the world. The Gold Coast is an area rich in waves and tourist dollars, and the constant tourist influx adds considerably to crowds, especially at the better breaks, where a talented bunch of locals are ready to fight for every wave.

North of the Spit, between the breakwall and Southport, there are seemingly endless banks along the beach with heaps of surf and uncrowded conditions. These breaks are offshore in N to W winds and are best in swells around 1.5 metres. The breakwall was built some years ago on the southern side of the Broadwater sea entrance to stabilise the entry to the Broadwater, and it brought a rare

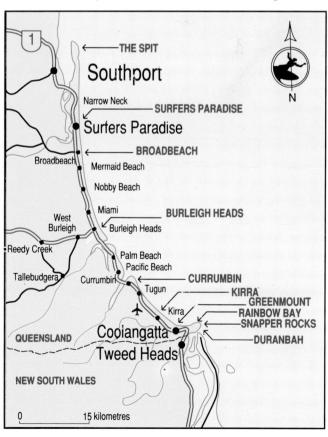

DICK HOOLE

53

significant gift to surfers. The sand built up on the south side and created a new spot with decent lefts on a bank close to the wall and associated peaks scattered down the beach in prevailing summer nor'-easters; it works best in NE to E swell (to 2 metres) and N to NE winds.

The long beach between **Surfers Paradise** and **Broadbeach** can have big waves which pound on the banks outside in huge closeouts. At those times the points all have ravenous crowds and the beach breaks are empty. However, when the swell is small and running at more of an angle there are some hot waves. Locals swear by their breaks and for hungry surfers there's plenty of waves. Close monitoring of the best sandbanks is necessary to catch these beach breaks with optimum conditions. Offshore in NW to SW winds.

On its day **Burleigh Heads** is almost flawless and its perfect cylindrical form, long barrels and guillotine lip have earned respect worldwide. A right-hand point break, Burleigh peels across a shallow sandy bottom formed at the southern end of the beach by sand piled up against the round boulders. On big days, the cove at the top end of the point can hold waves to 3 metres; best on S to SE swell and W to SW winds. With good banks and a clean south swell of 2 to 2.5 metres, Burleigh offers a sight rarely seen, and an experience even more rarely matched.

Another of Queensland's quality, sand bottom right-handers is **The Alley** at **Currumbin.** The waves start at the rocky outcrop which was once freestanding (now connected by a land bridge). The entrance area to the creek can become hectic at the weekends, with small fishing boats dashing through the break hopefully *between* the sets.

The area is also a haven for Hobie cats, sailboards, surf skis and all the other watercraft, particularly at weekends. Despite this, Currumbin offers a first-class wave on its day and well worth the hassles. Sometimes, when

the banks are shallow (just off the point), it becomes a top-to-bottom barrel for 20 to 30 metres then walls out into a total performance wave, often peeling all the way to the beach. Best in W to S winds and S to SE swell (to 2.5 metres).

The **first groyne** at **Kirra** would be just about the most prized break in Australia: a right-hander which peels over a sandy bottom in endless, top to bottom, freight train barrels. Some of the most impossible barrels ever made have happened here. The take-off is severe as the wave dredges on the shallow sandy bottom; make the drop and you're confronted with a jacking wall of Pacific Ocean. The wave is one of the thickest you'll find anywhere and the bottom seems to drop out, creating a 'step' in the ocean as tons of sandy water pitch over-head. Sections of up to 40 metres can fall in one huge slice and you've really got to step

MARTIN TULLEMANS

Burleigh Heads rarely holds much bigger than this

PETER CRAWFORD

PETER CRAWFORD

SEAN DAVEY

PETER CRAWFORD

on the gas to make it: maintain speed and line and you're inside one of the most awesome barrels of your life; make one mistake and you're in for a whomping you'll find hard to forget. This is the wave that surfers like Michael Peterson, Peter Townend and Rabbit Bartholomew cut their teeth on. Kirra is all quality when it works but it's an inconsistent break, requiring a solid swell to penetrate the bay to its take-off point. A second section of the wave bottoms out just off the weather shed, almost halfway down the point. Breaks best in S to SE swell (from 0.5 to 2.5 metres) and SW to S winds.

In Kirra, dreams come true. On its day, that classic point break provides endless barrels, one of the ten great waves to be found anywhere in the world. It looks as though Kirra is in for another battle as plans have been put forward for a marina right where the wave breaks. During the 1970s the waves at Kirra were ruined for two seasons by a rock groyne which was built to broaden Coolangatta's tourist sands. Until Coolangatta filled up with sand, Kirra was simply too deep to break except at low tides and large swells. Now the battle is on again as surfers and conservationists fight the developers and perhaps the council for the right to a very special piece of Australian coastline.

Top *Byron Bay's Gary Timperley in a no-lose situation during the Stubbies at Burleigh.*
Middle, bottom *Burleigh Heads perfection*

Kirra's second groyne was built in 1980. When the banks are established and the ocean currents right, this right-hander, although an all-sand bottom, can turn on a nasty little ride. Though not as long as Kirra itself it draws and stands up at the take-off point, sometimes making it almost impossible to ride; it works in the same conditions as its big brother and holds waves to 2 metres.

Often called the liquid fun parlour of Coolangatta, **Greenmount** is a gentle but satisfying wave and can, at times, deliver the goods, offering quality barrels. At other times Greenmount turns on long perfect walls, depending

55

SEAN DAVEY

Above *Purlingbrook Falls in the Gold Coast hinterland offers a drop so far unsurfed.* **Right** *Craig Wolgers on the kind of Burleigh barrel that leaves you picking the sand out of your Speedos for weeks, if you blow it.* **Below , opposite** *I Wanna Be There sequence*

DICK HOOLE

DICK HOOLE

DICK HOOLE

Right *Tom Carroll at Kirra*

on sand and swell conditions; an excellent place for less experienced surfers though the top surfers are often seen there. Needs a strong SE swell (to 2 metres) and SW to S winds.

Rainbow Bay is a similar wave to Greenmount, though slightly different in the way the banks form. When it connects right through to Greenmount, Rainbow Bay offers a wave so long and ever-changing that your legs feel what you have done before your mind tells you. The wave gets very hollow in the right sandbank conditions but is also a 'fun' wave, ideal for less experienced surfers. Best in S to SE swells (to 2 metres) and SW to SE winds.

The last of the great sand bottom point waves before the New South Wales border is **Snapper Rocks.** Another fun and performance wave which can, at times, launch you into Rainbow Bay (and on into Greenmount); if nothing else, your legs will feel the length of the ride. Then you get the choice between a marathon walk or a horrendous paddle back. Best in S to SE swells (to 2.5 metres) and W to S winds.

The glittering tourist centre of Coolangatta actually owes its name to a mountain peak some 2 kilometres west of Shoalhaven Heads, on the New South Wales south coast. This peak was called Coolangatta by the local Aborigines, a name adopted in 1822 by the area's first English settler, Alexander Berry, for his homestead. Berry was one of the first commercial success stories of modern Australia and by the 1840s his business interests extended as far north as

Top *Mark Richards, Kirra.* **Right** *Kirra.* **Below** *Rabbit negotiates the outside section at Kirra as the crowd scrambles for the shoulder, jockeying for the best drop-in point*

DICK HOOLE

the Moreton Bay settlement in Queensland. Berry named one of his ships *Coolangatta* but it was wrecked in 1846 on the deserted beach just north of the Tweed rivermouth, and the beach subsequently became known as Coolangatta.

Duranbah is a quality beach break that has saved many a dedicated local surfer from going insane. Queensland's Gold Coast has a habit of coming up with long flat spells which can go for weeks, if not months. But Duranbah never (well, almost never) lets the surfers down. Thebreak is situated to the north of the breakwall at the mouth of the Tweed River, which provides plenty of sand (drawn out of the river in the outgoing tide) for the quality sandbanks which are its feature. These banks create a series of quality peaks and the local 'hot rats' can be seen on any summer's day jockeying for position and busting down doors wave after wave. Duranbah is generally a short hollow wave which does its best on a S to SE swell (up to 2.5 metres) and W to S winds. The beach was named Duranbah after a local Aboriginal clan leader who defended this area against the European invaders. His grave, on a nearby hillside, survived until quite recently, when it was vandalised.

Duranbah is the last surf spot on the Queensland coast (situated at the mouth of the Tweed River — it's actually in New South Wales), but as the border into New South Wales is crossed the quality breaks continue. Surf on!

BILL McCAUSLAND

MARTIN TULLEMANS

Top *The inside section at Kirra.* **Above right** *Kirra.*
Right *Tom Peterson, Kirra*

STEVE TRIANCE

Top *Jason Buttenshaw at Snapper Rocks*
Below *Greenmount*

Below *Some surfboards perform upside down, even without a surfer*

MARTIN TULLEMANS

DICK HOOLE

PETER CRAWFORD

Above *Duranbah from the inside*
Right *American boogie -man Ben Severson inside Duranbah*
Below *Ross Phillips, behind the curtain at Duranbah*

MARTIN TULLEMANS

DICK HOOLE

61

Craig Pitchers at Duranbah

David Smith in sequence at Duranbah, where the consistent surf produces a competitive atmosphere

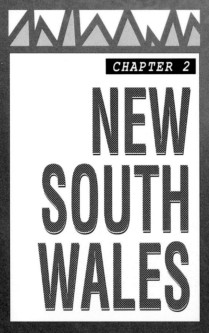

CHAPTER 2

NEW SOUTH WALES

It was in New South Wales, at Freshwater Beach on Sydney's north side, that surfing in Australia began. It was here that the Hawaiian master, Duke Kahanamoku, demonstrated the art in 1915, and from there the sport spread right around the coastline as more and more people discovered the thrill of speeding down (later across) a wall of moving water. Sydney remains the hub of contemporary Australian surfing, the base of most surfing magazines and the home — along with Newcastle and Wollongong — of many of our champion surfers. This coastline also contains the largest population of active surfers in the country, which has resulted in New South Wales becoming the most surfed coastline in Australia. Almost every kilometre has been explored and checked for surf potential and it's rare that quality waves go unsurfed, except after nightfall. From the perfect points of the north coast to the gnarly rock ledges of the south coast, the good waves are all hotly contested.

The legendary point power of New South Wales' breaks is typified by Dee Why Point

The golden hues of a north coast sunset at a spot called The Wreck, where an old shipwreck creates a great sandbank and, on occasions, the best waves in the area

THE NORTH COAST

The stretch of coast south from the Queensland border is home to some of Australia's most famous surf breaks. The major population centres of Brisbane and the Gold Coast in the north and Newcastle and Sydney in the south feed a hungry surfing population with some truly 'classic' surfing set-ups, particularly long right-hand point breaks.

In the 1950s and 1960s — when surfing really took off in Australia — the surfing sojourn or 'surfari' north became the thing to do, and many of these trips were well documented in surfing magazines, depicting seemingly endless lines of swell peeling

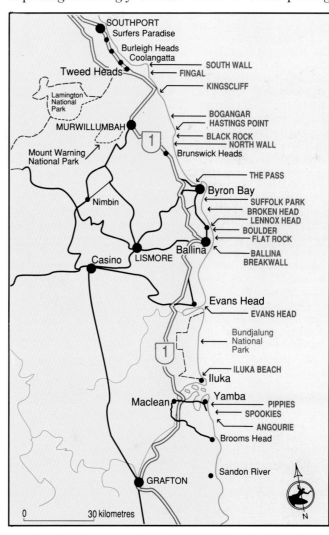

perfectly down long sand and rock points. These images attracted surfers from all over Australia and eventually from all over the world.

Today it has to be one of the most crowded stretches of coast anywhere, with 'locals' living at the well-known spots and visiting surfers constantly drifting through. The modern influence on some of these once remote spots has seen development of roads, industries, buildings and further urban growth. Some of the north coast, however, still holds the magic of yesteryear, though one suspects its days are numbered. The north coast is sliced by a number of huge river valleys — The Hunter, Karuah, Myall, Manning, Hastings, Macleay, Bellinger, Clarence, Richmond and Tweed (on the border). These river valleys support big rural industries and give the north coast a feeling all of its own.

The **North Breakwall** of the Tweed River is a popular surfing area for Gold Coast surfers, but there are good waves to be had off the **South Wall**. You can drive to it by turning off the Pacific Highway just south of the border, or if you're at Duranbah proper, then by a scary paddle across the Tweed River mouth. If you opt for the paddle, check for sharks first as they particularly like to trail the fishing trawlers. The surf is best at South Wall when the summer nor'-easters are screaming up the coast and the windswell is pushing past the Gold Coast breaks. Works best E to NE swells (to 2 metres) and NE to NW winds. A good escape but wave quality depends on sandbanks.

Fingal Point juts out from the coast far enough to offer some protection from the southerly winds. It tends to be an inconsistent wave, which is best in large SE swells and SW to S winds. If Fingal is good, then usually the points across the border (Snapper, Kirra, etc.) are firing. The Fingal beach break offers some reasonable lefts and rights in summer nor'-easters, but again the quality is dependent on shifting sandbars. Best on NE to SE swell, up to 1.5 and 2 metres, and NW to SW winds, with Fingal Point offering some protection on light NE days. There is a small local community of solitude loving people at Fingal and hoon behaviour is not recommended.

Kingscliff is the first town heading south on the alternative coast route. Primarily a tourist spot, it's a good fishing area too. There is a deadly right reef break at Kingscliff which can only be surfed on higher tides; low tide and it's skin-on-the-rocks material. Works best on ENE to large SE swells and it's offshore in W to S winds.

Bogangar can pick up a little more swell when the Gold Coast point breaks are small, but wave quality depends on shifting sandbanks. There is a patchy reef bottom and when the sand is right you can surf for up to 300 metres down the pandanus palm covered headland. Sometimes hollow, Bogangar is more often a fuller, even mushy kind of wave; works best SE swells up to 2.5 metres and SW to S winds. The headland offers some protection from the SE sea breezes. Shark sightings are not uncommon here. The back beach (**Norries Head**) offers a reasonable wave at times, usually in a nor'-easter.

At **Hastings Point**, Cudgera Creek enters the ocean near a low rocky outcrop. Deep gutters and strong rips along the beach on both sides of the

rocks can produce good quality left- and right-hand beach breaks up to 2 metres in NE to SE swells and NW to SW winds. Worth a look on small days. Further to the south **Pottsville Beach** works in similar conditions, again depending on the available sandbars on the beach which stretches all the way to New Brighton and Brunswick.

South of Pottsville, **Black Rock** is a good quality right-hander, sand over reef, which holds to 2 metres in SE to NE swell and is best in W winds. There are numerous other good beach breaks down the beach towards Brunswick Heads, but access is difficult and quality dependent on current sandbars.

Brunswick Heads has always been bypassed by surfers heading north or south in a rush to get to a more popular (and crowded) spot, but Brunswick has some excellent waves, created by sandbanks which form on both sides of the breakwalls at the mouth of the Brunswick River. The **North Wall** is best in 1 to 2 metre, E to SE swells and NW to SW winds. There is also a fishermen's co-op here for hungry surfers.

Byron Bay is the most easterly point on the Australian mainland and one of the world's top ten surf spots. The huge cape protruding out into the Pacific offers fantastic protection from the southerly winds on one side and from prevailing summer nor'-

A good day at The Pass, now measured not by whether there's a crowd, but by just how big a crowd

easters on the other, something of a rarity on the north coast. Byron Bay has a great little collection of surf spots and a colourful history. In the early 1960s this area became a haven for 'drop-out' surfers and the hinterland is, to this day, a centre of alternative lifestyles. The countryside has rich, green, rolling hills with remnant pockets of rainforest, streams and waterholes — one of the most idyllic stretches of coast in Australia.

Byron Bay supported a big abattoir until it was shut down in 1983, and stories are told of huge shark packs that once cruised by the Byron point-break on their way to the abattoir exhaust pipe, which ran the length of an old wooden pier on the main beach. The water would be red with the blood and offal pumped daily into the ocean. In the early part of the century, Byron Bay was a whaling town.

Today Byron Bay's main industries are tourism and surfing. The town also supports one of the highest percentages of welfare recipients in the country. There is only so much work to go around and people are constantly drifting through this beautiful place. As far as surf goes — Byron is holding!

The Wreck is on Byron's Main Beach, just north of the shopping centre. An old shipwreck, the S.S Wollongbar sticks its rotting hull just above the water at high tide and the sand gathered around the wreck has created an excellent right. It's best on either huge SE swells or solid E to NE swells (1 to 2 metre) and is offshore in SW to SE winds.

Main Beach occasionally gets good waves but depends on fluky sandbank conditions. Generally it's a long line of closeout but it can be very good in huge SE swells (when they're big enough to wrap around Cape Byron), but Main Beach tends to be best on small to medium NE to E swells and SW to SE winds.

The Pass is the most congested surf spot in the Byron area. When The Pass is working it's packed with locals, from bearded mountain folk to multi-finned grommets, as well as boogie-boarders and overweight surf ski riders, and getting very busy in holiday periods. A boat ramp at The Pass gives fishermen access to the ocean though their timing has to be perfect to dodge the swells and the surfers.

The Pass is at its best in an E to NE swell (to 2.5 metres) but can catch the bigger S to SE swells if they can wrap around Cape Byron. Offshore in ESE to SSW winds. The take-off is dangerously close to a jagged rock outcrop on the outside point and gets very tricky on crowded days as surfers push each other further and further inside. The wave peels for

TERRY WILLCOCKS

Mount Warning casting its spell over Byron Bay

up to 500 metres down the sandy point, depending on sandbanks and tends to get very hollow as it winds down the long point towards Clarkes Beach. Dolphins are often sighted in this area and sharks are common. It is extremely rare to see Byron uncrowded. Spaghetti arms are common at The Pass and spaghetti legs too, so it's sometimes easier to walk or run back up the beach to the take-off area.

The next and final spot out on the Cape Byron headland is **Wategos**, which tends to be a rather inconsistent wave breaking over a patchy sand and reef bottom. It's usually a more friendly wave and suits beginners or those needing a warm-up before tackling the more difficult breaks; it is more open to east winds than The Pass.

Access to **Tallows** is by a dirt road to the car park on the south-eastern tip of Cape Byron and then a long walk to the northern end of the beach. This spot catches just about any S to E swell (the NE swells tend to push down the beach) and is one of the few in the area protected from the prevailing summer NE winds. Tallows gets very powerful at times and the best banks are usually in the corner, tucked under the towering cliffs of Cape Byron. Because it's one of the only spots working in a nor'-easter, it does get very crowded.

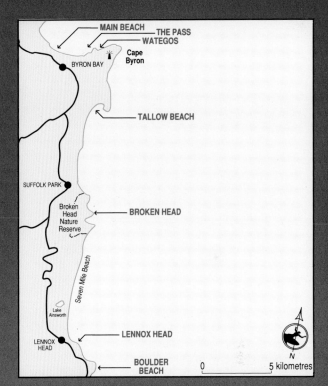

MAIN BEACH — THE PASS — WATEGOS
BYRON BAY — Cape Byron
TALLOW BEACH
SUFFOLK PARK
Broken Head Nature Reserve — BROKEN HEAD
Seven Mile Beach
Lake Ainsworth
LENNOX HEAD — LENNOX HEAD
BOULDER BEACH

0   5 kilometres

After heavy rain the sand banks off the river mouth at Suffolk Park form the spot known as Dereks, and when the other elements — sun, swell and offshore winds — come together it's a treat, as reflected in the face of a smiling Rod Anderson

It's worth keeping in mind that Tallows was the venue for one of Australia's most recent shark attacks. Marty Ford died from shock and loss of blood after having his leg mauled in a vicious attack in the northern corner of the beach. It's a pretty remote spot when it comes to seeking emergency help; no houses and no surf club.

The next spot heading south is Suffolk Beach, a long open beach which catches all the available swell, whatever direction, but needs NW to SW winds to be at its best. The wave quality depends on inconsistent and constantly shifting sandbanks; usually it's a mass of closeouts but can be very good when all the elements come together. During periods of heavy rain, when coastal streams break out on the beach (or when bait-fish are thick), Suffolk can get very sharky.

Broken Head is another of my top ten waves in Australia. A fast-peeling right-hander tucked inside the rocky headland and breaking inside the offshore rocky outcrops over a sand bottom, the quality of the wave is highly dependent on the condition of the sandbanks. On its day, Broken Head is a classic and challenging wave, breaking similarly to Burleigh Heads, and varying in character from one barrel to the next. Broken Head breaks best on NE to E swell but can be surfed in SE swells also. Offshore in W to S winds.

Broken Head is a beautiful spot with one of the quietest little camping grounds on the north coast. Thick forest palms — almost a jungle — surround the point. It's a popular fishing spot; the water rushes through the broken rocky outcrops outside the point and dolphins and big sharks are very common here, more often in summer.

Lennox Head is a great Australian wave with the classic point set-up; another break which rates in the top ten. Lennox is one of the prettiest spots you'll find anywhere and one of the most awesome waves on the coast: giant waves for those with giant hearts. The shoreline is littered with large round boulders, which offer a tricky entry into the water and require subtle timing on exit — not a spot for beginners. In the paddocks on the point, cows offer mute judgment on the performance of the many surfers who tackle this memorable wave. Lennox is at its best when the sandbanks are running a consistent distance from the rocky point and it needs a solid, clean, 2 to 3 metre S to SE swell (though it has been surfed at 4 to 5 metres) and is best in SW to S winds.

Paul Callahan at Broken Head

TERRY WILLCOCKS

SEAN DAVEY

The bottom section, towards the Lennox Head township, occasionally reels off with almost unmakeable speed. It also gets very crowded. Again, it's not recommended that you surf here if the bait-fish are running. George Greenough lives in this area for most of the Australian winter and filmed his memorable in the tube sequences for *Echoes* in the late 1960s at Lennox.

Lennox now has a major sealed road running the length of the point, south of Ballina, so it's easy to check from the top car park. The stretch of coast between Lennox Head and Ballina offers a variety of surfing locations but, to be honest, when it's good at **Boulder Beach**, **Skinners Head**, **Speedies Reef** or **Flat Rock** the classic point breaks like Lennox, Broken Head and Byron are usually 'off-the-richter'.

The opening of a major sealed road between Lennox and Ballina in the late 1970s made this previously 'secret' stretch of coast far more accessible to commuting surfers. Generally, most of the spots work on 1 to 3 metre E to S swells and are best in W to SSW winds. Most of the reef breaks are well offshore, at least 100 and up to 500 metres from the shoreline, and tend to deteriorate very quickly in sea breezes (NE to SE).

The **North Wall** at Ballina — the outlet to the Richmond River — is one of the more protected spots in a southerly and catches most available swell,

Top *Getting off the rocks at Lennox Head during a lull on a good days can vary from a character-building experience, to pure character assassination.* **Above** *Perfect swells line up and sweep down the point at Lennox*

Early morning at Lennox Head. The day is young but already the outside take-off zone is busy, but nothing like what it gets when there's really clean sets. Over about 3 metres, it becomes very interesting, the crowd thinning noticeably as it gets tougher to get off the rocks

although the quality relies on good sand forming out far enough against the huge boulders on the groyne.

Ballina's **South Wall** is one of the very few spots to offer anything even rideable when the nor'-easter sets in. Surfers can go crazy on this coast waiting for the legendary north coast perfection when all they're getting is NE onshore 'mushburgers'. South Wall works best in strong NE to E swells and W to N winds. Like it's mate on the other side of the Richmond River, South Wall relies on good sandbanks but can be really good to excellent. Access from the Ballina side is an interesting hassle, where a ferry trip (with your car) is required. Then, a careful drive, on a poorly maintained road, which deteriorates into the dirt track closed near the breakwall. Worth the adventure when the dreaded nor'-easter has set in.

One of the most unlikely places you'd ever expect to find waves is out in front of the new Missingham Bridge, in the Richmond River. To break in here, a massive SE swell must travel upstream between the breakwalls. Offshore in NW to W winds. Very inconsistent, good for learners, but definitely sharky.

Evans Head and **Woody Head** are not famous surf spots but can be worth the trip in from the Pacific Highway. However the real treats of this piece of the New South Wales north coast are to be found on the south side of the Clarence River.

Top *Usually at Lennox Head, the cows are outnumbered by surfers but Lennox is best when it's big and hard to get out; one of the most mongrel places to get 'out the back' anywhere in the world.* **Above** *Lennox on a big day*

DICK HOOLE

Paddle harder

Boulder Beach on a really good day

The Clarence is a mighty river, one of the biggest on the north coast, which supports a huge agricultural industry and is the first area, when driving north, that you run into huge fields of sugarcane. In my experience, finding good surf in areas in sugarcane regions adds a certain style of languid subtropical feeling; the warmth of the climate, rich river soil and plentiful rainfall make it a productive agricultural area. The Clarence is beautiful — small islands dot the river for kilometres upstream and the fishing here is legendary.

On the northern side of the Clarence River (turn off Pacific Highway at Mororo) you can sometimes find good waves in the corner of **Iluka Beach,** next to the breakwall. Needs NE to SE swell to 2 metres and SW to W winds.

After turning off the Pacific Highway near Maclean the road runs right along the Clarence to **Yamba**, a popular holiday resort supporting big caravan parks, motels and a classic old hotel at the top of the hill overlooking the Clarence River mouth. Yamba is my favourite north coast town; thankfully it has mostly escaped the big developers' creative effort, but it's been rumoured for years now that Japanese interest is high in the area.

Fishing is big in Yamba. Trawlers daily ply the offshore coast and the estuary provides excellent leisure fishing, but for the wave-hungry surfers fishing is only a fill-in activity for the Yamba area has some truly unique and demanding surf spots. In the town itself, **Pippies** is one of the best all round spots, working best in small to medium NE to S swells and NW to W winds. The very northern corner offers marginal protection from summer nor'-easters.

A short drive out of Yamba, past the light industrial area, brings you to **Angourie**, one of the classic

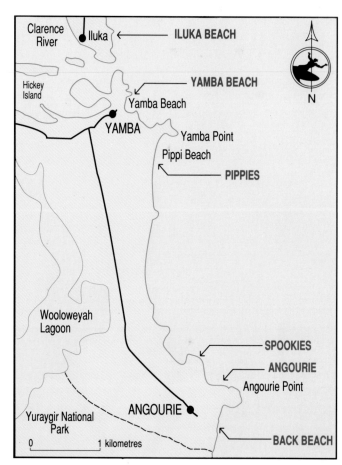

Angourie's neighbouring surf break, called Spookies, named for good reason

PETER SIMONS

waves of the world. A right-hand point break, Angourie is at its very best in a solid, clean E to NE swell and SW wind. The wave stands up over a rock shelf on the outside and the whole swell line tends to wrap in front of you. It then pivots on the island-style set-up and pitches thick on the inside, over a nasty rocky bottom. No sand here and no forgiveness; Angourie is a strong wave, particularly in bigger swells, and in no way is it recommended for inexperienced surfers. Many a surfer has felt the sensation of fibreglass on rock as his fins struck the bottom of a heavily sucking Angourie special.

Angourie can hold surprisingly large waves and becomes a real challenge when the swell gets over 2.5 metres, turning 'round' in the right conditions. When the swell is from the south Angourie is a little more forgiving but can close out on the inside across to the rocks just north, or tends to spill wide of the best part of the reef, wide of the take-off.

Locals here must be considered — their intimate knowledge of the tricky conditions usually sees them snaffling the best waves from deep inside and local ladies rip the waves on smaller days on their boogie-boards.

Just north of Angourie, some 500 metres around the rocks, is a spot called **Spookies**. The name is a giveaway, the appropriate word to describe this gnarly break; all-rock bottom but the take-off jacks up really quickly before the swell 'ledges' and the bottom drops out as the wave hits the shallow reef. It's a short ride but a true barrel, square from take-

On a smaller swell Angourie can be worth a session but the crowd can be a drawback, and the locals know the tricky outside take-off well enough to take the pick of the waves

off and holding across a shallow rock bottom, as hollow as they come. The wave ends after only 35 to 50 metres, petering out in deep water; occasionally a precisely timed cut-back will enable you to work the inside section a little but the best part of the wave is outside. Sharks are commonly sighted here (another good reason for its name). Spookies works best on NE to E swells and SW winds. It's a fluky spot and tends to be better on higher tides. Definitely a one person wave — drop-ins here are absolutely unforgivable.

The **Back Beach** at Angourie can get really good but nothing like 'Anga' proper. Generally a good spot in prevailing NE sea breezes, when the left on the rocky point is almost offshore. It catches all available S to E swells and rights and lefts can be found down the beach depending on sandbanks.

To the south of Angourie is the Yuraygir National Park (covering 40 kilometres of coastline and 13 000 hectares), containing several quality beach breaks. Most of these require a four-wheel drive and plenty of determination to find, with access by either the track around the back of Angourie in the north, or from Broome Head and Sandon in the south. Camping is permitted at some spots in the park, and the usual tourist facilities, as well as excellent beach and rock fishing, can be found around Broome Head.

THE BANANA COAST

Heading south from Yamba, the first readily accessible surf spot of any quality is **Arrawarra**. The highway diverts inland via Grafton and only comes near the coast again in the Corindi Beach–Arrawarra area. Arrawarra has a big caravan park ideal for camping overnight on surf trips and can occasionally be worth a stay for a few days, if the swell is happening.

This spot features a long point break along the same lines as Crescent Head (near Kempsey). It's a relatively weak wave, peeling over a rock bottom and on big swells tends to spill wide of the reef and 'fat-out' in deep water. It works best on E to SE swells (up to 2.5 metres) and SW to S winds but can offer some protection in a south-easter. The take-off is a long way offshore and can produce a good long ride when all the elements come together.

Just south of Arrawarra is **Mullaway**, where a grassy headland offers protection from southerly winds. Generally the beach breaks here are best in E to SE swells but it closes out in anything over 3 metres, with wave quality dependent on shifting sandbanks. Mullaway can get crowded, too, as local surfers from the Coffs Harbour area search north away from the crowded waves of Coffs itself.

Woolgoolga is the centre of a growing Indian population employed in the local banana industry. The area rarely produces any quality surf until you get down to **Back Emerald.** Tucked away just south of **Emerald Beach** (a developing satellite beach suburb of Coffs Harbour) you may find a long left peeling over a sand bottom. This break is a goofy-footer's paradise, but is totally reliant on good sandbanks. When the NE swells are pushing down the coast it can be one of the hot spots on the banana coast; works best on NE swells, as small as 0.5 metres up to 3 metres, offshore in NE to NW winds. A sewerage outlet was planned here.

Just a few kilometres further south along the Pacific Highway is **Moonee Creek**. The creek runs out at the top of the break, depositing sand which creates a beach break away from the rocky point. There's a beautiful tree-lined walk via a wooden foot-bridge over the creek to the point; a nice place to be, especially when the swell conditions are right. Moonee Creek works best on SE swells and W to S winds. It's best from 0.5 up to 1.5 metres and is a great hot-dog wave, reminiscent of a short Crescent Head-style wave; a good place to massage your ego with forgiving wave strengths. Moonee is great in small swells but doesn't handle real size very well and wave quality depends on rather fickle sandbank formations.

The banana coast is pretty barren wave-wise. The coast is rocky and seems geologically young — there could be hot waves in a couple of hundred thousand years after some heavy erosion. Now the area offers clean, aqua-coloured water, with the steep, banana tree covered foothills in the background and the solitary island formations scattered to the north-east.

The next worthwhile spot heading south is called **Diggers,** just north of **Macaulays**, Coffs Harbour's most crowded beach. Diggers is a beach break which can have average or great waves depending on the banks. It works best in SE swells up to 3 metres and S to W winds. The northern end can sometimes have a protected wave in north-westerlies.

Macaulays is the North Narrabeen of Coffs Harbour. Much of the area's growing grommet population is regularly out at Macaulays ripping it up. It's very open to virtually any available swell, particularly E to S. On big swells there is a left from the outside point all the way down the beach, connecting to an inside sandbank, and can hold some 3 to 4 metre days. Generally, the point break outside is separated from the inside bank where, on most days, there is a good right running into the corner. The bottom is sand but the wave has a considerable amount of power. Offshore in N to W winds.

The beach stretches south from Macaulays to **Park Beach,** which houses a busy caravan park with all the creature comforts. When the banks are good, peaky breaks are found on Park Beach up to around 1.5 metres and are usually best in NW to SW winds. At the very southern end of the beach the sand has built out to an island which can provide some good waves in southerlies.

At the mouth of the main port of Coffs Harbour are a series of huge breakwalls. On the north wall is a hairy right-hander which surfers flock to in big S to SE swells and S to W winds. The wave is quite sucky and right up against the wall; not recommended for the faint-hearted. At the entrance to the harbour there are waves on large E to NE swells and westerly winds. A sand bottom wave but relatively scary; when conditions are perfect a left breaks off the inside of the north wall.

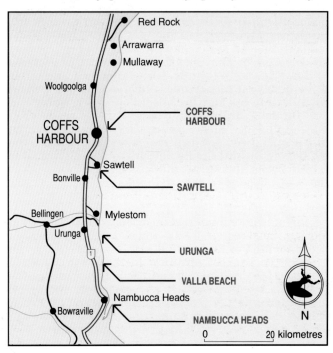

Red Rock
Arrawarra
Mullaway
Woolgoolga
COFFS HARBOUR
COFFS HARBOUR
Sawtell
Bonville
SAWTELL
Bellingen
Mylestom
Urunga
URUNGA
VALLA BEACH
Bowraville
Nambucca Heads
NAMBUCCA HEADS
0   20 kilometres
N

Above *Trapdoors near Sawtell*
Below *The beach break north of Crescent on a pristine day*

Further around, south of the harbour mouth, is one of surburban Coffs' heaviest waves, **Gallows**, which is open to any S to SE swell and needs a N to NW wind. It features an extremely heavy, sucking take-off over a rock bottom, and doesn't really get to be true Gallows until it's at least 1.5 metres plus, and holds up to 3 metres. You might be able to bluff it at some surf spots but not at Gallows — this one really sorts the men from the boys.

Boambee is a long stretch of beach which reaches from the man-made rock wall of Coffs south to the next rivermouth at Sawtell. Occasionally Boambee can have some good surf but it's pretty open and is more of a last resort spot. The northern end, however, can be fair in NE conditions, but the southern end of the the beach is the choice surf spot.

Trapdoors (another well-named surfing location) works best in S to W winds and handles huge southerly swells, up to 4 or 5 metres. A creek outlet runs sand out over a very patchy reef bottom with nobbles of rock sticking up and sand collected around. Under the take-off area is a huge rock platform which can make for some gutsy drops. When the sandbanks are right and the south swell is strong you can ride for a good 300 metres down the beach.

Sawtell Island is the last of the good surf spots in the southern Coffs region. At Sawtell a sand bottom has formed out to the headland or island. It's not a very consistent spot but to be fair can get very good when the banks are right. It's hard and fast on a medium to large SE swell and is offshore in W to S winds.

There are some areas in this section of coastline with good waves but the area is full of off-road adventure surfing. If you're willing to gear-up and look, you will find worthwhile waves. Further south, **Valla Beach** has some of the cleanest, clearest water you'll find. On a sunny day in S to SE swells and S to

SW winds it's a real pleasure to surf a good powerful beach break here. The waves break close to shore, making for a short but enjoyable wave. Valla is a pretty spot and has a caravan park worth a stopover at least.

Nambucca Heads has better fishing than surfing but sometimes there are good lefts on the side of the breakwall forming the entrance to the Nambucca River. A sharky spot, best in big E to SE swells and NW to W winds.

THE MID NORTH COAST

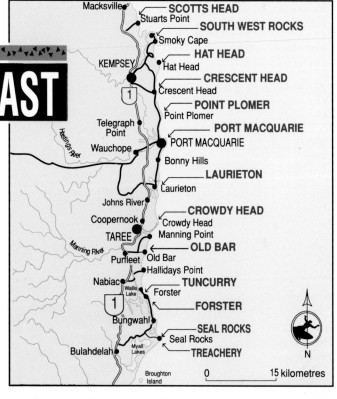

This section of the New South Wales coastline, with the exception of Crescent Head, is often bypassed by surfers in their hurry to get to better known spots. Typical of these spots is **Scotts Head**, just south of Macksville, which is worthy of at least a stopover to check the quality of the sandbanks.

Scotts works best on big SE swells (and sometimes E to NE swells), and is smoothest in lighter S to W winds. The take-off is close to rugged rocks under the headland and, after a relatively easy take-off, the wave walls up and runs down the beach. If the sand is right and the tide not too high, the wave links with banks way down the beach and your legs can get tired trying to pump your board to keep trucking down the line. It holds up to 2 and 3 metres but can section depending on tide and sand. Shark sightings are common. There's all the creature comforts at Scotts but the area has retained a beautiful natural environment. Generally a quiet little spot with good fishing, it gets busy during holiday periods.

Grassy Head is a grass-covered headland with a white sandy beach; a popular fishing spot, with scenic beach breaks at times. Trial Bay is an historic location, with the distinction of being home to the district's oldest prison; a beautiful area which can turn on great waves. Just around the corner, **Smoky Cape** is a wild, open point which catches plenty of swell but offers little in the way of worthwhile surf, though it often features in weather reports as the wettest place on the mid-north coast.

Like much of the surf on this stretch of coast, **Hat Head** is often overlooked. However, on its day, this wave — which literally runs down a huge rocky shelf dropping into the water at a 35° angle — can be a real treat. A right-hander, Hat Head works on NE to SE swells up to 3 metres and is best in SW to S winds. The sandy bottom and clear water make the rocky patches easy to see as the wave wraps down the point.

Crescent Head has been one of Australia's most famous surfing locations for many years. 'Discovered' in the 1950s, Crescent became popular with Sydney surfers as a first stopover on the long trek north, an ideal wave for the longer malibu-style boards except for the rocks lining the point which were responsible for so many dings before leg-ropes. Crescent Head is a special spot. As its name suggests the headland sweeps along a very long open beach from the north, right around in an almost perfect curve to a rocky point jutting out to the north-east. It turns on a long-walled easy wave. The golf course is a hazard for

surfers running out to the take-off, but at least it stopped the development of a lovely grass-covered headland. Huge weathered boulders line the point and disappear under the waves forming a basis for the sand to settle. On a good day, with a solid E to SE swell of 2 to 3 metres, Crescent goes off — from a rocky bottom take-off outside, it's a 300 to 400 metre wall of fun, linking up with the sand at the rivermouth on the inside to give you an incredibly long ride. Best in SW to SE winds.

On small south swells there are also good beach breaks on the northern side of the rivermouth. Sometimes Crescent can go for weeks without a decent wave but a good session here can do wonders for your cut-back, bottom-turn repertoire.

The sealed road from Crescent to the Pacific Highway does not continue south along the coast to

Scotts Head on a large day, when just getting out is a problem

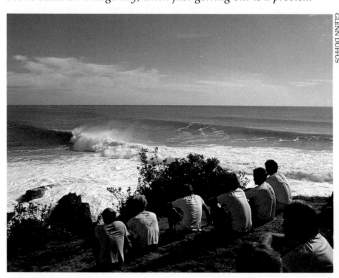

GLENN DUFFUS

Point Plomer, which might be a shame as the road deteriorates quickly into a rutty, potholed dirt track. However, when you consider that the real cost of a well maintained road would have been the continued rape of the coast by sandmining companies, it's worth the slow, bumpy ride. Parts of this coast were despoiled for their rutile in the 1960s and 1970s and the restoration program is going to take too long to ever let it happen again.

Point Plomer performs really well in big S to SE swells and SW winds, but it's usually a spot you head for when Crescent is over crowded although Plomer too can get a little hectic at times.

Back Plomer is a great spot in prevailing summer NE conditions. Beach breaks can be surfed here on smaller days as Plomer seems to stand up any available swell. It holds waves up to about 2 metres plus, and is smoothest in NW winds though it offers rare protection in nor'-easters. The water is clear, there's plenty of bush, but it's very isolated, andkeep in mind it's a long way to anywhere for medical help.

The long open stretch of beach between Point Plomer and Port Macquarie — which bears the scars of sandmining operations in its stripped trees and desolate dunes — picks up any available swell and will often have a beach break when all the points are flat.

Port Macquarie is not a particularly popular area for keen surfers. There are some breaks but the rugged coastline is generally too rocky and lacking in quality reef or beach breaks. The Port Macquarie locals — and the area boasts a considerable surfing population — would probably disagree, but better waves are found further south, especially south of Lake Cathie to North Haven. There's a variety of beach breaks which can produce excellent waves, usually in more westerly winds.

Flagstaff, in Port Macquarie itself, is right along-side the breakwater to the Hastings River and is one of the few local spots that can handle a sizeable swell; best in SW winds. Other popular spots in the area include **Oxley Beach, Flynns, Shelly** and **Lighthouse,** which all work in a variety of conditions — generally small to medium E to SE swells and SW to NW winds — but most keen surfers tend to use Port Macquarie as a fuel and food stop and move on to the better waves north and south.

At **North Haven** there is sometimes an excellent beach break right off the northern breakwall, which is the entrance to the estuary of Queens Lake, Watson Taylors Lake, Camden Haven and the Stewart River. The right stands up on sandbanks formed by the river, sometimes out beyond or level with the breakwall. Offshore in NW to SW winds, it's a relatively sharky area, but on big NE to SE swells it can provide great performance rights running down the beach. Again, very busy in holiday periods as many of these coastal hamlets rely on tourist dollars for their livelihood.

Point Perpendicular and **Diamond (Indian) Head** can be good, too, when the sandbanks are right (in southerly conditions) but they both need big swells.

Heading back to the Pacific Highway and south into **Taree**, there is a surprisingly healthy local surfing scene. One of the longest running pro/am surfing contests, The Capricorn Classic, is held every summer on the beaches immediately east of Taree.

Capricorn is the local surf shop and well worth a look as you head into the northern end of Taree's shopping area.

Old Bar is often the venue for the Capricorn contest. The beach breaks here can be really good, usually in small to medium swells, and they are best in NW to SW winds. But, like all beach breaks, the sand has to be right.

Uggs Reef (also known as **Saltwater** and **Wallabi Point**) is the choice spot when the swell is up from the east to south and can handle the size. It's reasonably protected in southerlies too and surfers head here from up and down the coast when it's cranking. The wave tends to section on different parts of the reef, but when it all links up it's really hot. The take-off is pretty hairy, over an intimidating rock bottom, so it's only recommended for more experienced surfers. The right peels up to 300 metres and, though it's not as soft as a Crescent Head style of wave, it's not super powerful either and lends itself to performance surfing.

Further south on the Pacific Highway is a very worthwhile detour. An excellent sealed road and picturesque scenery marks the Great Lakes Way and a link road runs through Tuncurry and Forster, bordering the mouth of Wallis Lake, Smiths Lake and, further south, the Myall Lakes National Park.

Top Crescent Head line-up. **Below** Hat Head

This is a beautiful area with great aquatic entertainment — excellent sailing, water skiing, fishing and, of course, surfing.

Black Head is sometimes worth a look in clean E to S swells. There's a beach break left into the corner which relies on sand build-up. The right-hander off the point is only short, about 100 to 150 metres, but can be good on its day and is offshore in W to SW winds.

The twin holiday fishing towns of **Tuncurry** and **Forster** are the biggest commercial centres in the Great Lakes area, which is packed in holiday periods, but the local pubs and restaurants provide good entertainment and tasty seafood. There's a surf shop here to provide any traveller's needs and occasionally, some classic waves, right in town.

Off the **North Wall** (Tuncurry side), in big NE to E cyclone swells and S to W winds, waves peel over the sand stacked up out beyond the tip of the northern breakwall. It's a 'down-the-line' wave, which stands up to a solid 2 to 4 metres and powers down towards Tuncurry for a long, demanding ride. When it's on, North Wall is the happening spot and gets crowded quickly. Often Newcastle surfers drive all the way from the Steel City just to catch it.

Further to the south-east is **Forster Beach** which also needs a big NE to E swell. The wave bends in, hits the outside point, moves past the pool and pivots onto the rock shelf, in much the same style as a little Angourie. Forster is offshore in SW to S winds and can handle light south-easters too.

One Mile Beach is the first good spot heading south out of the metropolis of Tuncurry–Forster. One Mile is a good nor'-east spot, handling the prevailing summer sea breeze really well. The best waves are at the northern end of the beach where sand gathers around a rock shelf, but you surf over sand and the wave quality is dependent on the shifting banks. There are left and rights, but mainly the left is better. It works best on W to NE winds and handles smallish days, up to 2 metres, but tends to break up over 2 metres. The lefts are best on pushing NE wind swells when most other places have only ordinary waves.

Heading further south, the Great Lakes Way continues along a narrow stretch of land between Wallis Lake and the Pacific Ocean. There's scrubby bush until the road goes through Booti Booti, where it winds through coastal hills and the vegetation changes to lush areas of forest and some beautiful beaches. **Boomerang Beach** is a well-known surfing beach which can produce excellent waves. North Boomerang catches E to SE swells and is offshore in light NE winds but best in north westerlies. It holds up to 2 metre swells and features assorted peaky lefts and rights. At South Boomerang there is a good right which works best on clean solid SE swells and is best in W to S winds. The right stands up on the outside over a reef shelf, then breaks over patchy reef and sand bottom. There is usually a left a little further down the beach which can be excellent when the banks are good.

Blueys Beach is a good spot in nor'-easters. That's the good thing about the surf spots on this stretch; there's such a variety of breaks to choose from in just about all conditions (except of course pure onshore E to SE winds). Blueys only really catches north-east swells and can produce surprisingly good waves on NE wind swells as they run

Perfect beach break

down the beach, creating predominantly left-breaking waves. North-west winds are pure offshore but it's quite decent in a nor'-easter.

Sandbar is a magnificent spot. The whole area was despoiled by sand-mining, except for a pocket of original lush rainforest which you walk through to get to the beach. The water is crystal clear and the sand soft and white, reflecting the sun's rays as you surf the beach breaks. There is a rocky outcrop at the very northern end of the beach which gives protection from nor'-easters, but this corner needs SE swells to produce decent waves. The nor'-east swells hit further down the beach, creating good little left and right peaks. Sandbar can hold up to 2 and 3 metre waves, depending on sandbanks. Occasionally, local authorities choose to bulldoze an opening through the sand into Smiths Lake to lower the lake water level and, for a short time, some good banks will form off the opening though all kinds of biteys will also be attracted.

Driving further south, the Great Lakes Way becomes an increasingly twisting and turning trip as it winds around Smiths Lake. At Bungwahl turn left to Seal Rocks, but only if you have a car which you don't mind taking over one of the roughest unsealed roads on this coast. It's sealed for a couple of kilometres, then turns to dirt and covers your car in dust or mud, depending on the weather. Big goannas and snakes are a common sight on this rugged bit of road as you head through the northern boundary of the Myall Lakes National Park.

Seal Rocks is being enthusiastically conserved by the loving locals as 'The Last Frontier' as developers continually eye off this beautiful piece of coast for 'bigger and better things'. Hopefully, their fight to save it from development will succeed and you can help by purchasing a bumper sticker from the local shop.

Seal Rocks is a point break tucked away at the very southern end of Sugarloaf Bay. It's rarely good but works best on either very sizeable SE swells or medium E to NE swells. The wave wraps around the rocky point and peels to the inside beach. It's a very short wave but can be a lot of fun and is very protected in southerlies. There is a caravan park right across the road. The beach further up the road is **Lighthouse,** which has good waves occasionally, but it's worth looking at the sleepy little fishing community here.

An extremely rugged dirt track takes you from Seal Rocks to one of the best locations (in north-east winds) on the mid-north coast — **Treachery Head,** or Yagen as it is sometimes mistakenly called. Treachery is a real treat. It's virtually offshore in a nor'-easter and sticks out further into the ocean than any other point on the coast, catching heaps of swell. When the rest of the coast is tiny or close to flat, Treachery can often have not only rideable waves, but really good waves. However, its reputation for producing such conditions means it gets crowded. The northern end of the beach features a beautiful rocky headland but it doesn't hold any surfable waves and the best breaks are just to the south of the headland. The water is always clear and clean and it can hold up to 2 and 3 metre waves depending on sandbanks. There is a small camping area behind the dunes at the northern end of the beach. Stories are still told of the 'Yagen monster' which was said to wander through the dunes at the back of the beach,

Top *Port Stephens.* **Middle** *Kempsey sunrise.* **Above** *Anna Bay sand dunes*

making a moonlight stroll hairier than the big outside sets.

There is a rough old rutile miners' road which runs from near Bungwahl on the Seal Rocks road down south through the Myall Lakes National Park. It's a beautiful (albeit slow) trip and there are some spots worth checking for surf potential. But generally, it's only open beach breaks and usually surf-starved travellers are too eager to get to more promising locations.

THE STEEL CITY COAST

The coastline surrounding Newcastle, from Port Stephens to Catherine Hill Bay, supports a huge local population of surfers. Port Stephens is one of the biggest (and most beautiful) natural harbours on the New South Wales coast and grandiose plans have been proposed for the area since early this century; recently, the area was even considered by the government as a naval port. For now the area has resisted huge development — its major industries are fishing and tourism.

Big towns have grown on both sides of the waterway which eventually becomes the estuary for the Karuah River. On the northern shore, Tea Gardens sits on the western side of the Myall River, so named after an unsuccessful attempt last century to grow tea commercially; and Hawks Nest rests on the eastern side. A long sandspit joins the mainland at Hawks Nest to Yacaaba Head which forms the northern head to Port Stephens.

On the inner side of the spit is one of the best lefts in Australia: called **Winda Woppa** or **Hawks Nest**. It only works (at its best) maybe a couple of times in one year. Winda Woppa needs a big to humungous S to SE swell and is offshore in NE to NW winds. This place will handle the biggest of

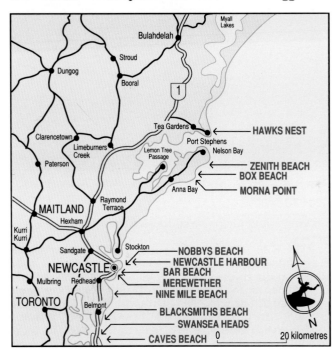

Simon Law, Newcastle practice session

southerly swells. The bigger the waves, the longer the ride — up to 400 metres when it's happening. Only recommended for experienced surfers. Needless to say, with all that deep water right next to you in Port Stephens, it's a shark-conscious paddle back out to the take-off.

On the open northern side of the spit at Hawks Nest there can be clean beach breaks in W to SW winds, but they're pretty unreliable. Strong currents are common here and it's not a place for inexperienced surfers when the swell is up or even in wind swell conditions sweeping the coast from the northeast.

On the southern side of Port Stephens is the town of Nelson Bay, tucked inside Tomaree Head which forms the southern headland of Port Stephens. There are some very good waves in this area but local surfers are very protective of them — understandably, too, as the voracious surfing population of Newcastle is only just south. **Zenith Beach** and **Box Beach** are two spots which can produce good waves, depending on sandbanks. Box Beach produces a really strong, wedgy wave in NE swells and needs W winds, but it's a heavy spot and definitely not for inexperienced surfers.

Fingal Bay occasionally produces reasonable waves too, but the almost enclosed bay blocks all but SE swells. It's a beautiful bay bordered by the Tomaree National Park and the whole area holds real potential for local surfers who are on the spot when the elements come together.

Further south, the coastal features carry promising names like **Boulder Bay**, **Snapper Point**, **Little Rocky**, **Big Rocky** and **Samurai Point**, but the coast is just too rugged to allow any good surf. About the only decent surf spot is **Morna Point** which is one of the few locations to work in NE winds, so it can be pretty crowded. Often, in small NE wind swells and prevailing summer nor'-easters, Newcastle surfers flock to Morna to get a wave.

Stockton Beach extends some 30 kilometres from Birubi Point in the north right to Stockton itself on the northern shore of the Hunter River mouth. Stockton has a huge expanse of beach breaks which occasionally get really good. Best in NE to SE swells and westerly winds. On occasions there are sandbanks formed around the *Sygna*, a Norwegian bulk carrier that was driven up on the beach in May 1974 by 165 kph winds. Half the superstructure remains stuck in the sand, secured to the mainland by a hawser.

Newcastle, a thriving city of some quarter of a million people, sprawls from the Hunter River mouth south and west. To outsiders, Newcastle is a dirty industrial centre built on the rich coal deposits of the Hunter Valley but to locals there's no other spot on earth. Four times world champion Mark Richards chooses to stay in his home town and the surfing scene here is possibly more entrenched in the average citizen's daily life than any other Australian city. There is an intensely competitive surfing population, the latest products of which are Nicky Wood and Luke Egan.

Newcastle Harbour, at times, has a hideous wave, which needs a big NE swell to wrap it in through the harbour entrance where the swells hit the inside of the eastern breakwall. The take-off is really heavy, before the wave barrels into a heavy tube. Wipe-outs can be fatal, with the bottom composed of huge concrete lumps, twisted metal and junk, with pieces of steel protruding through the concrete and several unfortunate surfers have been impaled on the sharp spikes. You have to be good to handle this spot. Best in S to SW winds.

Simon Law laying it down at Newcastle Beach

TONY NOLAN

TONY NOLAN

The Wedge, right near Nobbys Head, handles some biggish easterly swells. It's a left-hander which needs light offshore (westerly) winds to be at its best. **Stratts Spit** is immediately south of The Wedge and can be good on occasions, but is not a really consistent spot and needs light offshore winds to be at its best. Depending on the swell direction it breaks as lefts or rights, and it can be a pretty thick wave with reasonable power.

Nobbys Reef is outside the sandspit that joins the island to Newcastle proper and stands up in any S to E swell in ominous peaks which pitch in some places and spill out into workable mushy faces in others; offshore in NW winds. Diehard locals love the place but outsiders often find it hard to stay in position for the sets.

Nobbys Beach or **The Spot** has some chunky beach breaks in the southern corner which can be a saviour in strong southerly conditions. Generally there's a right outside, running down the beach and connecting to banks on the shore break on good days, while a left runs into the rocks in the corner.

The **Cowrie Hole** is hardly a beach. There is a small break in the rocky coast which indents into a reef which can produce some of Newcastle's best waves. A right stands up outside near the swimming pool, then pushes over the shallow reef and links up with a challenging inside section. The Cowrie Hole works best on medium to large SE swells and is smoothest in NW to W winds, though it offers some clean waves in light southerlies but is open to the ocean chop in sea breezes. **Flat Rock** is the left which breaks on the other side of the Cowrie Hole; it works best on a smallish NE swell and, like the Cowrie Hole, is offshore in westerly winds.

Newcastle Beach is the most popular with city people as it's only five minutes' walk to the commercial hub of the city centre. It has been the

venue for many surfing contests over the years, the most recent of which have been the 'BHP-Surfest' professional events. The beach faces straight south-east so cops all the swell from that quarter, but can produce decent waves on the outside in larger NE swells too. The rocky outcrop on the north-eastern end produces a reasonable left, depending on the sand, but sometimes right (in SE swells) stand up and run into Shark Alley in the very corner. The bigger waves often run into deeper water and reform for some heavy shore break action. It's straight offshore in NW winds, but is quite protected in nor'-easters too.

Bar Beach is the next surf spot south, situated at the northern end of the Dixon Park stretch with Merewether at the southern extremity. All these spots need NW to SW winds to be at their best and most of

Top 1987 BHP champion Tom Carroll. **Below** Mark Richards

PETER CRAWFORD

MARK SUTTON

the breaks depend on good sandbanks, turning on excellent waves when all the elements come right. Generally the waves stand up on the outside banks, and reforming inside sections are not uncommon. This is possibly one of the most densely populated surfing stretches anywhere in Australia, and when the waves are good the best banks are crowded all day.

At the southern end of the beach is **Merewether**, where Mark Richards can still be seen out surfing his favourite spot. Mark used the tricky reef and beach breaks as a training ground for his unmatched competition success. **The Ladies** is the nickname given to the reef break at the southern end of Merewether, because it's straight off the local ladies' toilet block. It offers some rideable waves in southerly winds, depending on the quality of the swell, but is best in SW winds. The Ladies handles real size, at times up to 4 and 5 metres on the outside, but is best at a solid 2 to 3 metres when the right peels through to the unpredictable inside sandbank. Merewether Boardriders Club is very active in this area. Whenever it even looks like breaking, it's crowded with a very young and aggressive crew; Nicky Wood, Luke Egan and Matt Hoy are just the tip of the Merewether surf talent iceberg.

On the southern outskirts of the Newcastle suburbs there are more good spots with difficult access offering far less crowded conditions. **Shallows**, **Leggy Point** and **Crosses Beach** all need westerly winds and any available swell. Leggy Point, just south of Merewether, is the best of these spots, where the rocky point and headland at the southern end of the beach offer marginal protection from a southerly. Leggy handles really solid SE swells off the

point and is perhaps one of the most underrated spots in the area.

Redhead is some distance further south and off the main Pacific Highway, but has some good waves particularly in nor'-east conditions. This was the home of former Australian Surfing Champion Col Smith, who tragically passed away in 1987 after a battle with lung cancer. The left off Redhead, to be at its best, needs a solid NE swell and is direct offshore in NW winds, but can handle the nor'-easters too.

Nine Mile Beach stretches from Redhead south to Blacksmiths and can have good waves in offshore (westerly) winds and smaller peaky wind swells but is dependent on shifting sandbanks. Nine Mile was once a beautifully vegetated strip of coast but sand-mining has reduced it to a rather desolate place.

Blacksmiths is a choice spot in southerlies as the swell (if it's big enough) sweeps along the breakwall at the mouth of the Lake Macquarie ocean outlet. The waves are dependent on sand build-up and work best in either huge SE swells or medium E to NE swells. Local surfer Michelle Donohue is now doing well on the international surfing circuit and there's a hot young crop of local surfers. Blacksmiths is a favoured fishing area too and the local seafood's worth a try.

Just south of the Swansea Channel there's a turn-off which takes you to **Crabbs Creek.** This little known break is the place to head for when everywhere else is out of control: it has a small beach under the headland offering a short, hollow left and a huge heart-stopping right, peeling 300 metres up the beach over a kelp-bedded ledge. This right-hander, which can hold waves up to 5 metres, has a wild bowl section and the kind of power rarely found outside the Hawaiian Islands. Definitely not for the inexperienced or novice surfer, and often not even for the experienced. Longer boards are recommended, especially to negotiate the horrendous take-off and bowl section. Works on all tides, depending on wave size, and is best in large S to E swells and W to SW winds. This is the kind of wave that provides some real stories for the locals.

The same road which led to Crabbs Creek also takes you to **Swansea Beach** and **Caves Beach** at the far southern end of this stretch of sand. At the northern end of Swansea Beach, some 80 metres past the end of the sand, is a left-hander which breaks 70 to 100 metres out behind the rocks. This break holds swells to 2 metres and is a good fun wave, breaking over a flattish rocky bottom. Works best in SE to NE swells and is best in NW to SW winds.

Slightly south of the rocks but still at the northern end of the beach is **Frenchmans**, a V-shaped sandbank which creates consistently good lefts and rights. This break is the popular spot for the Swansea locals, who will all be jockeying for the glamour peak of the day. These breaks tend to be best during the summer months.

Further south are more channels and sandbanks which create left and right peaks in swells up to 2 metres. At the far southern end of the beach, if you're very lucky, you'll get to experience the **Caves Beach** right-hander. Since the construction of the long breakwall this break requires a very large swell to get into the area. Once upon a time a shallow bank created consistent barrels breaking left into the southern corner during the winter months. Those days of perfect cylindrical forms are now rare, and often come when they are least expected. Caves Beach needs a giant SE swell and is best in SW to W winds.

Left *Dixon Park.* **Top** *Luke Egan.* **Above** *Nicky Wood at Merewether.* **Below** *Dixon Park*

THE CENTRAL COAST

What we know as the central coast is bounded in the north by Catherine Hill Bay and stretches south to Broken Bay and the mouth of the Hawkesbury River. Despite being flanked by huge surfing populations in Sydney and Newcastle, the central coast has relatively uncrowded waves and often turns on world-class quality. This area represented my home breaks for several years and holds some treasured surf spots, from fun summer beach breaks to wonderfully powerful reef breaks.

Catherine Hill Bay is the kind of spot you hit when the swell is small in the hope that there's a good sandbank somewhere on its length. At the southern end is a huge alien-looking pier built by the coal mining industry for loading the black stuff from local mines. There are rarely any decent waves at the southern end of the beach but just south in the next bay is **Moonee,** which can produce less crowded waves. It's a walk to get in and, though it's offshore

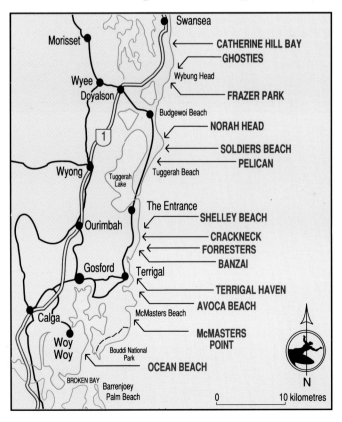

in westerly winds, further up the beach is **Ghosties**, which can handle light sea breezes on clean small to medium (up to 2 metres) swells, depending on the sand formation.

Further south, in the Munmorah State Recreation Area, is **Frazer Park**. There is a road off the Pacific Highway that takes you right to the beach, but Frazer is a bit like Moonee: fickle. The banks, when they're right, can usually only hold 1.5, maybe 2, metre swells. The beach is tucked away in a beautiful little bay which can resist sea breezes just that bit longer than the open stretches of coast. In larger swells there's a lot of water moving quickly and strongly in both Moonee and Frazer Park, so inexperienced surfers should be careful.

Norah Head offers several challenging reef breaks, which work best in big NE to huge SE swells and W to S winds; all are heavy spots and recommended for experienced surfers only. **Soldiers Beach** is another place that offers good protection from the summer nor'-easters and catches most available swell. A good left breaking over a rocky bottom with a steep take-off; tends to be best in NE to SE swells up to 2.5 metres and NW winds.

Pelican is a spot which catches most available swell and can be an excellent break in small NE swells, depending on sandbanks. Best in NE to NW winds; closes out on bigger swells. **Blue Bay** turns on a heavy, thick wave that breaks over reef and sand;

TERRY WILLCOCKS

works best on E to S swells from 2 to 3 metres and W to S winds. Not for the inexperienced.

At the southern end of **Shelley Beach** good beach breaks are found in the right conditions (S to E swells and SW to S winds), but the north end tends to offer better value. North Shelley works best on NE to SE swells, providing consistent waves when the sandbanks are right. There's also an excellent left found occasionally at the very north end of the beach, which can hold swell up to 3 metres. Shelley Beach is often good on typical summer days and can be an excellent spot for learners and novices.

A little imagination will quickly tell you how the spot known as **Crackneck** got its name: a secluded, left-hand reef break, which works best on NE to E swells and NW to W winds (at low to medium tides) and tends to be hard to catch in the optimum conditions. This wave breaks fast over a shallow and unforgiving bottom; access is by foot from Blue Lagoon.

Forresters is a beach with infrequent good sandbanks and so only has memorable waves on rare occasions. But the outside reefs make Forresters one of the foremost big wave spots on the east coast of Australia. This reef is broken up into three different sections, all for experienced surfers. At the southern end of the beach is a heavy take-off, short right which stands the swell up almost bottomless and barrels over a sharp and shallow rock platform in

Above *Wamberal.* **Below** *Brett Warner at Copacabana*

TONY NOLAN

front of dangerously close rocks. Called **Banzai** (for obvious reasons), this wave works best on S swells 2 metres plus, NW winds and higher tides and can hold swell up to 4 metres. The **Forresters Left** is a deepwater, shifting peak take-off, some 700 metres offshore, which stands the swell up over a surprisingly shallow reef and peels left. Works on S swells from 2 to 6 metres, breaking further out as the swells get bigger and with a power rarely found outside the Hawaiian Islands. The wave also breaks right, luring many natural-footers into a thumping inside section and a frightening paddle back out. Forresters also offers another right-hander, which walls up to the north side of the exposed island of reef and dies out in deep water: works best on S to E swells and tends to be less crowded.

Wamberal is a long stretch of beach which sometimes offers excellent beach breaks depending on sand and swell conditions. It catches plenty of swell action and sometimes produces excellent waves. Breaking over the rocky outcrops at the northern end of the beach is a series of consistent waves which offer marginal protection from light to moderate N to NE winds. The central part of Wamberal can also produce good beach breaks and is offshore in W winds, but the sandbanks have to be in good shape.

Terrigal Haven is one of the area's more famous spots and a special place for those who enjoy powerful, grinding right-handers. When the big SE to E groundswells hit the eastern coast, Terrigal Haven offers a true test for the most experienced surfers. The wave holds very big swells, which peel and dredge some 250 metres over an irregular bouldered

Above *Crackneck.* **Below** *Banzai Backhand.*
Right *Sydney's Rod Kerr lets loose at Avoca Beach*

94

bottom. Mostly it's a long wall, with hollow sections and a few stretches which suck out square. The Haven can be surfed at all tides, though mid-tide seems the most consistent. The wave usually works all year round but tends to be best in huge E to S swells and SW winds, the general conditions found more often in winter. The Haven is one of those places where it's worth carrying a spare leg-rope (unless your board breaks first). The Terrigal beach breaks are mostly gentle and good for learners, but close out heavily in NE swells.

North Avoca picks up plenty of swell and turns on lefts and rights, which work best in N to NW winds. When good banks coincide with wind and swell conditions, this break can turn on some excellent waves. **Avoca Beach,** open to most available swell, is one of the most consistent beaches on the central coast. When the swell is E to SE, the point at the southern end produces an excellent right that breaks very close to the rocks all the way (drop-ins here can be deadly). Holds up to 3 metres, and is best in W to S winds. A left in the centre of the beach runs into the rip and every now and then — on huge E to S swells — a giant peak stands up level (if not further out) with the point, producing a big left and a long right. The beach break offers good waves in offshore conditions or glassy mornings; ideal in peaky, small waves and NW to SW winds.

At **Copacabana Beach,** right in front of the lake's entrance at the northern end of McMasters Beach, perfect waves can be found when the conditions and sandbanks are right. This is a deepwater wave which catches most available swell and works best in N to W winds. A good, 'suckey' left can also be found off the northern point, breaking over a rocky bottom; best in NE to NW winds.

McMasters Point is one of the many excellent point breaks on the central coast; a unique right-hander, requiring a big E to SE swell or a giant S swell (at least 3 metres). The take-off is close to rocks, then the wave walls out over an irregular rock bottom before entering a bowl section midway and ending in a closeout as it links with the shore break left. Sea eggs and sharp rocks await the unwary; definitely only for experienced surfers. Best in W to S winds and higher tides.

Bouddi National Park extends from McMasters Beach south to Broken Bay, covering 1150 hectares and encompassing some beautiful beaches and reefs. There is surf to be had on this coast, which generally works on medium to large swells from any direction and NW to W winds. However for all but the most experienced surfers it's a dangerous area; it is unpatrolled and there is no help within immediate reach. A long walk faces the adventurous surfer and the reefs are fickle, which means it can be wasted time.

Broken Bay lies at the mouth of the Hawkesbury River and Brisbane Waters lake system. **Ocean Beach** or **Box Head**, lying just north, receive substantial deposits of sand which create excellent banks and, in a southerly swell and NE winds, some memorable lefts up to 1500 metres in length. One of the suckiest spots you'll find, so recommended only for experienced surfers. The paddle back out is a deterrent — spaghetti arms are common here as are shark sightings. The Box varies greatly, from a suckey low tide break to a fatter, soft high tide wall. The current on falling tides can be strong and often takes unwary surfers way out between the sets. This spot is popular with boating surfers from Sydney and it can get incredibly crowded. If you decide to surf it remember that it rarely breaks here and the locals can go for long spells without *any* surf.

SURFING SYDNEY

Bordering the area which supports the heaviest concentration of people in Australia, Sydney's sandstone cliffed coast has much to offer its huge surfing population. Competition for waves is fierce and constant. Every spot is more than covered with its own committed crew and demand for waves is high. Yet Sydney has a range of quality beach, reef and point breaks to offer. Apart from the crowds the only major drawback in Sydney is the polluted water. The surf is consistent, particularly on the beach breaks, though it can take a while to get conditions wired. When there's a sizeable east swell and offshore winds, Sydney's point breaks are only surpassed by the perfection of points outside the metropolitan area.

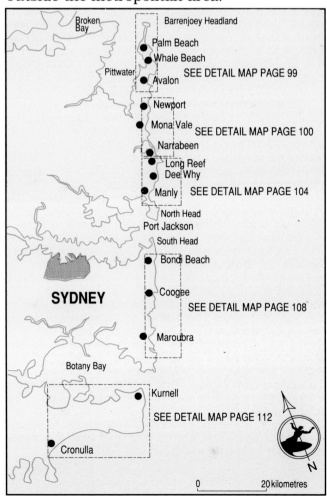

Broken Bay

Barrenjoey Headland

Palm Beach

Whale Beach

Pittwater

SEE DETAIL MAP PAGE 99

Avalon

Newport

Mona Vale   SEE DETAIL MAP PAGE 100

Narrabeen

Long Reef

Dee Why   SEE DETAIL MAP PAGE 104

Manly

North Head

Port Jackson

South Head

Bondi Beach

SYDNEY

Coogee

SEE DETAIL MAP PAGE 108

Maroubra

Botany Bay

Kurnell

SEE DETAIL MAP PAGE 112

Cronulla

0   20 kilometres

Martin Potter making it all look so easy

The northern beaches

Sydney's stretch of northern beaches represents one of the finest sections of surf coastline to be found anywhere in the world. Over the years these beaches have been the training ground for many of Australia's international surfing champions. In the 1960s, it was Midget Farrelly and Nat Young; more recently, Tommy Carroll, Simon Anderson, Barton Lynch, Pam Burridge and Damien Hardman have all achieved worldwide success based on a training in these breaks. Some 15 beaches stretch over 50 kilometres, from Palm Beach to Manly and the northern headland of Port Jackson.

In the lee of Barrenjoey headland is **Palm Beach,** a long and scenic beach which can be a bottleneck on summer Sundays, but offers a series of options that turn on some quality beach breaks. The clean water and mostly uncrowded sands and waves offer plenty. Also a good spot for beach fishing and sailboarding, which is popular on both sides of the spit of sand that stretches out to the Barrenjoey headland. If the surf is really off you could try a walk up to the lighthouse, where a memorable view of the beach and Broken Bay can be had. The path is reached from the end of the sand on the west (Pittwater) side, in the SW corner of Barrenjoey.

The **Barrenjoey** break is one of Sydney's least accessible surf spots — shock, horror, you actually have to walk to this one, about 1 kilometre north of the car park at north Palm Beach over soft sand. The headland offers good protection from the nor'-easters in the corner but the break is fickle, dependent on sandbank quality and swell direction. When it all comes together the wave breaks as a pitching, outside peak with long lefts, short rights and a rip along the rocks to paddle out in. This is an isolated spot, so recommended for more experienced surfers.

The beach breaks along this open stretch of some 2 kilometres can be good from time to time, depending on sandbanks, wind and swell direction. The beach is open to all wind and swell, but there's nearly always a shore break when you're keen. Best in SE to NE swells and offshore winds.

Above *On the very northern tip of the Sydney coast Barrenjoey can be a relatively uncrowded spot when the sandbanks are in good shape.* **Below** *The Whale Beach wedge*

Right *Little Avalon.* **Below** *The original locals. Every year in late winter or early spring, migrating pods of dolphins put on spectacular surfing displays along Sydney's beaches.* **Bottom** *Jeff Gibson at Little Avalon*

GUY FINLAY

PETER CRAWFORD

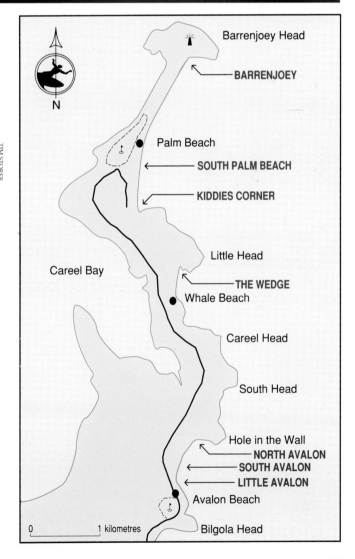

TIM STORER

Right in the southern corner of the beach is Kiddies Corner, which is an ideal learner's spot with a gently sloping, sandy bottom and easy access. Note, though, that there's nearly always a rip in the very corner running out next to the pool. During cyclonic storms from the E to SE, south Palm Beach is one of the few rideable spots in Sydney.

Whale Beach generally offers good protection from the summer nor'-easters and, depending on the sandbanks, produces good quality beach breaks at times but more often small, fun waves. A popular sunbaking beach with good fishing off north and south points. **The Wedge,** in the northern corner, offers some excellent waves at times. It is so called because of the way a solid NE swell refracts off the north point, creating a heavy pitching break and fast left-hand wall, especially at lower tides. (When it's real Wedge, you don't go right.) Only works in solid (at least 1.5 metres) N to NE swells and not recommended for the faint-hearted. The rip, which runs along the rocks, offers an easy way out, but can be a problem for the inexperienced. On smaller days fun, peaky lefts and rights can be found in the north corner. Best at mid to low tides and NW to NE winds. Only the southern corner of Whale Beach offers any protection if the wind is from the south. Occasionally there's a good right in the corner and suckey lefts

Barrenjoey Head
BARRENJOEY
N
Palm Beach
SOUTH PALM BEACH
KIDDIES CORNER
Little Head
THE WEDGE
Careel Bay
Whale Beach
Careel Head
South Head
Hole in the Wall
NORTH AVALON
SOUTH AVALON
LITTLE AVALON
Avalon Beach
0   1 kilometres   Bilgola Head

back into the rocks, depending on swell directions and the build-up of the sandbanks.

Avalon has come to be known worldwide for its quality waves. These can happen at each end of the beach, or off the rocky ledge at the southern headland known as Little Avalon. This beach tends to have coarse sand and a steep rise, creating a formidable shore break. On its day **North Avalon** can be one of the great waves of Sydney. When it's working — and the swell is big to huge from the E to NE — North Avalon produces some classic lefts, peeling from outside the north point to the southern corner of the beach. It is very difficult to get out in these conditions and is *only* for experienced surfers. On smaller days you can find excellent lefts in closer to the boulders and suckey rights closer to the beach. Works best on those days in S to E swells and offers optimum protection from the summer nor'-easters, which blow almost offshore.

South Avalon can vary from near perfect to horrible closeouts. Often it stands the south swells up higher than any other beach on the north of Sydney, and when the sandbanks are right it turns on some classic beach breaks. The lefts are short and hollow and the rights can peel all the way up the beach, with some truly testing sections. When the swell is big, getting out can be a problem and jumping in off the rocks on the point can be a nightmare first time. In those conditions it's experienced surfers only. Best in swells from NE to S, depending on banks and W to S winds.

Little Avalon, or LA as it's affectionately known by the locals, breaks over a shallow rock ledge on the southern headland of the beach and offers one of the hairiest take-offs you'll find anywhere. The wave sucks and jacks up as it hits the ledge and requires expert timing and real courage, especially when it's got some size. The reward is one of the roundest barrels to be found anywhere, but look out for the lip which is thick and allows little argument. The character of this short but memorable wave has been known to rearrange the ego of several surf stars. Works on S to NE swells and requires W to S winds. Higher tides are recommended and definitely only for experienced surfers.

Bilgola Beach is one of the most beautiful beaches in Sydney, surrounded by some of the most evocative real estate and hairiest corners, along the

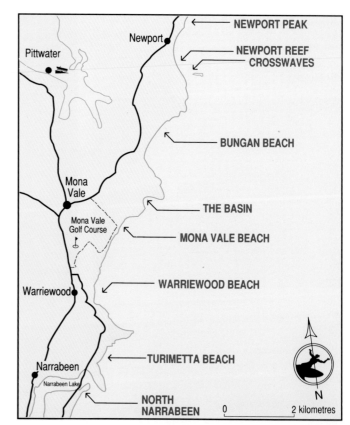

famous 'Bilgola Bends' of Barrenjoey Road. The beach catches most of the available swell and the northern corner offers good protection from the nor'-easters. Occasionally producing a quality beach break at the north or south end of the beach, depending on sandbanks, it has mostly small shore-break waves and great sunbaking. The north end is an ideal learner's spot in small swells.

Newport Beach is the home break of twice world champion Tom Carroll and the famed Newport Plus Boardriders Club. Several breaks are accessed here, from the patchy northern headland, where sometimes an uncrowded left-hander stands up, to the long thin reef at the southern end of the beach and the break known as Crosswaves. Newport is also a

Newport reef

CHRIS ELFES

popular sailboarding spot, especially in strong southerlies. **The Peak**, situated at the northern end of the car park, is the most consistent break on the beach: a compact take-off, peeling left and right, over patchy reef and sand. Usually better at mid tides and can be good in swells from S to NE. There is a heavy local crew, so be polite. Occasionally, good rights can be found on a bank just south of The Peak known as **Thompsons.**

At the southern end of the beach, right out from the pool, there's a right-hander called **Newport Reef.** A gently sloping rock bottom stands up S to SE swells (of at least 1.5 metres), creating long walls after a relatively easy take-off. This makes it an ideal place for novice surfers to ride big waves for the first time. Watch out for several big rocks in the shore-break, which have claimed more than one unwary

surfer's new board. Depending on size, best at mid to low tides and when the swell is true SE and is best in W to S winds.

The long, low island reef at the southern end of Newport is one of the landmarks of the peninsula. The reef catches swell from all directions but the only rideable waves are on the northern side, when an E to NE swell squeezes in on the reef and jacks up a powerful and often hairy right, known as **Crosswaves** (also known as The Path, The Pass and The Island). The wave peels down the northern face of the reef with bowling sections and appropriate points to get

Above *Tommy Carroll at Newport peak.* **Below left** *The right-hander known as Crosswaves on the northern side can hold the huge south-east swells.* **Below** *Warriewood, one of the northern beaches most inconsistent surf spots*

PETER CRAWFORD

MARK SUTTON

out of the wave, especially at the far end of the island (otherwise you'll find out why it's called Crosswaves). Mid to low tides only. The outside section can hold S to NE swells of humungous size and requires Hawaiian gun-style boards and real courage. Definitely only for experienced surfers.

Bungan Beach is one of Sydney's least accessible ocean beaches, which once kept it uncrowded. Take a packed lunch for this one. A very open beach, catching most available swell, and good protection from the nor'-easter in the northern corner. Wave quality can vary from awful to excellent, depending on sandbanks, wind and swell direction; it's easy to check from Bungan Head Road, without even getting out of the car.

A long and open beach, **Mona Vale** is open to most available swell and has several beach breaks which can be excellent on their day. At the northern end of the beach is **The Basin**, a small sheltered cove with a right-hander which breaks over the rocky bottom on the north side of the swimming pool. A fast, right-hand wall, finishing in a bonecrunching, fin-snapping shore break. Works only in N to NE swells and S to SW winds, at high tides. On the south side of the swimming pool (at the northern end of the beach) there's a left which

breaks over patchy reeef and sand. Best in NE to SE swells and N to W winds. Right in front of the clubhouse — and often inside the flagged area — there's usually a sandbank which can produce quality lefts and rights, but there is usually a strong rip bordering the sandbank.

On smaller days good peaky lefts and rights can be found down the beach to the hospital, depending mainly on sandbank quality. One particular area — known as **Cooks Terrace** — is accessible down the cliff in front of the hospital and has consistent, uncrowded peaks, especially on glassy mornings and offshore winds.

Warriewood is a relatively narrow beach which attracts a lot of swell, offering protection from S to SW winds and consistently providing a decent rideable wave. On big days, a right breaks from the southern point down the beach; on small days a left runs into the rip in the south corner. The north end of the beach occasionally turns on good lefts and rights, depending on swell and sand conditions.

Turremetta Point is the home of one of Sydney's most recent sewage outlets and produces some good lefts and short rights in N to NE swells at a break known as **Sheepstation** or Little

Greg Anderson attacks the Narrabeen left

*In winter when the crisp westerlies blow and there's a decent east swell,
North Narrabeen can have some of the best lefts on the Sydney coast*

GUY FINLAY

PETER CRAWFORD

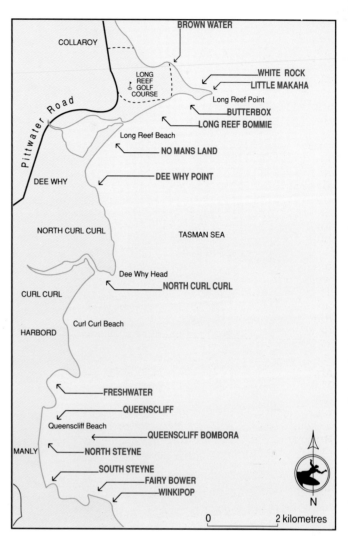

Top *High density home units obscure the beach south of Narrabeen. The left breaking outside is near a spot called 'Tea Gardens'.* **Above** *Tea Gardens, from the north*

Narrabeen. Access is difficult and the beach is unpatrolled, so recommended only for more experienced surfers.

Commonly acknowledged as the most consistent wave in Sydney, **North Narrabeen** is a rivermouth surf break which can turn out beach breaks of exceptional quality. Narrabeen Lagoon empties into the ocean at the far northern end (also known as 'Shark Alley') and provides a steady flow of sand for the banks which make this classic left so consistent. The beach is exposed to most available swell, particularly from the SE, and usually works best in a solid E to NE swell. On smaller days, the Alley has a peak with good lefts and rights: the rights can be excellent in SE swells and NW to NE winds. There is always a fast-moving rip in the northern corner of the beach and surfers are constantly pulling unsuspecting campers (from the nearby camping area) out of the water just before they disappear around the point. The name 'Narrabeen' comes from the story of a local Aboriginal woman of the same name who once travelled a great distance through the surrounding bush to bring a message of importance to the first white settlers in the area. Her story was, in my childhood, depicted in a huge mural on the wall of the local milk bar in Waterloo Street.

The area has undergone substantial change since the first attempts to reshape the shores, dunes and hills surrounding Narrabeen Lake, the source of North Narrabeen's famous sandbanks. At one time trees completely covered the sandy peninsula dividing the lake and the ocean, but now it is suffering an infestation of high-rise development. Warringah Shire Council is currently investigating a proposal to build a breakwall at Narrabeen Point to avoid the cost of continual silting up of the mouth of the lake. Such proposals ignore the real value of North Narrabeen as a surf break, one of the best beach breaks to be found anywhere in the world and one that must be preserved.

The Point at North Narrabeen produces a left with one of the hairiest take-offs in Sydney. A rock ledge stands up swell from almost any direction into a short, pitching and mean barrel, which can link up with the left in the centre of the beach on classic days.

Halfway down the beach to Collaroy is a break known as **Tea Gardens**, sometimes producing an excellent, uncrowded wave. It is very open to swell and wind, so works best in offshore winds and only when the sandbanks are established. Otherwise it's Closeout City. Many spots of this beach can turn on quality breaks when the banks are there.

Collaroy provides an ideal learner's wave, especially in the big southerly swells, so it's sometimes referred to as Powderpuff Point. It's gently sloping bottom provides easy waves in most conditions and often turns on quality beach breaks. NE swells here also tend to create Closeout City. Access is easy, with local shops close at hand. The point has a gently sloping rock bottom and produces small, peeling rights. The sharp rocks near the shore need to watched, as well as the accompanying rip. Ideal when swell is big and from the SE, with S to W winds.

Just outside the pool is a more advanced break called **The Kick**, which produces a hollower wave. Further along the rocky shoreline towards Long Reef are several reef breaks known as **The Natural, Brownwater, Fisherman's** and **White Rock**. All these breaks are relatively inaccessible (and unpredictable), breaking over lava reef, so recommended for experienced surfers only. Best conditions are a big NE to SE swell and SW to S winds.

The **Long Reef** area of Sydney's northern beaches offers a wide selection of reef and beach breaks that work in a wide variety of swell and wind conditions. There are plenty of reef breaks to be found in this area, which can produce powerful waves on their day; however all of them have difficult access. The best known include Little Makaha, Butterbox and The Bommie.

At the NE tip of the reef is a break called **Little Makaha**, but access is very difficult. The Little Makaha reef lifts almost any swell, before the waves die out again in deeper water, but is a disjointed wave unless the swell is over 3 metres. It tends to be a scary spot; best in SE swells and SW winds. **Butterbox** and **The Bommie** are best on a 1.5 metre plus S to SE swell and NE winds. Butterbox, situated on the SE corner of Long Reef and requiring a long walk in from the car park, can turn on excellent lefts. **The Bommie** is formed in a series of undulating reefs and the bigger the swell, the further out it breaks. The depth of water off the reef is critical and mid to low tides tend to produce the best waves, depending on swell size.

The long beach that stretches from Long Reef to Dee Why often turns on quality beach breaks, the northern end of the beach offering excellent protection from the nor'-easters. The section in the centre of this stretch of beach is known as **No Man's Land**, which tends to be relatively uncrowded (because of the walk in) and can turn on some good fun waves in swells from S to SE, particularly in offshore winds.

Dee Why is another of Sydney's best known beaches, mainly for the point break. But Dee Why offers several options. In the southern corner of the beach (**Kiddies Corner**) there's usually a great learner's wave in the protected cove with a gently sloping bottom. Take care, however, of the rip which runs out along the rocks. Up the beach (north) is a break known as **Dee Why Centre**, which occasionally produces classic rights on big SE to S swells, peeling toward's No Man's Land. Almost always a good left here, but often a heavy closeout finish. Dependent on banks and best in S to W winds.

Dee Why Point is one of the great point breaks of Sydney, but this wave is not recommended for powderpuffs. If you survive the heavy take-off at 'The Chair' (which is very close to the rocks) you will find you're in 'The Suck-up', which offers either a spectacular barrel or a bonecrunching wipeout, but you might find you have to back door it. This wave has a thick and unforgiving lip and, in big S swells and SW to S winds, offers a truly spectacular sight from the

Above *The Long Reef golf course frames a busy scene of surfing recreation. Wavesailors utilise Long Reef's exposed swells in ever increasing numbers, hang-gliders and model aeroplane enthusiasts take up air space on the cliff and surfers can almost always find a good wave on the adjacent rock shelves*

Above *No Man's Land.* **Below** *Dee Why Point*

viewing gallery on the point and in the pool. It tends to be easier to paddle out from the beach than risk a dangerous (and possibly embarrassing) entry off the rocks. The greatest hazard you face here is likely to be Dad, out on his new surf ski cracking a big one from deep on the shoulder.

The beaches from Curl Curl to Manly tend not only to be more crowded than those further north but also more polluted, especially when the winds are S to SE. It's much cleaner when the winds are NE. **North 'Curlie'** is ideally protected from the summer nor'-easters and can produce quality waves on its day. Even on the smallest days, there's always a fun wave to be found here, with plenty of competition from the local juniors, and it can also hold size on the outside banks in bigger swells. The middle of the beach is more open to the wind, but can be good on offshore days.

South Curlie is exposed to most available swell and wind (and pollution in SE winds) and the waves are usually powerful, with a tricky rip in the corner. At its best South Curlie produces good rights from outside the rocks down the beach, with a left-hand shore break.

Harbord, also known as Freshwater, is a small beach which offers maximum protection from the nor'-easters and was the site of the Duke's famous surfing demonstration in 1915. Open to swell and wind from the SE, it gets a bit 'woofy' when the wind is S to SE and carrying pollution from the North Head sewage treatment works. When it works Harbord can produce good left and right peaks in the south corner, the left running into the rocks. Tends

Below *Merrick Davis slashes his weight through a Queenscliff shorebreak.* **Right** *Damien Hardman at North Steyne*

to work best in an E swell and NE to W winds. There are occasional good waves at the north end of the beach, depending on sandbanks; a good learner's wave and a popular body surfing beach.

The once great beach of **Manly**, for so long one of Sydney's tourist attractions, is sadly now one of the city's most polluted beaches. But it still produces some great waves.

At the very north end of Manly beach is **Queenscliff**, another rivermouth set-up, with plenty of sand build-up on the banks. Every now and then there's a good left off the point, but rights into the rocks are more common with a strong rip along the rocks. This wave can be excellent, depending mainly on sandbank conditions. There's also a good left several hundred metres south of the point and usually a good, reforming shore break. Queenscliff Boardriders Club tend to be very active on this break and so it should be approached with caution.

Around 1 kilometre off the beach at Queenscliff is a huge, open ocean wave — virtually unridden these days — known as the **Queenscliff Bombora**, which breaks on swells over 3 metres and is a true test of anyone's courage.

North Steyne, situated just south of Queenscliff (although there's no clear border) can turn on some excellent beach breaks but also goes through times of horrible closeouts. Generally better on higher tides and during times of good sandbanks and offshore winds, North Steyne can produce excellent waves. When the swell is giant you'll usually find protection from the south winds and a good reform shore break here, though rips can be a problem. Usually best in E to NE swells and W to S winds.

The **South Steyne** section of the beach often features a good left-hander, running into the rocks, with a rip at the south end. It also offers a good peak on the outside, when the swell is big to huge.

Fairy Bower is one Sydney's best, and most famous, point breaks. The wave is accessible from the beach at the southern end of Manly, via the car park at the top of the headland. Access is difficult, parking a problem, rip offs likely. The reef around the point is strewn with boulders which have an insatiable appetite for foam, fibreglass and flesh. Not a break for the unwary, even if it looks small from the car park. Breaks very hard and best on 2 metre plus NE to ESE swells. On bigger SE to S swells, the wave tends to wrap around the point and lose power, spilling wide of the inside section of the reef (called 'Racecourse'). The outside take-off pivots around a suckey rock, known as 'Surge Rock', which has been known to suck bone-dry on big swells and low tides. Despite this, the wave tends to be better at lower tides. For experienced surfers only.

Outside, and around the corner, is **Winkipop**, which links through to the Bower on favourable days. A heavy, dredging take-off and thick lip provide the clifftop gallery with amusing spectacles of the inexperienced surfers disappearing over the falls, embedded in the lip. A short wave with the rocks very close: one of the hollowest waves on the north side of Sydney. Best in E to SE swells and W to S winds. For experienced surfers only.

Further around the point is an extremely hairy spot called Blue-Fish Point which has been surfed, but only by madmen years ago. These days no-one regularly braves this awesome reef break

Top *Barton Lynch takes the drop at Queensie bommie.*
Above *The Norfolk Island pines along the Manly beachfront have been losing their battle with pollution. However Manly can still turn on some great waves.* **Below** *Fairy Bower and the wrapping nature of the swell can be seen from the air.*

The city beaches

These beaches, stretching from Bondi to Maroubra, service a huge eastern suburbs population and tend to be crowded most of the year. Quality waves are found here, although with two sewage outlets in this section of coast (Ben Buckler and Malabar) all these beaches suffer from pollution in some wind and current conditions.

Bondi Beach is Sydney's most famous beach, which can produce quality waves but is sadly one of the most polluted beaches anywhere in Australia. The beach faces directly SE which gives it access to all available S to SE swell, but little NE swell. **North Bondi** is well protected from the NE winds and has gently sloping banks, which makes it ideal for beginners and families but rarely does it produce any quality waves. No surfcraft are allowed. The break at **South Bondi** usually separates on two or three sandbanks, especially in winter. The sandbanks tend to deteriorate in summer, but when the swell is SE and the winds N to NE, Bondi can turn on some excellent beach breaks. The walk to and from the surf during the summer months, particularly at the south end, across a carpet of sizzling flesh can be hazardous, hectic and heat-inducing. Works best in E to SE swells to 1.5 metres, but occasionally holds rights and lefts to 2.5 metres.

In the midst of Sydney's most urban stretch of coast, Tamarama, or 'Tamma' to the locals, remains a bastion for bodysurfers and boogie boarders. Surfboards are only allowed out there before the flags go up at 7am

SEAN DAVEY

Just south of Bondi is **McKenzies Bay,** with a very small beach that can disappear completely at times (usually after big storms) but occasionally produces good, wedgy lefts and smaller rights. A short wave, which works best in E to SE swells and mid to high tides. The break is reasonably protected from NE winds, so it can be good in summer when the surf is small.

Tamarama is one of the most popular sunbaking spots among the city beaches (also known as 'Glamarama'), which also provides small fun waves over a left-hand reef break. The beach is restricted to Boogies and Coolites which means you'll see some of the oldest Coolite riders in the world here, especially during summer. There's also a body-surfer's left off the north point and a few peaks in the middle. A small and exposed beach, Tamarama picks up all available swell and can be dangerous any time the swell gets over 2 metres.

At the southern end of **Bronte Beach** there's a right-hand reef break known as **Bronte Reef,** which can turn on excellent waves especially in winter. The wave breaks over a patchy sand and reef bottom and the wave usually works best on mid to high tides and E to SE swells in SW to W winds. In the middle of the beach there's also a left-hander, which breaks into the channel.

Thomsons Bay is an extremely suckey peak, breaking left and right over a dangerously shallow rock ledge. The left is the slightly safer way to go. Works best in big SE to NE swells, and W to SW winds. Surf this break only at high tides and only if you are an experienced surfer.

Coogee Beach has limited access to swell, as Wedding Cake Island shuts out most of the action. A small reef at the southern of the beach can produce small rights, but only when the general swell conditions are big. **The Southy** is an offshore reef, situated between Wedding Cake Island and the

Above *The Southy might not be the most original name for a reef break at the southern end of Coogee but in big swells it provides adrenaline pumping drops for locals sick of surfing city beach breaks.* **Below** *Out off Coogee Beach, Wedding Cake Island on rare occasions produces rideable waves for the more experienced locals.* **Bottom** *Matt Elks at Bronte*

109

southern tip of Coogee Beach. An extremely powerful wave which only breaks in big S to SE swells, it is best at mid tides and W to SW winds. A ten minute paddle from Coogee Beach will get you out there, but only experience will get you back.

Tucked quietly into **Lurline Bay,** just north of Maroubra, is a heavy reef break which holds the largest waves found anywhere on the south side of Sydney, has a liking for inexperienced surfers, and a reputation for breaking boards and bodies. This ferocious right-hander breaks over a bottom consisting of three separate reefs which start working when the swell is 2 metres and then the waves break on the outer reefs as they get bigger. Access over the rocks and barnacles (there is no beach) can be hazardous; getting back out of the water can be a nightmare. An ultimate challenge but fitness and experience are a must. Best in S to SE swells and S to W winds. Low tides are usually required, unless the swell is humungous. Longer boards recommended.

Maroubra Beach is one of the most consistent beaches on the south side of Sydney, and regularly produces quality peak and rip breaks. At the northern end of the beach, a consistent right-hander breaks into 'The Toilet Bowl', which is best in S to SE swells. When the swell is E to NE, there's usually a quality left, often real perfection, when the banks are there. Winter is usually the best time as the banks tend to deteriorate during summer. In S to SE winds, effluent from the Malabar Treatment Works makes this beach one of the most 'woofy' in Sydney. Maroubra Boardriders Club, a source of many quality surfers over the years, is active on the beach.

The break known as **Maroubra Reef** is a hollow right-hander, which breaks over an irregular rock bottom at the south end of the beach. Only works in E to NE swells and mid to high tides. Can be an excellent wave but often inconsistent.

Malabar or **'Club Med'** as it is affectionately known by locals, can produce good waves but it would have to be the most polluted water anywhere in Australia.

Right *Maroubra's beach breaks can hold true size. Here kneeboarder David Parkes wraps it off the bottom.*
Far right *The reef at the south end of Maroubra holds challenging powerful waves on larger swells*

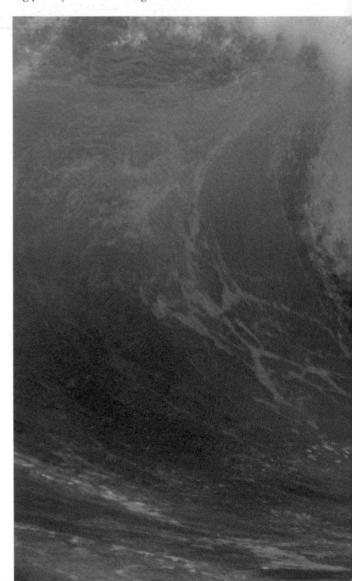

Top *'The Stormy' showing clean morning offshore conditions. Maroubra attracts surfers from all over Sydney as the graffiti indicates.* **Above** *On many East to North-East swells Maroubra's lefts can be the best on the Sydney stretch.*
Right *Maroubra's 'Toilet Bowl' sometimes turns on waves that are cleaner than the name would suggest*

110

SEAN DAVEY

GLENN DUFFUS

SEAN DAVEY

The southern beaches

Botany Bay creates a natural separation from the rest of the Sydney coastline. This southern stretch of beaches has consistently produced some of Sydney's hottest surfers, the most famous being Cronulla's favourite son Mark Occhilupo. As Cronulla remains the only metropolitan beach accessible by rail, surfers are attracted from all over Sydney to these beaches, which tends to make the waves crowded and competitive.

Voodoo is one of the more popular and gnarly lefts on the south side of Sydney. The wave starts with a radical suck-up as it jacks incredibly over a shallow rock ledge then walls out over a kelpy bottom. Leaving the surf in big swells can be a problem and summer months tend to be the most consistent. For experienced surfers only. Access is by car — preferably a four-wheel drive.

Marys Reef Boatharbour is an area offering a variety of small reef breaks over a kelp bottom, but access is difficult, requiring a boat or a long paddle. Works best in small NE to SE swells and offshore winds, and is an excellent escape from the madness of other spots. For adventurous, experienced surfers.

A walk or four-wheel drive over the sandhills at Kurnell to **Green Hills** is often the answer to crowded surf and sand. This area offers a variety of small beach breaks which tend to be consistent all year round. Works best in a S swell and NE to W winds.

The beach breaks at **Cronulla** stretch from Green Hills in the north to The Alley in the southern corner of the beach, with the quality dependent on the condition of the sandbanks; it can vary from excellent lefts and rights right up the beach to Closeout City. Cronulla Beach faces south-east so it is exposed to all the swells from the south but tends to miss a lot of the north swell during summer. Consequently, the waves tend to be better during the winter months.

The best known of these beach breaks are **Elouera** (at the north end), **The Wall** (just south of Elouera) and **The Alley**, which is about the only place on the beach you'll get the NE swells. There's also a left, just outside the pool, which works in bigger swells. Just south of Cronulla Point is another break, known as **Sandshoes** because of the sea urchins which inhabit the weedy ledge over which the wave breaks. A short right-hander, but any more than three surfers and it's packed.

Cronulla Point is the most spectacular point break on the south side of Sydney. The reef consists of two major break-ups. First Reef is a hollow fun wave which breaks over a relatively flat rock bottom. The real face of the point is Second Reef, a rock ledge 30 metres out from First Reef which comes into play when the swell is about 2 metres. But it's not till the point gets up to 3 metres that it shows its true form, jacking, pitching and barrelling along the ledge. Hawaiians have called this wave a cross between Backdoor and inside Sunset. When conditions are over 4 metres, a third reef comes into play. This wave has a habit of breaking boards and lacerating bodies: definitely only for experienced surfers. Best on mid to low tides in big SE swells and W to SW winds.

Above *An unfortunate time to blow it for this surfer as Voodoo pours on the magic.* **Below** *Cronulla Point.*

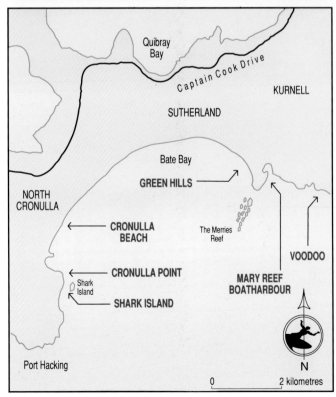

Shark Island is a barnacle-encrusted outcrop of rock, some 100 metres south-east of Cronulla Point and only visible at low tides. It is home to one of the roundest barrels you'll find anywhere; the real jaws of Mother Nature. The main wave is the right, though there's an equally hollow left. The right peaks up at the southern corner of the island and then horseshoes onto a rock known (and respected) as Surge Rock, which is always in the mood to lacerate given half the chance.

Bundeena is not a consistent surf spot by any stretch of the imagination. Access is via Port Hacking, near Gunnamatta Bay at Darook Park (a popular sailboarding spot) near the Department of Fisheries building, and then a paddle out into the middle of the bay — way out. The break works best on very big N to E swells but sometimes catches humungous SE swells. The swell has to be really big and the tide low, and it's best in light westerly winds.

The first part of the break is off Cabbage Tree Point, the second across the sandbanks in the middle of the bay. Predominantly a right (but occasionally producing a short left), it runs way down the sandbank which is formed regularly inside Port Hacking. The wave is extremely powerful and although it breaks over a sand bottom it is not a place for the inexperienced. Locals say it breaks with the power of a reef break, dredging up a merciless thick lip. Like all rivermouths, this place is very sharky and local fishermen reckon the surfers are crazy just going in the water. These sandbanks form a hazard for boats and dredging is a constant process, sometimes ruining the sandbanks for surfers. There are currently plans to build a breakwall to curb these drifting sands.

Top *Elouera beach break.* **Above** *When Cronulla lit up for the international surfing world nearly everyone was impressed... except the local council.* **Below left** *Shark Island juice.* **Below** *Martin Potter amongst some Shark Island power*

Getting it right. *If you notice how quickly this surfer's trail rips back up the face behind him you get an idea how steep and dangerous Shark Island can get, but with rides like this as the lure plenty of surfers are prepared to take the risk*

Shark Island, getting it wrong. There are many easy-to-discover methods of getting it wrong at Shark Island. **Right** *Surfer Number 1 has either caught a rail in the thick face of the wave or he has spotted the biggest lobster he's ever seen and he's off to get lunch (no doubt about who is getting lunched).* **Below** *Surfer Number 2 has been smart enough to enter the face of the wave rather than head butt the rock bottom, however a terrible trip over the falls is likely to follow.* **Below right** *Surfer Number 3 has bailed out the back of the wave where he knows it's not too shallow. Extra points for style, especially the pointed toes.*

SOUTH FROM SYDNEY

To those who surf the area regularly, the New South Wales south coast represents one of the richest sections of surfing coastline in the world, offering a variety of long point breaks, rivermouth perfection and quality beach breaks. In the explosion of surfing in the 1960s every surfer dreamed of those uncrowded country waves and almost invariably headed north (from Sydney) in search of warmth and waves, leading to the mythology of breaks like Crescent Head, Angourie and The Pass. But silently, more and more surfers headed south in search of waves, and found them; particularly as board design and performance criteria demanded hollower, faster waves.

The south coast is truly rich in ferocious barrels, some of which break almost square. There are also a couple of rivermouth breaks which, when they work, are as good as you'll find anywhere in the world. So jealously guarded were these waves by the locals — many of whom had moved into the area just to surf the waves — that when a photo of the Pambula rivermouth break (showing endless perfect barrels) appeared in *Tracks* magazine in 1981, the locals went looking for the photographer who had released the photo even though there had been no indication where the wave was. Just showing outsiders how good the south coast could get was enough.

The south coast is littered with great reef breaks

PETER SIMONS

TERRY WILLCOCKS

The Royal National Park

Just south of Sydney is Australia's first national park, 15 000 hectares which includes some 20 kilometres of coastline, backed by high cliffs and extensive forest and heathlands, offering many surfing options. The only serviced camping areas are at the northern end of the park, at Bonnie Vale near Bundeena.

The most popular beach in the park is **Garie Beach**, at the end of winding roads and native bush scenery. Some 15 kilometres south of Cronulla, it offers an assortment of fine beach and reef breaks. There's often an excellent left at the northern end of the beach, in E to NE swells, which peels across a patchy sand and reef bottom. This break is at its best in NE to W winds. The rest of the beach is sand, except for a rocky shelf at the southern end of the beach which sometimes produces a small right. Garie is a great place to get away from the city. The waves tend to be consistent all year round and it works in NE to SE swells; best in NW to SW winds and mid to low tides. Access is by car, through the park — there's ample parking near the clubhouse.

North Era is another of the quality breaks to be found inside the Royal National Park. Access is gained by a 20 minute walk south from the Garie Beach car park. After walking for 15 minutes, you'll come across a tiny beach (**Little Garie**) with no more than a 50 metre stretch of sand. In swells up to 2 metres from the SE to E you'll find right-handers off the southern point of this beach, at mid to high tide. A further 5 minute walk brings you to

A useful lookout

Around 1.5 kilometres from the Garie Beach turn-off, on the right, is the Governor Game Lookout. This spot looks down on North Era and offers the chance to judge whether the waves are worth the walk. Also, don't forget to take food and drink with you if you're planning more than a quick surf.

PETER SIMONS

118

North Era, where a quality left-hand point break works in NE to SE swells up to 2 metres. A secluded spot, with few people, just the odd fishing or holiday shacks. At the southern end of the beach, right-hand waves (which can get very hollow at times) are found in a straight south swell forming off the rocky platform at the point. In the middle of the beach, peaky waves — with right and lefts — are common when the swell is below 2 metres.

East of the small town of Otford lies a tiny reefy bay known as **Bulga Bay**. Access is via a narrow goat track which drops over the 150 metre cliff offering an adrenalin-rich crawl to the bottom. A little mountain goat or skydiver in the blood can be helpful. At the southern end of the bay is a short suckey right-hander (best in SE swell), breaking over a shallow rock platform. At the northern end of the bay a short left breaks over a rock and kelp bottom in NE swell conditions. Best in swell to 2 metres and NE to S winds. The elusive 'shack men of Bulga' can often be observed around their shacks at the base of the cliff, where they are reported to spend all their spare time. And don't forget to leave some energy (or Staminade) for the horrendous walk back up the cliff.

Above *Bulga Bay seascape.* **Below** *Terry Richardson at one of his south coast haunts.*

Left *Garie Beach, so close to Sydney and often with perfect empty beach breaks*

THE COAL COAST

The high cliffs of Stanwell Park mark our entry into this coal-rich section of the New South Wales coast, which has created an industrial base for the coal centres of Wollongong and Port Kembla. The Stanwell Tops area was the site of Australia's first adventures in flight: it was here that Lawrence Hargrave conducted his early experiments and, in 1894, managed to get 5 metres off the ground using a train of four box kites. More recently, hang-gliding enthusiasts have adopted the area.

The first beach in this section of coast is **Coalcliff,** which offers several surfing options in varying conditions. At the southern end, around 200 metres off the beach, a bommie works in N to NE swells to 2.5 metres. This wave peels as a gnarly left-hander, which grinds some 100 metres down the beach. At the southern end, behind the pool, a short right sucks onto a shallow ledge. This wave can be deceptive: you may take off on a 1 metre wave only to find yourself pulling into a square barrel over 2 metres — what some would call an 'in and out' barrel. Only breaks at low tide and in SE to E swells under 2 metres. This can be a fickle wave, best in W to SW winds. In the middle of the beach a variety of peaks can be found in swells under 2 metres.

Scarborough Beach has a variety of beach breaks in swells up to 2 metres. Best in NW to SW winds.

After a period of prevailing north winds and swell — usually during the summer months — the sandbanks at the southern end of **Nombara Beach** can produce quality rights in a new SE to S swell up to 2 metres. April and May are usually the best months, after the long summer sand build up. Best in SW to S winds.

At the southern end of **Coaldale Beach** is a right-hander that breaks when the sand build-up is established. This tends to be an average break at most times but produces quality waves when the conditions are right. At the northern end of Coaldale Beach is a rock platform known as **Thommos** which produces a left-hander, breaking over a patchy reef and sand bottom. This wave only works in strong NE swells, from 2 to 4 metres and can produce quality waves in the right conditions.

North of Austinmer there's a reef break known as **Headlands**, a real test of skill and courage and a true sister to Shark Island. Breaking over a very sharp and irregular bottom (with a few barnacles to tickle your fancy if given half the chance), Headlands is an

Above *Stanwell Park.* **Below** *Sandon Point on the kind of day most surfers would be in too much of a hurry to stop and take this photo from Bulli*

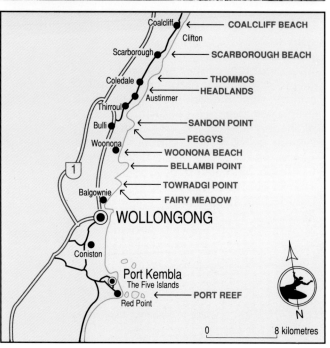

unforgiving wave. When the swell gets over 1.5 metres the take-off is vertical as the wave jacks on the north-east corner of the reef then pitches all the way down the length of the reef. Headlands works on NE to E swells to 3 metres and is best in NE to E swells. High tides only, and this wave is off limits to everyone but the most experienced.

Right in the middle of **Austinmer Beach** a good right-hander can often be found which tends to work best in a small NE swell; a great summer fun wave. In an E to SE swell (up to 2 metres) another right often breaks at the southern end of the beach. Best in NW to SW winds, though a light nor'-easter can be tolerated without great loss of wave quality.

On the north side of the 'tackle-buster', Sandon Point, lies **Thirroul**, which in SE to E swells can provide a respectable right-hander in the southern corner. The rest of the beach offers an assortment of right and left beach breaks, which work best in offshore winds and swells under 2 metres.

Sandon Point is considered to be one of the best point breaks anywhere on the New South Wales coast, holding swells over 4 metres with distinction and real power. The wave can work in swells as small as 1 metre, but it's when the swell conditions get over 2 metres that Sandon shows off its magic and muscle. A mean wave at times, Sandon has a habit of snapping boards and holding underwater those who exceed their limit. The wave peels right over an ever-changing weed and cunji bottom, with sea eggs layering the inside section. Ever since a local surfer drowned at this break some years ago, its power has been held in great respect. Tends to be best in big S to SE winter swells, with S to SW winds and mid to low tides. Recommended for cautious, experienced surfers.

Just south of Sandon Point a peninsula of rock, known as **Peggys,** juts out some 600 metres into the ocean. On the north side of this rock shelf, some 400 metres out from the beach, is a right-hander which sometimes has the power of ten waves and offers a ride with changing character, lifting and dropping as it winds down the reef. Best in a strong SE to E swell and SW to SE winds. On the south side of the peninsula is the break known far and wide as **Banzai**: an extremely fast and very hollow barrel and

a testing challenge for those with the heart to tackle her unforgiving power. Close to Banzai is another left which is 'almost' too close to the rocks to be surfed. A gnarly and dangerous wave, which works best in 2 to 3 metre swells and NE to NW winds.

Probably Wollongong's finest beach break, **Woonona** picks up NE swell better than anywhere else within 10 kilometres, north or south. It has lefts and rights in a variety of peaks, barrels and down the line-type waves. Best in swells from 1 to 2.5 metres and better in NW to SW winds. A great summer beach break.

Further south **Bellambi Point** has rights in small E to SE swells and there's a bommie about 250 metres out from the centre of the beach which has awesome lefts in moderate NE to SE swells and light NW to SW winds.

The Wollongong beaches are divided either side of Flagstaff Point. To the north of the boat harbour (on the northern side of Flagstaff Point) is **North Beach**, where there are often waves to be found right in front of North Beach International Hotel; lefts and rights over a sand on reef bottom. Works in SE to NE swell to 2 metres and best in SW to W winds. This is a popular beach, with board manufacturers and surf shops nearby, so it tends to get crowded.

South Beach is on the southern side of Flagstaff Point and it gets good beach breaks in NE to SE swells under 2 metres and is best in NW winds. The point offers South Beach protection from the summer nor'-easters, which means it gets very crowded at those times.

Towradgi and **Fairy Meadow** sometimes have good beach breaks in small NE to SE swells, depending on the availability and condition of the sandbanks. Best in NW to SW winds.

Around Port Kembla there are reef and sand breaks that maintain the quality waves of the coal coast at its southern extremity. South of the harbour, towards Windang (and visible from the car park out near the end of Red Point), **Port Reef** is a classic hollow wave which works in E to SE swells and is best in NW to NE winds.

Below *While the tankers queue up outside Port Kembla the boys go surfing at Woonona*

PETER SIMONS

THE SOUTH COAST

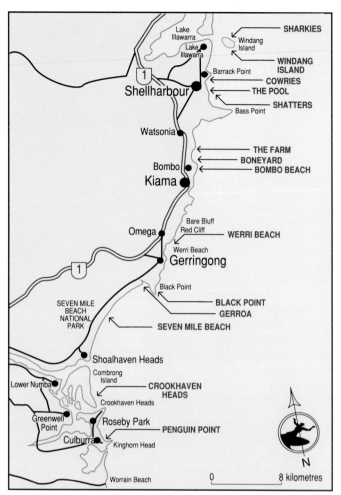

S outh from the coalfields of Wollongong and Port Kembla, the true character of the south coast — sandy beaches and rolling hills — becomes apparent. This area has become a popular tourist and retirement centre and the coast offers a variety of protected bays and rocky headlands, with good fishing and great surfing.

Some 10 kilometres south of Port Kembla and straight out from the entrance to Lake Illawarra is **Windang Island**, which offers a great left wrapping down the southern side of the island and has a well-deserved reputation as the premier big wave spot on the south coast. A small, grass-topped and cliff-ringed island, with access via a narrow sandy spit, Windang has a big jacking take-off close to the rocks on the southern side of the island, grinding and peeling with long workable walls towards Warilla Beach. Works in big NE to SE swells and best in NE to NW winds at lower tides, Windang is capable of holding waves to 5 metres and is only for experienced big wave surfers; its power and size can be intimidating as are the committed locals. On the northern side of the island is **Sharkies,** a patchy reef some 50 metres offshore which offers quality lefts and rights. It breaks in most swell conditions and is best in W to SW winds.

Shellharbour has surf beaches either side of its small horseshoe-shaped bay and boat harbour. On the northern side of Shellharbour's northern point there's a hollow right-hander called **Cowries** which breaks over a shallow rock ledge in E to SE swells; best in SW winds. The point at the southern end of the bay has breaks on both sides. On the north side, there's a good right called **The Pool** which works in E to SE swells and is best in SW winds. The break on the south side of the point has a habit of destroying boards, hence the name **Shatters**. This powerful left breaks along the point in towards the beach and works in NE to SE swells and is best in W to NW winds.

Further south **Bass Point** protects the rocky coastline to its north from all but the biggest SE swells. Along this shore there are a couple of reef breaks and bommies which work on big SE and moderate E to NE swells and are best in S to SW winds.

Heading south towards Kiama there are a couple of spots which are accessed through private property, so good manners are a must; shut the gates, don't chase the cows and no wheelies. The first and best of these spots is a break called **The Farm**, which lies in

Dotted along the nook-and-cranny coast in southern New South Wales are numerous reefs which are sensitive to swell changes but perfect on their day

PETER SIMONS

a small protected bay accessed via a turn-off about 3 kilometres south of Bass Point. The beach here tends to have excellent sandbanks, and quality beach breaks can be had in SE swells to 2 metres and are best in W to NW winds. Just south of The Farm is a good left-hander called **Mystics**, which works in NE swells and is best in N to NW winds; but remember, this is private property so ask permission to enter and shut the gates behind you.

Closer to Kiama, just 2 kilometres north of the town, is a break known as **Boneyard**, which is reached via a winding road back north from the turn-off. This secluded bay is surrounded by steep cliffs and has a rocky outcrop about 100 metres off the shore. The reef holds big S to SE swells and is best in SE to SW winds.

Just north of Kiama the highway overlooks a long sandy beach called **Bombo**, which sometimes gets good beach breaks in either the southern or northern corners. This beach picks up any available swell and is best up to 2 metres in SW to NW winds. Closer to town and breaking the rocks next to the pool just north of Blowhole Point is a left known as **The Pool**, which works in large NE to SE swells and is best in SW to W winds. South of the blowhole car park is a heavy-breaking left called **The Wedge** which grinds along the rocks towards Storm Bay, the small beach visible from the highway. Works in SE to NE swells and best in NW to SW winds.

Heading south from Kiama the Princes Highway winds through lush, green, undulating farmland, where dairy cows graze right down to the coast. The coastal regions through here have a series of headlands and secluded bays but access is difficult and usually involves a long walk.

North of Gerringong the long stretch of **Werri Beach** picks up plenty of swell and can have good beach breaks, especially at the northern end, where there's usually a good left-hand sandbank; best in N to NW winds. **Werri Point**, at the southern end of the beach, gets quality right-hand barrels and long walls in clean NE to SE swells. The wave breaks off a shallow reef right off the end of the point and can be powerful, so inexperienced surfers should stay clear — a head plant into the reef here could have dire consquences.

Above Near Kiama, Boneyard didn't get its name without reason. **Below** South coast quality

PETER CRAWFORD

PETER CRAWFORD

Geroa, to the south of Gerringong, overlooks the long stretch of Seven Mile Beach, but the quality waves are found out off **Black Point** at the northern end of the beach. The best of these breaks is a long-walled left at the end of the headland which works in SE swells and N to NW winds. Around the point to the north there are left and right reef breaks which work in smaller NE to SE swells and are best in N to NW winds.

Seven Mile Beach has become a popular spot in recent years with a hot crew of sailboarders who are seen regularly out there ripping the place to pieces with forward loops, barrel rolls and slashes, especially in strong nor'-easters.

Shoalhaven Heads has little to offer the travelling surfer, except for a right at the breakwater at the southern end of the beach at the mouth of the Shoalhaven River. Access is difficult (four-wheel drive over a rugged dirt track) and the effort is hardly worth it. Further south **Penguin Point**, at Culburra, often has a right on the north side of the point during big E to SE swells.

The Jervis Bay area offers a variety of options for surfers. **Plantation Point** (4 kilometres east of Vincentia) forms the southern headland to the bay and offers an excellent, though inconsistent, right-hander which only works on the biggest SE to E swells. Plantation Point is one of the places the locals turn to when everything else is closing out; best in S to SW winds. Inside Jervis Bay, at the mouth of Moona Moona Creek (near Huskisson), is an excellent right-hander which breaks off the point at the mouth of the creek and works in similar conditions to Plantation Point.

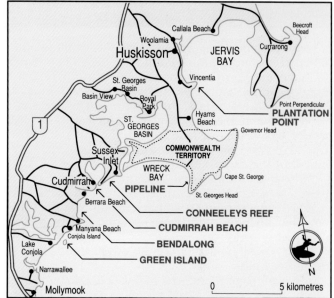

Top *Mark Occhilupo stretches into afternoon Pipeline.*
Below *Barton Lynch barrelled at Black Rock*

PETER CRAWFORD

Australia's only 'real' locals

South of Jervis Bay is Wreck Bay, the site of an Aboriginal settlement and home to one of the classic south coast waves. Right off Summercloud Cove is Pipeline, a perfect left-hand reef break that gained its name as a compliment and comparison with Hawaii's famous north shore break, though it's known by many other names including Black Rock, Summercloud or Wreck Bay. Pipeline is one of the hollowest and most photogenic waves in Australia, with surfing magazines dedicating many pages to its perfect barrels over the years. Pipeline features a thick and fast-moving peak, which pitches with surprising speed over the shallow, sea urchin-infested reef. It breaks left and right on smaller days, but only left when the swell gets over 2 metres. Pipeline spits out perfect barrels with monotonous regularity. The relatively short ride has surfers hungry for more and this break can get crowded on good days. Works on SE to S swells to 4 metres and best in NE winds.

Right *One of the most surfer envied pieces of New South Wales south coast real estate — the Aboriginal settlement at Wreck Bay.* **Below** *No question as to who the locals are here*

Michael Mackie showing how this spot earned its nick-name Pipeline

Mark Occhilupo slotted at Pipeline

Very short but very sweet. Summercloud Cove

Two bays to the west of Summercloud Cove is **Caves Beach**, a small sandy beach that often has good beach breaks in small south swells and N to NW winds. It's worth a look when Pipeline is too small or crowded.

Sussex Inlet, at the entrance to St Georges Basin (the turn-off is 3 kilometres south of Wandandian), is a popular holiday and retirement town, with **Bherwerre Beach** and **Cudmirrah Beach** offering a variety of peaky beach breaks in S to SE swells and W to N winds. There's also a good right and left reef break called **Conneeleys Reef**. Robert Conneeley was one of the earliest surfers here, but the reef was actually named after his father who had a fishing hut and set his craypots on this reef.

At Bendalong (11 kilometres from the highway along Red Head Road) you'll find a number of sand and reef breaks, scattered along the coast from Berrara south to Red Head. The area's big drawcard, however, is the quality beach breaks to be found on **Bendalong Beach** itself, which pick up most available swell and offers hollow peaky barrels in E to SE swells (to 2 metres) and almost any tide. It can get crowded but there are usually plenty of peaks along the beach.

At the mouth of Lake Conjola and south-east of Manyana Beach (5 kilometres from the turn-off at Yatteyattah), **Green Island** has long been respected for the quality of its left-handers, which peel off the southern end of the island. Breaking over a shallow reef (covered with sea urchins and weed), Green Island has a long, fast, take-off section before the wave wraps into deeper water towards the south-west tip of the island. Working on big SE to NE swells and

Below Richard Cram at Ulladulla. **Right** *Green Island*

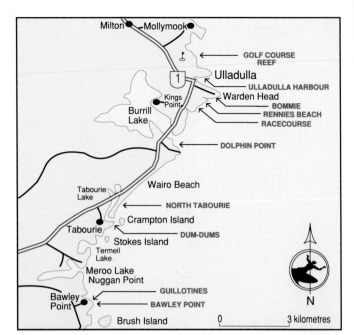

N to NW winds, Green Island is well worth checking out when the swell is up.

Just north of Ulladulla is a turn-off back north to Mollymook. A further turn-off through the middle of the golf course leads to a car park in front of **Golf Course Reef.** This reef produces excellent lefts with long hollow walls, breaking over a shallow bottom. Golf Course gets better as it gets bigger, holding up to 3 and 4 metres on SE to NE swells and best in W winds. It's a long paddle out, which can be quite punishing on big days.

South of the golf course is another break, which produces quality rights over an extremely shallow reef. This break is often just as good as Golf Course—

Above *Ulladulla.* **Below** *Richard Cram at Ulladulla Reef*

129

without the crowds — and offers hollow barrels to 2 and 3 metres as it grinds off close to the rocks and into the small bay. Works on smaller NE to SE swells and SW to NW winds.

Mollymook Beach is popular with tourists and a variety of surf craft are seen in its beach breaks, the quality of which depends on the availability and shape of the sandbanks. Bannisters Point, to the north, offers some protection from the nor'-easters and the beach is open to swells from E to SE, with N to W winds offering the best conditions.

For an unforgettable experience, turn off the Princes Highway in Ulladulla towards Warden Head Lighthouse. Follow the road to the car park overlooking a small beach to the south. Right off this point is the infamous **Ulladulla Bommie**, a thick, unforgiving right-hand reef break with a sucking, shifting peak and numerous heavy bowl sections. This wave works best on a heavy swell (to 4 metres) and a light NE wind. There are numerous locals who surf the wave (they're all hot) and plenty of raw power in the wave, as it breaks over a shallow rock bottom all too ready to chew up the unwary surfer. There are heaps of boils and ledges with strong rips: a true, all-round challenge. Definitely a break for experienced surfers only.

Further south of the car park, **Rennies Beach** offers a variety of breaks — a right-hand reef break in the southern corner, and left and right peaks up the beach. This break can turn on a fine wave, breaking over a sand-covered rock bottom; best on small days, mid tides, in a S to E swell (to 2 metres) and NW to NE winds.

Just south of Ulladulla take the turn-off at Racecourse Creek and follow it to the northern end of the beach where there's a hollow left-hand barrel known as **Racecourse**, which starts outside behind the rocks and breaks across to the beach. Racecourse can be a quality wave in NE to SE swells (to 1.5 metres) and W to NW winds. Good in summer, before the nor'-easter gets up.

Just over the bridge across Burrill Lake take the turn-off to **Dolphin Point** for an excellent left-

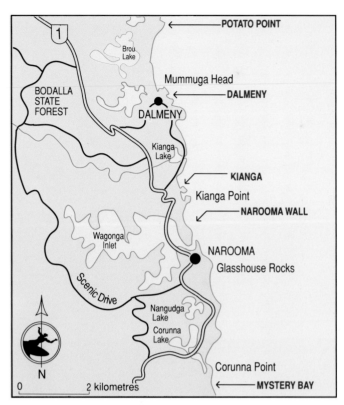

hander. Breaking left over a shallow, tapering ledge on the southern side of the point, Dolphin Point has a shifting take-off which sucks off the edge of the rock ledge and walls out with several hollow sections along the way. A changeable wave which works best in a NE to E swell (to 2 metres) and W to SW winds. A right can sometimes be had on the northern side of the point in smaller SE swells and NW winds. Peaky beach breaks can be found up the beach to the north in smaller SE to NE swells and NW to SW winds.

An offshore reef, combined with several excellent beach breaks, make **North Tabourie** a spot worth checking when the swell is at least 2 metres and the winds offshore (NW to SW). The outside reef jacks the

Left *Vetea David.* **Below** *Durras coastline*

TONY NOLAN

swell up into a series of shifting peaks, which can create great lefts and rights. The breaks are some distance from the car park, making vehicle break-ins and rip offs a constant problem.

On the southern side of Crampton Island (also known as Tabourie Island) is a small bay with a right-hand reef break called **Dum-Dums**. This is a fast, hollow wave breaking over a very shallow reef bottom, only surfable on certain tides (depending on sand build-up); it offers real quality when the sand between the island and the mainland has been chewed out. Best on a small NE to SE swell and NE to W winds, it is a good summer break when the swell is under 2 metres.

South of the island are a variety of sometimes good beach breaks, which work best in NE to SE swells (to 2 metres) and NE to SW winds. Lefts and rights; shifting peaks over a sandy bottom.

Around 20 minutes drive south of Ulladulla (and 252 kilometres south of Sydney) at Termeil, the Bawley Point turn-off is a 6 kilometre drive to a helluva wave. The point is an open flat area, with slabs of razor-sharp platforms which melt into the sea. The break known as **Bawley Point** is situated at the outer platform and will hold swell to 3 metres or more. The wave is a short and powerful one, starting very close to the flesh-eating outer platform and barrelling with the punch of Mike Tyson. Getting out of the water when the swell is over 2 metres can be as harrowing as the wave itself. Definitely for experienced surfers only.

On big days when the swell is 3 metres plus those with big hearts turn to **Guillotines,** an awesome experience. This is truly a mean mother of a wave, with jaws as hungry as a pack of starving white pointers. This spot was named after its habit of

Matt Cattle

decapitating those surfers who, after taking the elevator drop, couldn't quite tuck inside quick enough. Peeling only metres from the dry rock ledge, the wave folds down the ledge taking the surfer closer and closer to disaster before a final deliverance back over the shoulder of the wave. The only place the wave can be ridden is behind the curtain of this square-jawed barrel, which requires liberal helpings of guts, skill and experience. Breaks best in large SE to NE swells and is best in S to SW winds. Take a spare leash for your heart.

Just north of Point Upright, on the Durras North Road (the turn-off is at East Lynne), take the turn to **Depot Beach**, a very pretty holiday settlement with excellent rock fishing and diving. Depot Beach and the immediate environment offer many surfing options but there's lots of walking required. Many waves can be found on this almost inaccessible stretch of coastline which extends north from Ulladulla to Batemans Bay. This coast has some of the prettiest spots to be found anywhere in New South Wales and there are dozens of bays, reefs and beaches (including Pebbly Beach, Pretty Beach, Kioloa and Merry Beach — that's only a few), as well as tame kangaroos and excellent camping grounds. Well worth a visit, even on the flattest of days.

Back along the winding track through the thick bushland of Murramarang National Park and Kioloa State Forest brings you to the small town of **Durras North**. South of Point Upright and out from the usually closed Durras Lakes entrance is a large reef extending out from the beach, producing excellent lefts and rights due to the heavy rip action on either side. Best in NE to SE swell and NW to SW winds.

Further south on the Princes Highway, some 280 kilometres south of Sydney, is the town of Benandarah and the turn off to **Durras** (a sealed road) where you'll find a variety of beach and reef breaks. On the southern side of **Beagle Bay** is a small right-hander breaking over a shallow reef bottom, which works in NE to SE swells and SE to SW winds. Further north (where the road first meets the coast) is a car park overlooking the bay. Right in the southern corner of the main beach small, shifting beach breaks are found from time to time, usually in small NE to SE swells and offshore winds.

Further south, Batemans Bay is a busy tourist town at the mouth of the Clyde River with several beaches offering beach breaks along George Bass Drive. Along this coast there are several small bays which sometimes offer good waves; the best are usually found at **Mackenzies Beach**, just south of Malua Bay. There's a quality left at the northern end, breaking along the rocks; best in SE swells and W winds. **Rosedale Beach**, between Mackenzies and Guerrilla Bay, also produces good beach and reef breaks on smaller days.

George Bass Drive continues south to Broulee and back to the Princes Highway. Some 2 kilometres north of Broulee is the **Tomalga rivermouth**, which offers a good left- and right-hand sandbank in E to SE swells and holds waves to 2 metres; best in W to SE winds. On bigger days good reform waves can also be found here. Further north along the coast road, towards Batemans Bay, there are over a dozen small bays which can produce good waves when conditions are suitable. Worth a check on big days.

At the southern end of the bay is **Broulee Island**, accessible from the beach via a short paddle. Once on the island, a long walk to the north-east corner brings you to an horrendous right-hander known as **Pink Rocks**. This fearsome break can be exceptional in large, smooth, SE groundswells and S to SW winds. On smaller days (around 2 metres), the wave starts with a dredging, grinding take-off over a shallow rock ledge before walling out through a series of bowling sections with plenty of wall to spare. On larger days, the shallow take-off rock becomes an awesome bowl section, where you get a really good look at the rock as you drop from the peak. At these times the take-off point moves further out around the point but remains very critical. Can be a truly excellent wave, but definitely only for experienced surfers.

At the mouth of the Moruya River there are several breaks that are worth checking out. Turn off the highway on the north side of the Moruya River bridge and follow the road for 5 kilometres, where you'll find a long rocky breakwall and a break known as **The Wall** offering good quality right-handers which are best on NE to SE swells (to 2.5 metres) and W to SW winds. Further out, in the entrance to the river between the breakwall and the southern point, is a good left-hander known as **The Entrance**, offering long, hollow and fast waves over a sand bottom in similar conditions. Best on low to mid tides, though currents and sharks can sometimes be

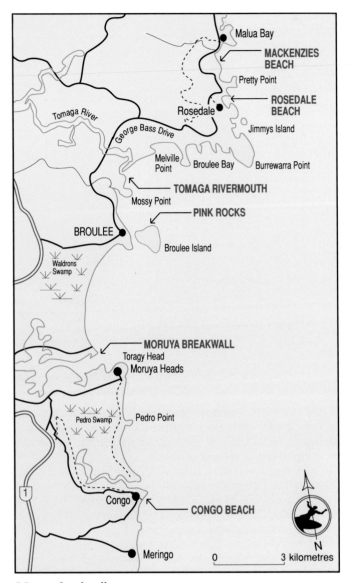

Moruya breakwall

a problem. An occasional right-hander also breaks here. Further to the south of Moruya Heads is a variety of small shifting beach breaks, which all work in similar conditions to The Wall and The Entrance depending on sand banks. The best of these is often found at **Congo**, about 5 kilometres south of Moruya Heads.

Just south of Bodalla is the turn off to **Potato Point**, about 7 kilometres of partly sealed road. On either side of the grassy headland are small bays which offer protection either from NE or SE winds, easterlies being the only winds that can get into both sides of the point. Works in swells from S to NE, which offer shifting lefts and rights on each side. Just north of Potato Point on the north side of Blackfellows Point there's a right-hander called **Blackfellows**, which is best in S to W winds and swell conditions similar to Potato Point.

About 8 kilometres north of Narooma there's a turn-off onto the coast road through **Dalmeny Point** and Kianga. Opposite Dalmeny Point caravan park is a sand-covered reef which offers lefts and rights, depending on shifting sandbanks. The left, towards the rocks, tends to be short and hollow, whereas the right is longer and works up the beach. Best in NE to S swells to 3 metres and SW to W winds.

South of Kianga there are waves to be found at the **Narooma breakwall**, usually right-handers which barrel over the build-up of sand adjacent to the wall. Best at mid tides in NE to SE swells to 2.5 metres, with NW to SW winds. Further north, a series of small sandy bays offer protection from the NE winds

and produce good waves on swells to 1.5 metres. South of Narooma, several rocky bays offer good waves from time to time.

Some 9 kilometres south of Narooma and 3 kilometres from the highway — in front of Cape Dromedary — is **Mystery Bay**. Take the first right turn as you come into Mystery Bay and follow the dirt road over several grassy headlands and past a series of rocky bays, where you will find several sand-covered reefs and beach breaks. Left- and right-handers are available, which work best in NE to S swells to 2 metres and SW to NE winds. Some of

Above *Rob Bain finding some south coast solace.*
Below *Moruya beach break*

133

Map labels:

Tura Beach
Short Point
Merimbula
Merimbula Point
MERIMBULA BAR
Merimbula Lake
1
Merimbula Bay
Pambula
PAMBULA RIVERMOUTH
Pambula Beach
Haycock Point
Ben Boyd National Park
N
0   2 kilometres

Merimbula occasionally has quality left-handers but is usually very crowded and fickle.

these bays offer good protection from the summer nor'-easters and quality waves go unridden often.

Camel Rock, some 6 kilometres north of Bermagui (opposite Wallaga Lake) protects the quality beach break from nor'-easters. Usually a left-hander with long walls, though there is also a short, suckey right. Best in NE swells to 2 metres and NE to W winds, but also works in E to SE swells. The sandbanks here tend to be permanent, which makes it a consistent wave. Further north of Camel Rock is the entrance to Wallaga Lake, which turns on good right- and left-handers to 2.5 metres. Best in S swells to 2 metres and S to W winds.

Bunga Head, situated 20 kilometres south of Bermagui, is accessible over a partly sealed road at the southern end of Murray Beach. Works best in big southerly swells (usually during winter), mid to high tides and W to S winds. Access is either from the rocks, part of the way out to the point, or on smaller days from the beach. Bunga Head offers a quality right-hander with long walls. The wave starts with a heavy take-off section, then walls out before the fast suckey bowl section which breaks over an extremely shallow rocky shelf. It is situated on private farming land, so shut the gates

after you. There are no facilities or camping and no dogs are allowed, but it is a good fishing and diving area. This spot gets very crowded by a tight local crew; definitely not recommended for inexperienced surfers or those with faint hearts.

Tathra Beach, with the entrance to the Bega River at the north end, offers a variety of quality beach breaks which work in NE to S swells to 2 metres and NW to SW winds. At the southern corner of the beach there's a surf club and kiosk, with a camping area offering accommodation. Good beach, rock and river fishing. North of Tathra is a series of small rocky bays and sandy beaches, most of which are accessible from the Tathra/Bermagui road and offer good waves when the sandbanks are there. Best conditions similar to Tathra.

Located at the entrance to Merimbula Lake, 460 kilometres south of Sydney, lies a classic left-hand rivermouth break over the **Merimbula Bar**. Big S to SE swells produce hollow spitting barrels, which run for up to 200 metres along the shallow sandbar at the northern end of Merimbula Bay. A wave that offers everything: a fast, dredging take-off, followed by a series of bowl sections, providing an experienced surfer with the chance to try a full

range of manoeuvres from deep tube rides to roundhouse cutbacks and slashing re-entries. Due to its position in the lee of Green Cape, the majority of south swells are usually only seen marching up the coast way out on the horizon. And the close proximity of Merimbula (a thriving resort and holiday town) guarantees the bar is usually packed out with a large and assorted crowd of surfers, whatever the time. You get it all here: surf skis, malibus, sailboards, boogies and even jet skis. The Merimbula bar is renowned for its 'one-day wonders' — fantastic one day and then flat the next, just when you were really ready for more. This usually creates heavy competition for the set waves on the good days and the normally placid locals have been known to get very possessive about 'their' waves. Best in S to SE swells and NW to NE winds. Despite the obstacles, a very picturesque and pleasant spot.

East of the Princes Highway some 470 kilometres south of Sydney is Pambula Beach, a small holiday and retirement village which overlooks the **Pambula rivermouth** and Merimbula Bay. At either end of the bay, red-ochre coloured cliffs signal danger to the unwary seafarer: treacherous, ever-changing sandbars and shallow bommies off Haycock Point hinder access to the sheltered water inside. These sandbars, which makes the rivermouth so dangerous for boats, are what creates the famous sandbar barrels of the rivermouth which, on their day, can match anything in Australia. Sadly, these days have

Above *The perfect sand bar barrels at Pambula rivermouth, a rare but much sought after event.* **Below** *Mark Occhilupo carves into another south coast beach break*

become few and far between in recent years as inland drought conditions have not produced the floods needed to move the sand at the rivermouth. When it does turn on, in a heavy NE swell (preferably a cyclone off the New South Wales north coast) and S to SW winds on a low or incoming tide, the rivermouth is an unforgettable barrel; similar in character (especially the length and depth of the barrels) to some of the classic point breaks of southern Queensland, without the consistency.

Those lucky enough to surf the rivermouth in its classic days (and still young enough to remember) will tell you with wild eyes of the magic 300 metre long crystal-clean tubes, spinning and grinding at freight train speed along a knee-deep sandbar, usually just a bit faster than your board will go. It's one of those breaks where you rarely need to think about cut-backs. From the fast, sucking take-off — which tends to be easier to get into than out of — the wave quickly draws and throws, hissing and spitting sand and spray, before spinning with machine-like precision down the line getting hollower and faster as it goes. The challenge is to hold your edge high and tight, seeking that sweet spot in one of nature's true wonders — the perfect barrel. Making a wave from start to finish is a real bonus here and ten second tube rides are common. The adrenalin really pumps deep inside these barrels, with the shore obscured by a racing curtain and the only way out at the other end of the tunnel. Even the wipeouts (especially with

a sand bottom) can be fun. It's a difficult line-up to master due to shifting banks, inconsistency and lack of any real landmarks. Generally not favoured by goofyfooters and crowds are a problem when the place is working: definitely a one-man wave.

Leonards Island is a right-hand wave which wraps around a rocky headland in the northern section of Ben Boyd National Park 5 kilometres north of Eden, access being via a rough bush track. The wave starts with a suckey take-off, followed by a series of cut-back sections before the wave bowls over the shallow weed reef which is usually strewn with sea urchins. Leonards Island works in NE to E swells to 2.5 metres and W to S winds, though it's at its best in a NE swell, S winds and mid tides. Tends to be best in the summer months as the southerly winter swells often pass right by. Wetsuit booties are highly recommended. (Anti-rubber purists can try it without booties, in which case a decent pair of tweezers and heaps of magnaplasm are a must.) No camping or dogs allowed. Further north are numerous sand-covered reefs and beach breaks, where conditions vary with the sandbanks which can change radically from week to week. Good beach fishing and diving here, with barbecue and toilet facilities at Haycock Point.

Eden, set on picturesque Twofold Bay, is the centre of many great breaks and also the home of New South Wales' largest fishing fleet (and most controversial chip mill). It was once the centre of a thriving whaling industry, where killer whales worked in tandem with the whalers to drive the larger migrating whales in close to the shore and within range of the harpoons of the hunters. This is the only recorded instance of whales working with humans to kill other whales. Eden's main surfing beach is **Aslings Beach**. Turn off at the 'Garden of Eden' caravan park and continue on past the high school and playing fields. At the southern end of the beach, off the old sea baths, there is often a quality right-hander (when the banks are right), which is best in NW to SW winds and SE swells to 2.5 metres.

Saltwater Creek is reached via the Eden Chip Mill turn-off some 20 kilometres south of Eden. The road quickly deteriorates into a rough dirt track winding its way through the thick eucalyptus forests, most of which are a part of the southern section of the Ben Boyd National Park. The roads

Rob Bain has spent so much time on the south coast that he's greeted like a local

Saltwater

bordering the park are used by heavy logging trucks, so extreme care should be taken on these roads. After some 30 kilometres the track ends at a small, unobtrusive camping area next to an unspoilt, white, sandy beach. At either end of the beach are two small creeks, the entrances of which are usually silted up. To the north lies a rugged, rocky headland; to the south, a low, boulder-strewn point, thick bushland, and (hopefully) excellent right-hand waves.

This break, known as **Saltwater**, is capable of holding waves to 4 metres, although it's more usual to surf here in 1.5 to 2 metre swells. The take-off point varies according to swell size and direction, but is usually over the large, sand-covered boulders. On bigger days the wave starts further out, on the edge of the reef. Saltwater features a steep, jacking take-off followed by a bowling inside section before swinging towards the beach in a series of cut-back sections and extinguishing itself in the dredging shore break to the north. On big days this shore break becomes a mass of rip-torn white water smashing with great force against the rocks, the spray dwarfing the 15 metre cliffs behind. Although it works on all tides, Saltwater is hollower, and better, at lower tides. Jumping in from the point is usually the way to go, until you mistime things and face a whirlpool ride over the razor-sharp, barnacle-encrusted rocks on the point. Camping is permitted, but forward bookings are required. There's little if any fresh water available, no dogs allowed, and the mozzies are plentiful and bloodthirsty at night. Apart from the low fences and log parking bays Saltwater remains almost as it was 200 years ago — unless the swell is up, when the area is invaded by an eager, assorted crew who, with spaghetti arms, surf until the sun sets in the west.

CHAPTER 3

VICTORIA

Occasionally the butt of north-of-the-border jokes, Victorian beaches and surf breaks are now respected worldwide for their quality and power. From Mallacoota, just south of the New South Wales border, right around to South Australia, the Victorian coastline cops plenty of swell action, especially the awesome west coast, where one glance at the shredded coastline gives an indication of the relentless power of the southern ocean swells. The area also breeds a hardy brand of surfer, well adapted to the cold southern waters. In fact the cold Victorian waters and great waves acted as an incentive to the fledgling wetsuit industry and a rubberised life support system built up along the Torquay coastline, where Rip Curl and Piping Hot have been pioneers in the development of thermal surfing. Rip Curl is now the biggest wetsuit company in the world. As a teenager in the mid-1960s, Victorian junior champion Wayne Lynch shook the surfing world with his radical free-flow surfing style, developed in the powerful southern ocean breaks. Lynch was raised on adventurous surfing, and Victoria to this day retains much of that exciting open surf spirit.

Andrew Flitton at Elevators on the west Victorian coast

THE EAST COAST

South of the New South Wales border — 575 kilometres south of Sydney and 520 kilometres north of Melbourne — is **Mallacoota**. Surrounded by rugged bushland, inaccessible coastline and open to the full force of Bass Strait's notorious winds and seas, Mallacoota offers challenging sailboarding and fishing as well as several good surf breaks.

Situated at the entrance to Mallacoota inlet, **Bastion Point** offers the pick of the local waves. Best in SE to E swells and W to NW winds, this long right-hander breaks over a sand bottom and holds waves to 2.5 metres, depending on the sandbanks. One of the local highlights is the sight of the abalone divers' shark cats launching themselves skywards over the set waves on the sandbar.

South of Bastion Point past the golf club is **Tip Beach**, which offers quality beach breaks at times. The beach features sand-covered reefs that create great waves, depending on sand conditions. The water here seems to flow straight from Antarctica and full-length wetsuits are a must in the winter months. Best in S to E swells to 2 metres and W to NW winds. Further south are a number of reefs and beaches which offer similar conditions, though not usually as consistent as Tip Beach. All in all, well worth the 25 kilometre drive along the winding (sealed) road from the highway at Genoa. Be cautious on this road, especially during summer when caravans can offer big hazards on the narrower sections of the road.

At Cann River turn off the highway to **Point Hicks** (also known as Cape Everard). After some 40 kilometres of dirt road you'll come across a camping area at the entrance to Thurra River. This very spot was Captain Cook's first Australian landfall in 1770; in fact it was at dawn on 20 April 1770 that Lieutenant Zachary Hicks, a member of Cook's crew, sighted the point which bears his name. The area remains almost unchanged to this day: the lighthouse on the point is the only obvious sign of civilisation. This wave is best in S to SE swells to 2 metres and NE to NW winds. On larger days there is sometimes a rideable wave to be found on the outside reefs. Camping is permitted but bookings are essential, through the National Parks Service Office in Cann River. No services are available and dogs are not permitted. Tends to be best in the summer months.

The next surfable waves, heading south, are found at **Cape Conran.** Turn off the Princes Highway just north of Cabbage Tree, then follow the dirt road some 20 kilometres to Cape Conran. Quality left-hand waves are often found off the boat ramp, though sometimes it can hold larger swells. Best conditions are found in S swells to 2 metres and SE to NW winds. The wave breaks over a mixture of reef

Above *Tip Beach at Mallacoota. It's almost always full-length wetsuit weather with cold water and long deserted stretches of coast.* **Bottom** *Wilsons Promontory beach break*

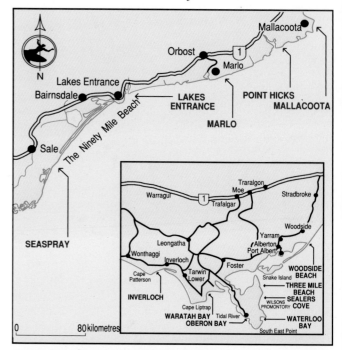

and sand bottom, running along the point into a sandy bay. To the east of the cape is a small bay which turns on a right-hand reef break in S to SE swells and NW to NE winds. Further east, around a small point, there's a bombora which, when the sandbanks are established, provides good right-handers up to 1.5 metres. Camping is allowed, though bookings are required through the National Parks Service. No dogs and no services, except toilets and water. Best in the summer months.

Some 732 kilometres south of Sydney and 314 kilometres east of Melbourne is **Lakes Entrance**, a busy fishing port and tourist town. Just north of town a sealed road leads to **Lake Tyers**, a small settlement with three camping grounds plus a boat launching ramp and good prawning. **The Bluff** offers one of the few waves in the area, a left-hander which works best in E to S swells and N to NE winds. The wave breaks over a sand and reef bottom and can offer a long ride in the right conditions. Many services available, but waves can be a long time coming. Best in summer months.

Ninety Mile Beach, which stretches from Lakes Entrance all the way to Wilsons Promontory, has little to offer surfers; no points and not even any consistent sandbanks, though it's often worth a check at **Seaspray**. But better waves are found on Wilsons Promontory. Access to Wilsons Promontory is gained from the Gippsland Highway at either Foster or Meeniyan. Characterised by rugged windswept sand dunes, long sandy beaches, massive granite outcrops and steep inaccessible sections of coastline, Wilsons Promontory National Park (covering 49 000 hectares and 160 kilometres of coastline) is the most southerly point of mainland Australia.

The possibility of finding good waves here is restricted by most of the coastline and surf breaks are accessible only on foot. The road, however, does take you to the park headquarters settlement at Tidal River (store, laundry, camping area and even a doctor), and from here it is only a short walk to **Oberon Bay** which sometimes (in W to S swells and NE to SE winds) gets good beach breaks. To get to the other beaches, bays and reefs requires more effort and planning, but for the keen adventurer the rewards for undertaking the long walk (with its rough, steep trails extracting a heavy toll — especially if you're carrying a surfboard as well as a backpack) can be good quality and definitely uncrowded waves. **South East Point** and its lighthouse, **Waterloo Bay**, **Sealers Cove**, **Tongue Point**, **Picnic Point** and **Daisy Beach** offer a wide variety of spectacular scenery and waves in almost all conditions. Camping restrictions make booking essential during holiday seasons.

Seek (and walk) and ye shall find.

Heading west for Melbourne on the South Gippsland Highway there's a signposted road to **Inverloch**, also accessible via the Bass Highway. Located between Cape Paterson and Cape Liptrap on the shores of Venus Bay, and the western shores of Anderson Inlet, Inverloch and surrounding areas produce a variety of good quality waves. The best of these are often found at the entrance of Anderson Inlet. On its day, classic right- and left-hand barrels can be found here.

To the south east of Inverloch and past Tarwin Lower (alternatively you can turn off the South Gippsland Highway at Foster) you will come to

Wilsons Promontory

Waratah Bay, with the small sleepy township of **Sandy Point** nestled behind the high scrub-covered sand dunes. On smaller S to SW swells and N to NE winds you can sometimes find good quality beach breaks here, both back towards **Walkerville** and to the south-west towards the entrance of **Shallow Inlet**. There are good beach breaks to be found along the shifting sandbars at this entrance, though paddling out on larger days can be a problem. These breaks work on S to SW swells and are best in N to NE winds (also popular with experienced wave sailors) on mid tides. Further along the beach to the east (access is difficult) is a variety of beach breaks — conditions needed depending upon the sandbanks and how far you go south-east towards **Cape Liptrap**.

Around to the south-west of Inverloch (towards **Cape Paterson** with its craggy shores and numerous reefs and small beaches) you can sometimes find good waves along the road which loops around to **Wonthaggi**.

Heading west from Inverloch along the Bass Highway you will find some good waves at **Eagles Nest** and the beaches around **Kilcunda** towards San Remo and Phillip Island. Eagles Nest has good shaped right-handers working on SW to SE swells and NW to NE winds, while the beaches around Kilcunda work on smaller south swells and are best in north winds. Although these beaches are usually uncrowded, the travelling surfer is probably better off heading for Phillip Island despite the crowds.

PHILLIP ISLAND

Some 140 kilometres south-east of Melbourne and outside Westernport Bay, Phillip Island is a popular surfing spot for hordes of resident surfers and the regular influx of visitors from surrounding areas. The island has a diverse history, having once been shared by sealers with banished Tasmanian Aborigines and being the site of the first Australian Grand Prix Championships. Wildlife is abundant, with migrating mutton birds and seals regular visitors. The island is also host to a large koala population and the world's smallest penguin (*Eudyptula minor*) draws many tourists to the island to watch the daily parade to their burrows after sunset. But the largest species of wildlife present — and the one that most concerns surfers — is the shark.

Phillip Island became known outside Victoria for its quality waves after the island hosted several successful surfing contests in the 1970s. The Alan Oke Memorial was one of the key events in the first years of the professional world circuit.

Access to the island is gained via the bridge that runs from San Remo, on the mainland, across to Newhaven. The island has some 25 kilometres of coastline facing south and catching the swell out of Bass Strait, offering a variety of ideal beach and reef breaks, and is almost guaranteed to have waves somewhere in most conditions. The island also attracts considerable surf industry activity, from board and clothing manufacture to surf shops.

At the eastern end of the island, **Woolamai Beach** offers some of the best beach breaks to be found anywhere in Victoria and is a remarkably consistent spot. Along the 8 kilometres of beach there are a variety of shifting sandbanks and sand-covered reefs, which offer plenty of chances to ride hollow, peaky barrels. Some of the best of these breaks are usually found right out from the Woolamai Surf Club. Works in S to SW swells to 2 metres; best in NE winds.

West of Woolamai are the **Forest Caves** beach breaks, which are similar to Woolamai in character, with S swells and N winds being best. To the west of **Surf Beach** (where you'll find more good beach breaks) is Sunderland Bay and **Surfies Point**, a right-hand reef break with a peaky take-off and a fast wall; a fun wave, rather than a classic. Best in S swells (to 2.5 metres), mid tides and N to NW winds.

Directly across Sunderland Bay is **Express Point,** a quality right-hand reef break and probably the best wave on the island, often with crowds to suit. This wave has an extremely heavy take-off as the wave dredges off the shallow reef, followed by an intense

Above *Gary Judd at Right Point.* **Below** *Greg Cox, Express.* **Right** *Express Point, short but strong*

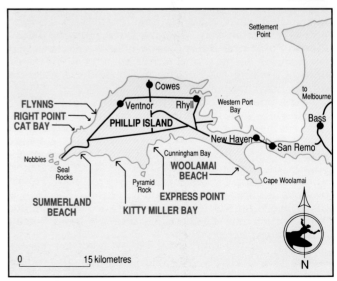

144

inside bowl section. Holds swells to almost any size, but best in S to SW swells 2.5 to 4 metres and NE to NW winds; high tides only. As the tide drops, numerous rocks appear to claim all but the most experienced surfers. Drop-ins are a definite no-no and won't be tolerated by the heavy local crew.

Express Point has, for a long time, been accessible from the eastern end via a walk around the outside of a farmer's dairy paddock. Photographer Peter Crawford was one of many enthusiastic surfers who chose to take the short cut across the paddock and jumped the fence. The startled cows watched silently before moving away to reveal a large, aggro bull who chased Peter across the paddock. Reaching the fence, Peter dived over without even slowing down, landing with kneeboard, flippers, wetsuits, towels and cameras. And an unforgettable memory of Express Point. Go around the paddock; the waves are gnarly enough without taking on the local stud bull.

Back Beach Road will take you to **Pyramid Rock,** where you could find right and left peaks over a sandy bottom with quality dependent on sandbank buildup, though there's no beach. Access is over the rocks. Best in NE winds.

Berrys Beach offers a right-hand reef break (access via Berrys Beach Road) which can produce quality waves, breaking over a shallow reef that holds swells to 2 metres. Best in NW winds and high tides only.

A short walk from the car park brings you to **Kitty Miller Bay.** Off the western end of the tiny beach is a right-hand reform break, which squeezes between a small rock island and Kennon Head, then reforms. A good fun wave, which works best in NW winds (though Kennon Head offers protection in light winds from NW to SW) and swells to 1.5 metres.

Summerland Beach is the home of the famous penguin parade. Off the west point is a right-hander, breaking over a patchy reef and sand bottom. This wave, which requires large swells to work, is essentially a good fun wave, although the jacking take-off provides some interesting drops. There are also some good beach breaks to be had up the beach.

The western tip of the island, Point Grant, has a small seal colony serving as something of a beacon to the local white pointers. Queensland shark hunter Vic Hislop recently proved the point by catching a 7 metre monster right off this point. This shark is now on display in Hislop's Shark Museum in Hervey Bay, Queensland. It is also worth noting that 90 per cent of the catch from the fishing fleet operating out of San Remo is — yes, you guessed it — shark.

Around the corner from The Nobbys is **Cat Bay,** which gets surprising access to the big SW swells bending around the western end of the island. Right out the front of the car park (access from Ventnor Road) is **Right Point** which, believe it or not, is a left-hander. This place produces a powerful wave and can turn on classic walls and barrels on its day, breaking over a patchy reef bottom. The take-off features thick-lipped peaks, especially on big days. Best in big SW swells and half tides (incoming) with E winds. Access to the break is difficult at low tides on big days because of the rugged shoreline. On smaller days, the wave also breaks right and there is another left off the point at the western end of **Sherry Beach.** Both of these breaks are more suitable for beginners.

At the eastern end of Sealers Cove the shoreline turns to the north, and at **Flynn's Reef** there is a good right-hand reef break which can turn on classic walls with a fleeting bowl section. Crowds tend to be a problem here with plenty of competition for the waves when it's good. Best in large SW swells (to 2.5 metres) on a half tide (incoming) with NE winds. Rocks appear out of the water on falling tides and many fins have been lost here.

THE MORNINGTON PENINSULA

The Mornington Peninsula forms the eastern side of Port Phillip Bay and catches plenty of swell on its southern side. To the east of Cape Schanck swells squeeze between Phillip Island and the cape. To the west, the stretch of beaches from Gunnamatta to Portsea are open and exposed to the southern swells.

From the east, the first real waves for surfers are found at Balnarring Point and Merricks Point, south of the town of Balnarring. **Balnarring Point** is a classic, small wave right-hander, which starts with a horseshoe peak and then tapers quickly away, breaking on a sand over rock bottom. A high tide wave that works best in S to SW swells to 1.5 metres and NE to NW winds.

When the wind goes cross-shore from the SW and there's a big swell, **Merricks Point** offers one of the most protected waves around, though it requires a long walk in. Holds swell to 2 metres and high tides only.

The right-hand break at Point Leo is known as **Suicide**, holds swells as big as you'll want, and offers the most consistent reef break in the area; works best in S to SW swells and SW to NW winds at high tide. The wave has an awesome, sucking take-off (hence its name), before walling out in long workable sections. Just up from Suicide is a small reef break known as **First Reef**, which offers lefts and rights to 2 metres and works best in NE to W winds.

Honeysuckle Point offers a small wave break, which peels over a shallow, rocky bottom with a reputation for devouring foam and flesh. Sometimes an excellent wave, it works best in S to SW swells to 2 metres and W to SW winds. Off the point is a bombora which can hold swell to any size, but works best in 1.5 to 2 metres, peeling over a sand over rock bottom. Usually a right, and often a very long ride. Best in W to NW winds.

Pines is one of the classic set-ups of all time. A perfect right-hand reef break which works in swells over 2 metres. Best in big swells and W to SW winds, often when everywhere else is blown out.

Meanos is a break situated directly below the guns of the Flinders Naval Base at West Head that offers lefts and rights over a reef bottom. The left is very hollow and dangerous, the right a little more forgiving. A high tide wave, which works best to 2 metres in a N to NW wind. Just west of Meanos the break known as **Gunnery** offers lefts and rights in small conditions (to 1.5 metres) on lower tides and N to NW winds. Further west, there's a right hand reef break called **Cyrils,** which works best in large swells, very high tides and NW to NE winds. This wave has a

somewhat notorious final section which sucks out very hollow and likes to hurt people.

When the swell is moderate and the winds are strong and south-westerly, **Bushrangers Bay** turns on a small right-hand point break at the end of a scenic walk. Low tides are preferable and often the spot to check when the SW winds have blown everything else out. The left-hand reef break at **Cape Schanck** can hold swells to 3 metres and works best in SE winds and low tides, but involves a long walk in and a steep climb down the cliff.

Gunnamatta Beach offers quality left and right peaky beach breaks, which work best in swells to 2 metres though sometimes larger swells can work, depending on tides. Along this strip of beach, when the winds are SE through to NW, you can find some of the best beach breaks you'll see anywhere.

Breaking in similar conditions to Gunnamatta, **St Andrews** offers a series of beach breaks which are usually a little larger and hold the bigger swells (to 2.5 metres) better. The sandbanks determine quality and best winds are SE through to NW.

There are excellent beach breaks to be had at **Rye**, which break in similar conditions to Gunnamatta and St Andrews. Directly off the prominent clump of rocks is a quality right hand wave which tends to be best at low tides and SE to NW winds. The swell and currents around here can be strong and dangerous; it was in these waters that Australia's prime minister Harold Holt drowned on 17 December 1967. The beaches at **Portsea** are also exposed to the big south swells and this region of the coast picks up plenty of swell.

Spooks is a fearsome wave located inside a prohibited army area, which means you run the risk of being ejected at gunpoint. When it works, Spooks would have to rate as one of the hollowest, meanest, double-up waves you'll find anywhere. This break peels right over a sand on rock bottom, and holds swell to 2.5 metres. Best at low tide.

STEVE TRIANCE

Quarantine, or Corsair, is situated just inside the heads of Port Phillip Bay. This left-hand point break is one of the all-time classics: breaking over sand, Quarantine wave holds swells to 3 metres and breaks extremely hollow and fast — a real pile-driver. Situated in a prohibited area (soon to be opened to the public) and only accessible by boat, Quarantine works best in SE winds. The tidal movements here are magnified by the bulk of Port Phillip Bay and if you're not familiar with the conditions it can be a dicey place to surf.

Above *Gary Green at Gunnamatta.* **Below** *Entry at Corsair.* **Below left** *Tom Carroll at Corsair*

PETER CRAWFORD

MARTIN TULLEMANS

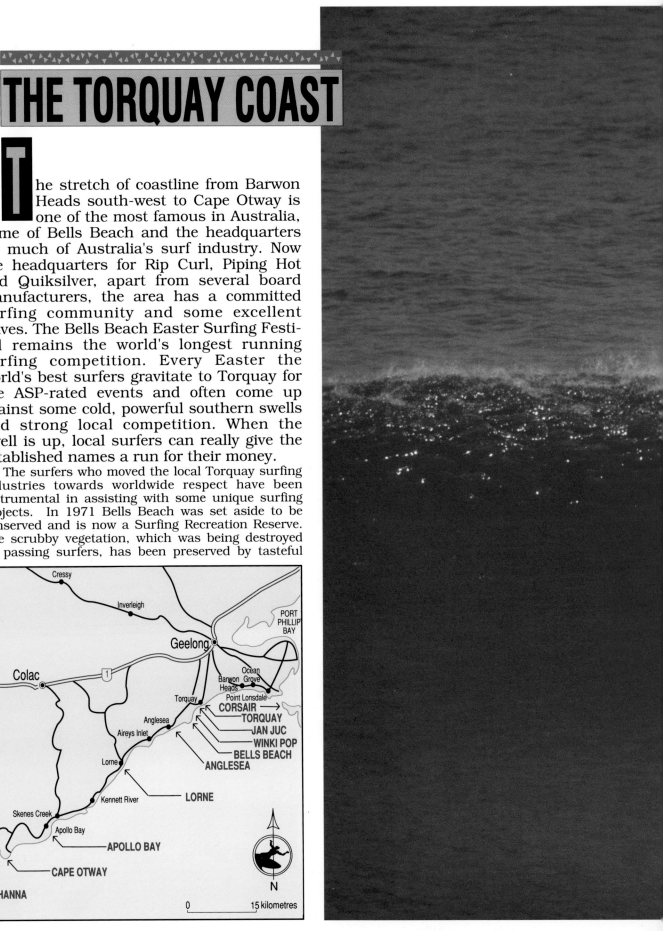

THE TORQUAY COAST

The stretch of coastline from Barwon Heads south-west to Cape Otway is one of the most famous in Australia, home of Bells Beach and the headquarters for much of Australia's surf industry. Now the headquarters for Rip Curl, Piping Hot and Quiksilver, apart from several board manufacturers, the area has a committed surfing community and some excellent waves. The Bells Beach Easter Surfing Festival remains the world's longest running surfing competition. Every Easter the world's best surfers gravitate to Torquay for the ASP-rated events and often come up against some cold, powerful southern swells and strong local competition. When the swell is up, local surfers can really give the established names a run for their money.

The surfers who moved the local Torquay surfing industries towards worldwide respect have been instrumental in assisting with some unique surfing projects. In 1971 Bells Beach was set aside to be conserved and is now a Surfing Recreation Reserve. The scrubby vegetation, which was being destroyed by passing surfers, has been preserved by tasteful

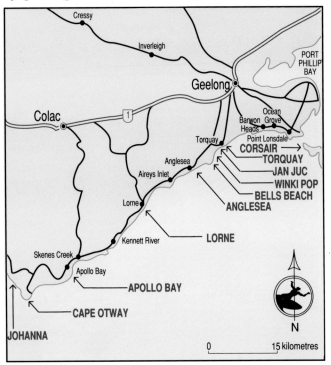

Pete Johnson at Winki Pop

timber walkways and access stairways lead to Winki Pop and Bells. Trees have been planted and development will now never touch these unspoilt coastal cliffs and rugged headlands.

More recent has been the construction and opening of Australia's only 'Surfworld Museum'. Queensland's Peter Troy is the head historian of this unique government-backed centre which features a community hall, theatre, offices for the governing body of amateur surfing (the Australian Surfriders Association), and a special education development including a computerised filing system with every issue of every surfing publication ever printed and a complete surf film library. Also included in the building is a Surfing Hall of Fame to honour the sport's champions.

Torquay has everything a travelling surfer would desire: the world's best products in the surf shops; a diverse range of local surf spots; entertainment; sailboarding; fishing; good restaurants; health food takeaways; and friendly people.

At the northern end of this coast, around Barwon Heads, there are long sandy beaches which sometimes get waves – in SW swells and N winds – depending on the condition of the sandbanks. Heading south-west along the coast there are point breaks at **Bancoura** and **Point Impossible**, but the real waves on this coast begin around Torquay.

At the mouth of Port Phillip Bay there is the Point Lonsdale Lighthouse and around the corner is the start of one of the more consistent stretches of surf in Victoria, including **Barwon Heads** and Thirteenth Beach. There are several interesting reef breaks off the rocky platform at **Point Lonsdale** that are fluky and vary widely with tides and wind, but worth trying to catch. A huge species of kelp covers the intertidal zone and often wraps up unwary surfers.

Top *Damien Wilson, one of the many hot young locals, pulls in at Bird Rock.* **Above** *Thirteenth Beach.* **Below** *Greg Brown at Torquay Point.* **Right** *Tony Ray at Jan Juc*

Thirteenth Beach stretches away from the rocks at Barwon Heads in an almost continuous curve to Torquay in the west. Thirteenth is considered by some surfers as the spot to go as there's always a rideable wave, but when this beach has offshore winds and anything over a half a metre of swell it can produce some great little waves. Rocky outcrops rise above sand and water level right along the eastern end of the beach, and provide excellent reefs on larger SW swells and with small to medium straight S swells; NE winds are offshore. The more famous Torquay–Bells area can be flat and Thirteenth will still have some good waves.

North of Point Danger, **Fishermans Beach** is only rarely surfed, mainly because it requires a huge south swell and is only ridden when other, better quality waves are closing out. Breaking over a sand-covered reef on SW to NW winds, it is generally too protected from the swell. A good wave for learners, as is the inside part of Point Danger.

At **Point Danger** you can find some fair quality left-handers breaking quite a considerable distance out from the point. In recent years Point Danger has been taken over by the keen local crew of wave sailors, so paddle out on windy days at your own risk as these guys are usually moving so fast that they won't see you until it's too late. And the waves are usually better at several other spots along this coast anyway. Works on NW winds and S swells, up to 2 metres.

Perhaps the best learners' waves in the area are found between Point Danger and the surf club on **Torquay Beach** (the numbers usually found out here are proof enough). Various sand-covered reefs produce lefts and rights along the beach, and there's a slow right-hander off the point. Holds up to around 2 metres, on SW to NW winds. (The surf club patrols here from December till Easter.) Further around, in front of the golf course and car park, you can sometimes find good beach breaks at **Jan Juc** (2 kilometres to the west of Torquay) which works on S swells to 2 metres and NE to NW winds.

This area features shifting sandbars which will determine quality, but worth a look on small days although it can get crowded. Between Jan Juc and Winki Pop there are a number of good quality reef breaks all breaking on smaller S to SW swells up to 1.5 or 2 metres and being a bit more difficult to get to, but they rarely get as crowded as the more popular breaks around Bells. The first of these is **Bird Rock**, on its days one of the finest waves in the area. A steep, jacking, hollow barrel, working on mid to high tides and best in NW winds, it's well worth the effort to surf this break. Bird Rock is a unique wave: the rock shelf has been pushed up out from a horizontal position by some incredible earth movement and the swell wraps down this almost artificial-looking reef. More than six people out here is a crowd unless they're locals; three 'in tune' locals can take the place over and it's definitely a one

PETER CRAWFORD

person wave.   Some surfers, obsessed with the uniqueness of the spot, are totally dedicated to surfing it, so keep that in mind when you check it out from the cliff-top car park.

Further south and visible from Bird Rock is a sister wave, **Sparrows**; a flatter wave, nowhere near as hollow as Bird Rock, though it works in the same conditions. **Steps** is the next wave, a right-hand reef break, which works in N to NW winds but like all these spots closes out on bigger days. **Boobs**, a hollow right- and left-hand reef break, is surfed on smaller S to SW swell days at higher tides (on lower tide, it's too hairy as the reef becomes exposed);

Above *Sydney professional Damien Hardman loosening up at Bells Beach.* **Below** *Sunrise over Winki Pop.* **Top right** *Greg Brown is one of Victoria's best surfers and here he shows local knowledge of the lip zone at Winki.* **Below right** *Andrew Flitton ripping*

PETER SIMONS

offshore in N to NW winds. Access to these spots is time-consuming; an old dirt track at the top of the cliffs seems to always be washed out and it is often impassable by car. It's a long walk and climb but is often worth the effort, particularly on those glassy smooth, medium to large days.

Located below the top car park at Bells, **Winki Pop** produces some of the best, longest-walled waves to be found in Victoria. Breaking for up to 200 to 300 metres along a shallow reef bottom, Winki holds up to 3 to 4 metres but is usually best on 2 to 3 metre days. A steep critical take-off off the outside point is followed by a seemingly endless series of sections grinding faster and faster down the point. Another section to this wave is called **Lowers**, which needs a large, clean, S to SW swell and N to NW wind. Like all breaks around Torquay it gets incredibly crowded — especially on holidays and weekends, with the hardcore local crew dominating the outside take-off and set waves. Needs a mid to high tide, as low tide makes the wave too critical and dangerous.

Bells Beach is the world's only Surfing Recreation Reserve and a concrete wave greets you at the entrance to the reserve on the Bells road. Bells is one of Australia's renowned big wave spots but doesn't need huge swells to produce enjoyable waves. At high tide on small swells, the rock platform right around the base of Bells — **Rincon** — produces fast walls. Best on SSW to S swells, up to 2 metres and, like Bells, is offshore and best in NW to W winds.

Above *Aerial view of Bells beach coastline*

Above *Great Ocean Road.* **Below** *John Darby*

Above *'The Sultan' himself, speeding through the Bells bowl*   **Below** *Bells Beach line-up*

The reef at Bells is very much tide affected and on lower tides and clean, medium to large swells **The Bowl** breaks at its best. Occasionally, it's possible on clean, large to humungous swells to surf all the way from outside Rincon through the Bells Bowl to the shore break, and that's when Bells is booming, with lines of swell stacked up like corduroy to the horizon.

Further around the reef at the base of the cliff are several very good spots. **Centreside** works on small to medium swells and typically provides a fast sectioning right. Further around a suckier left, which wraps and runs down a reasonably sharp reef, is called **Southside** and provides some relief for frustrated goofy-foots with most of this area producing right-hand waves. Southside is a good wave on medium S to SE swells and can handle a touch more west in the wind direction.

Further south-west, is **Point Addis** and **Anglesea** another coastal town much smaller than Torquay but supporting a keen group of local surfers. There are a couple of breaks around here worth catching on their day, but if the swell is up most opt for the Bells area to provide some famous waves. Anglesea has become a very popular holiday spot during vacation periods and, again, has a commited local group of active surfers. The sport has been so well promoted in the area that almost every kid who lives within cooee of the water is committed to becoming a fully fledged surf nazi. Anglesea has some good beach breaks, particularly for less experienced surfers and beginners, too, who find the waves at **Point Roadknight** perfect for their needs. It's a slow, gentle wave down the long, sandy point and ideal for kids. Point Roadnight is extremely protected from S to SW winds and while it is safe, the bottom is too shallow for more experienced surfers to find any really challenging waves. It's also a favourite area for longboard and malibu riders. However, the Anglesea breaks can become surprisingly crowded when good conditions coincide with holiday periods.

Hut Gully or **Guvvo's** (so-called as it's situated right off Government Road) is crowded whenever it breaks — the locals have it well covered; best in N to NW winds.

The next town south, **Airey's Inlet,** was one of many in the area devastated by the bushfires of Ash Wednesday, 1981. There are some good waves in the area but again, there's usually more value at the better known spots during good swells. At the Airey's Inlet restaurant — run by an ex-seppo named Butch — you'll find great tucker and Butch is a keen surfer. In holidays a reservation is necessary. Butch is just one of many locals who frequent the beach breaks south of Airey's from **Fairhaven** past **Moggs Creek** to **Spout Creek**, which are generally all offshore in NW to NE winds but only handle smaller swells. On calm, glassy mornings when the swell is only 1 to 1.5 metres, these spots provide some great waves. The bottom is patchy sand and reef but if the swell is up, **Cathedral Rock** can handle it. The only worry is that the Rock might manhandle you. It's a strong, gutsy wave in much the same style as Winki Pop; some believe it's even better. The Rock is not good until the swell is over two metres, so obviously less experienced surfers should be content to watch the action and avoid becoming the star stuntman in some local

Greg Brown at Point Addis

STEVE TRIANCE

horror feature. But if you're into size, Cathedral can handle it.

The Great Ocean Road can be a tortuous test of your driving proficiency, especially when you're on a surf mission. The road twists and turns around steep headlands and hills and you only get into top gear on the straighter, flatter stretches on the river plains which carve up this rugged coast. Don't underestimate this road — it can be a killer — but if you take your time it's a magnificent piece of Australia to explore.

Lorne is one of Victoria's prettiest coastal towns with all the comforts a travelling surfer would require. The hills which surround Lorne are covered in forest and tree ferns, an almost tropical atmosphere when the sun is out. The town is tucked behind a long rocky point which produces some great waves on really big SW or medium SE swells, protected from winds in the west right around to the south. The **Lorne beach breaks** often produce fine waves on calm, smaller days, but be warned: there is a very tight local scene at Lorne. The Point is best on low tides and more SE swells as it moves more evenly down the rugged point, and on the bigger, better days the sections are linked to one helluva long, fast, challenging ride. More often the sections are separated by dead spots or unmakeable chunks of rocky wall.

A huge pier juts out of the coast at the top of the point on this little tourist town; fishing was the original industry of this area. **Vera Lynn** is the name of the left- and right-peaking reef break at the top of Lorne Point (though no one knows why). It handles any swell but the wave tends to spill out onto a flatter shoulder and generally could be considered somewhat of an overrated spot, ideal for intermediate surfers. The Great Ocean Road continues very close to the coast with rock falls common, occasionally blocking the road after heavy rain. The cliffs are majestic but the road is a slow down model, otherwise you could suffer the ultimate drop-in hundreds of feet to the ocean below. The only chance of decent surf is at the rivermouths that dot the coast. **Jamieson River** can be very good. Other spots worth checking include **Cumberland River**, **St George**, **Wye River**, **Kennett River**, and **Skeenes Creek**. Beaches are rare on this stretch of coast and rocky caves are sometimes all you will see. However, on N to NW, even SW winds at some spots and even SW to S swells, there can be some worthwhile waves. The water, of course, is cold in this area; kelp grows thick at most spots and can be a problem on legropes. Kennett River is about the best of these spots. Offering more protection in southerlies, it is not a classic wave but can get surprisingly crowded.

Apollo Bay, further down the coast, is yet another of Victoria's quaint coastal towns. The main industries are tourism, farming and fishing but it was once a whaling station before becoming a timber town. The harbour at the tip of the point protects the commercial fishing boats from a very active ocean. The beach breaks can produce good waves on their day with protection in northerlies at the Lorne end of the coast, while in big swells southerly winds are blocked by Point Bunbury.

Just around the corner at **Marengo** there are some excellent spots in clean, medium swells and N to NW winds; access is generally via private farming properties. As you continue along the coast, the Great Ocean Road cuts away from the ocean west

through the Otway National Park. The forest here is absolutely beautiful — huge straight trees and lush fern covered gullies give the area a tropical feeling which is rather surprising so far south.

Cape Otway itself is the site of the Australian mainland's first lighthouse. The mountainous topography extends right to the rugged coast: too rough for quality waves, yet at **Crayfish Bay** on the eastern side of Cape Otway there is protection from the arctic-born south-westerly winds which sweep this part of the world.

Above *Mark Clift at Anglesea.* **Below** *Wayne Lynch at Cathedral Rock*

THE AWESOME COAST

The awesome power of the Southern Ocean is clearly seen on the stretch of coastline between Cape Otway and Portland. Carved in an erratic pattern of gorges, archways, caves and offshore stacks, the limestone cliffs have proven no match to the ocean's relentless might. Along the Great Ocean Road lookouts and vantage points give spectacular views of London Bridge, Loch Ard Gorge (named after the most disastrous of six shipwrecks near Port Campbell, where of 54 people aboard the *Loch Ard* in 1878, only two survived) and the Twelve Apostles, as well as the many excellent big wave locations, although these are somewhat harder to find and are suitable only for the most experienced and dedicated big wave surfer. The waves down here extract a fearsome toll on boards and bodies. Confidence in your ability, as well as your equipment, is essential. Here, unlike Hawaii's north shore, there are no helicopters on standby to perform rescues, and drowning becomes a distinct possibility.

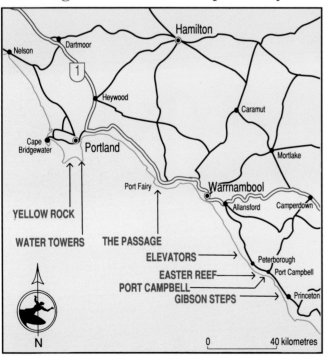

Andrew Flitton at Easter reef

Leaving behind the virgin forests of Cape Otway National Park, the country opens out into lush farming land. The first good spot you hit is **Castles**. One time it was secluded by difficult access, but a relatively new section of sealed road means you can check Castles from the car park on top of the cliff. Castles features a left and (better) right reef break. It's offshore in northerly winds and is open to heaps of strong swell action — often the problem down on this stretch of coast is that there is too much size in the swell. Castles is a very powerful wave and is not for the inexperienced or faint-hearted.

Johanna is Victoria's equivalent to Byron Bay, where once dairy farming was the main rural industry. The big rolling hills have been cleared of their original forests and, like huge green waves, they roll the length of the coast. There is no town at Johanna, not even a shop; the nearest supply centre is up the road at Lavers Hill. The only structure at Johanna car park is the old tennis court where, between surf sessions, John Witzig once tried to teach me the finer points of the game.

Like Castles, Johanna can often be too big to surf, or the swell will jump from a perfect 2 metres to an unrideable 3 to 4 metres in a matter of hours. The beach is about 4 kilometres long, with assorted breaks created by sandbanks formed around rock clusters on the beach or offshore reefs. The waves are strong and inexperienced surfers should exercise care or they could be in trouble with medical help a long way off.

The cowpats can be a hazard in this area. Sometimes when you rush from the campsite early, bleary-eyed and barefooted, a warm, squishy surprise awaits. One surfing animal (who will remain

Top right *Wayne Lynch, Gibson Steps.* **Below** *Along this coast there are some big boots to fill.* **Below opposite** *Johanna*

STEVE TRIANCE

Left *The Apostles off Port Cambell National Park.*
Above *Port Campbell.* **Right** *Gibson Steps coast.*
Below *Greg Brown at Gibson Steps*

nameless) invented a novel method of warming up cold toes after surfing the chilly Johanna waters — standing in a fresh cowpat! The local farmers have been very kind to passing surfers over the years and the area has been kept clean, considering the number of surfers who have visited Johanna since it was exposed to the world during the 1970 World Championships (a long flat spell at Bells Beach forced the finals to be relocated in the seclusion of Johanna). You can be sure that when the Bells area has any sizeable swell, Castles and Johanna are maxed-out.

West of **Princeton** the first surfable waves are found a short distance from town, along a dirt track off the Great Ocean Road. Access varies from difficult to impossible. Working on NE to N winds and S to SW swells, the waves here are dependent on current sandbar formations, but usually offer quality left and right peaks up to around 2.5 metres. Over this size, the inevitability of being cleaned up by bigger sets makes surfing at one of the reef breaks in the area a wiser choice.

From Princeton the road takes you through Port Campbell National Park, which extends along this rugged coastline all the way to Peterborough. Just before you reach the Twelve Apostles there is a long sandy beach called **Gibson Beach**, where ever-moving sandbars produce excellent quality, powerful peaks. Strong rips and the long paddle out make surfing this beach a real challenge. Even getting to the beach (down the steps cut into the cliff by early settlers at the western end of the beach) is a challenge. On smaller days, and at low tide, there is a tunnel through the cliff to the beach at the foot of the Twelve Apostles.

Just to the south of **The Jetty** at Port Campbell there is a shallow rock shelf, off which a fair quality left-hander breaks. Best in smaller S to SW swell, up to 2.5 metres and NE winds. Check it out from the road at the top of the cliff.

South-west of the small sheltered harbour at Port Campbell — where the cray fishing boats are regularly winched up onto the jetty to escape the mountainous seas — is another of Australia's premier big wave locations.

Easter Reef is capable of holding waves bigger then you'd ever want to surf and on huge SW swells it has been known to break up to 7 metres. An awe-inspiring, power-packed right-hander, with steep take-offs (no matter how you look at it, a 7 metre wave is going to have a steep take-off) and long walls, Easter Reef demands respect. Best in N winds.

Don't surf this break unless you are absolutely sure you can handle it. The crayfish which live in the caves around here may welcome the feed your body would give them, but think of how your friends and family would feel when you don't come up after that humungous clean-up set or wipeout.

Closer to **Peterborough** (to the east of the bridge over Curdies Inlet) is a small beach ringed by sand dunes, which is worth a look on small days when the reefs aren't firing as it sometimes gets good banks. One of the only waves on this stretch of coast even remotely suitable for the less competent surfer.

Situated to the south-west of Peterborough is the body-crunching right-hander called **Massacres** — an apt description in anyone's terms. Featuring a thick-lipped pitching peak which moves rapidly out of deep water, the steep elevator like take-off (the break is also known as **Elevators**) is followed by a hollow

Below *Easter Reef.* **Right** *Andrew Flitton at Easter Reef*

PETER SIMONS

Top *The west coast is rich in ocean reefs.* **Above** and **right** *Greg Brown at Elevators.* **Below** *Andrew Flitton at Black Cloud*

bowl section which grinds off the shallow reef towards a sharp, inhospitable coastline. Breaking best on large S to SW swells and N to NE winds, Massacres holds waves as large as most surfers could hope for (or have the guts to take off on). But it's generally best from 2.5 to 3.5 metres. It's a long paddle out through deep spooky waters to these heavy breaking waves, which usually ensures they are only ridden by experienced surfers. The less competent don't last long out here as the inevitable wipeout is followed by a terrifying hold-down.

Further to the west, and way out to sea, there is another offshore reef which breaks in only the biggest of swells and defies anyone to surf it. Holding perhaps the largest waves to be found anywhere in Australia this wave is usually a right-hander, though the left also looks good at times. Requires the same approach needed to tackle Waimea Bay — big boards, extreme fitness, total confidence in your ability, long leash, huge heart (and even bigger balls) and preferably a pick-up boat or helicopter, as an unplanned burial at sea is a distinct possibility out here. Don't even consider it unless you've ripped Sunset apart or have a death wish.

Between Peterborough and Warrnambool the Great Ocean Road cuts inland through lush green farmland. Local knowledge is required to just reach the coast here, let alone pinpoint and surf the many beach and reef breaks in the area. Most of these spots work in S to SW swell to 2 metres and NE winds, and require time and determination. West from here, the Great Ocean Road connects with the Princes Highway near Allansford, 10 kilometres east of Warrnambool.

There are waves to be found along the beaches to the east of the **Hopkins rivermouth** and in **Lady Bay** itself. To the west of Warrnambool there are several powerful offshore reef breaks, which work in S swells and N to NE winds but are suitable only for experienced surfers. **Port Fairy** gets its share of good waves, with the eastern end of Griffiths Island, past the breakwall, able to hold good right-handers to around 2.5 metres; works on large S swells and W to SW winds.

Around to the south of Griffiths Island, **The Passage** is a heavy right-hand reef break which holds the biggest surfable swells in the area; works on S swells to 3 and 4 metres and N winds.

From Port Fairy the highway follows the coast around Portland Bay to **Portland**, where you can find good beach breaks on smaller S swells and N to NE winds although the beaches close to Portland are usually too protected for real swell action. Better waves are usually found at **Crumpets Beach** and **Point Danger**, where there are sometimes excellent right-handers breaking along the low rocky shoreline. These breaks require a heavy S to SW swell and W winds.

South of Portland is Nelson Bay and Cape Nelson, where the coastline is exposed to the full fury of the southern ocean swells, with sheer cliffs overlooking the quality waves at **Yellow Rock**. This reef break offers lefts and rights in S swells to 2.5 metres and N winds.

Bridgewater Bay also has waves at times, again requiring S swells and N winds. The stretch of coastline from Cape Bridgewater to Nelson and the South Australian border holds numerous possibilities for good waves, from the dangerous reef breaks, **Blacks**

and **Whites**, which work on S to SW swells and E to NE winds, to the many beach breaks found along the shores of Discovery Bay.

A reliable four-wheel drive and a non-caring attitude towards the ravages of rust makes this coastline more accessible and will offer more waves. Crowds are unlikely to be a problem on this coast, but cold water, together with heavy rips and huge swells could be. And the local march flies are so ferocious they might just eat you before the sharks get a chance.

Before you reach South Australia, the last spot is near Nelson, where the Glenelg River meets the sea. Here, shifting sandbars and strong currents sometimes produce good quality rights and lefts on smaller S swells and N winds.

Strong winds, heavy swells and freezing water ensures that this coast is only surfed by keen, well-equipped and experienced surfers, who maintain their respect for Southern Ocean power.

Top Southern Ocean juice. **Right** *Wayne Lynch, the pioneer of surfing on Victoria's west coast, finds another perfect barrel*

George Wales eyes off a nice Daley Heads hook

CHAPTER 4

SOUTH AUSTRALIA

The surf on South Australia's coastline is one of the country's best-kept secrets. Apart from the better known spots such as Cactus, Granites and Victor Harbor, South Australia has a wealth of surf spots hardly known outside the state. The swell is strong — straight out of the south — and the water is cold. And white pointer sharks are never too far from the surfer's thoughts on this coastline.

PETER SIMONS

WEST FROM VICTORIA

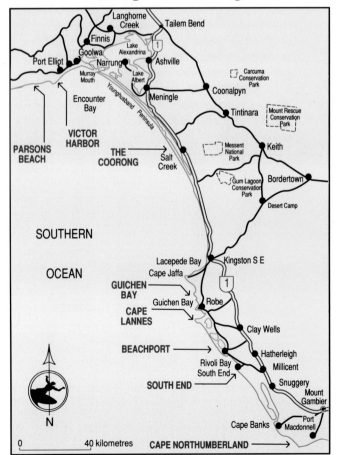

The south-eastern coast of South Australia — stretching from Port MacDonnell (and the Victorian border) to Victor Harbor — offers some of the least-known waves in Australia. Open to most of the southern swells as far as Kangaroo Island, this coastline offers some isolated beach and reef breaks where crowds are unlikely to be a worry. Sharks, however, could be.

Heading west from Victoria on the Princes Highway (Highway One), a 28 kilometre detour south from Mount Gambier brings us to Port MacDonnell, where there is a bunch of surfing options to celebrate our arrival in South Australia. Just east of the original Port MacDonnell lighthouse is **Posties**, a powerful, hollow and often excellent right-hander considered by most to be the best break in the area. Works in S to SW swells to 3 metres, and is best in NE winds. Following the Point Douglas road north

there are several beach and reef breaks which can be reached by following the tracks to the coast.

Cape Northumberland and **Point Douglas** are both capable of turning waves on at times. The cape has an outside reef which works in huge S to SW swells (only for the very brave) and E to NE winds. On the east of the cape there are also lefts and rights. At Point Douglas there can be waves on either side of the point, the best usually being the right-hander on the eastern side. To the north of Point Douglas there is further surf to be found by the adventurous — in four-wheel drive vehicles — but inaccessible to most.

Further east on the Princes Highway (back through Mount Gambier) take the turn-off at Millicent, where it's 33 kilometres to **Beachport** and **South End** at either end of Rivoli Bay. Beachport is a small crayfishing port which once operated a whaling station; now it's better known for its Pool of Siloam, which offers the bizarre experience of swimming in water six times saltier than the sea. Fed by underground springs, the pool is about the closest you'll ever get to walking on water.

Just inside Cape Martin and Penguin Island (a sanctuary for the little black-and-whites) there is a reef called **Ringwoods Reef** which can turn on long, hollow right-handers. This break is popular with the local crayfishers who often pull up here in their crayboats on their way back to the pier.

To the north of Cape Martin the coastline is characterised by sand dunes and rocky outcrops, some of which are under water creating reefs which turn on waves at times, but access is difficult. In Rivoli Bay

MARK SUTTON

An empty wave sneaks through at Victor Harbor

there is a popular beach break east of the pier, though it requires a solid swell to enter the bay. At the eastern end of the bay is South End, situated inside Cape Buffon. On the western side of the cape **Lighthouse Reef** turns on good waves; best in big SW to S swells and SE winds. Around the cape is another reef break called **Cullens Reef**, a powerful, hollow left which is best when the winds are NE.

To the south of South End is the Canunda National Park, which offers some 40 kilometres of sandy coastline with secluded surfing, excellent fishing and plenty of seals to keep you company (and the white pointers handy).

Further west, around 35 kilometres west of the Princes Highway, is Robe on **Cape Dombey**. To the north of the cape is **Guichen Bay** and in the inside corner at the boat ramp is a left-hander. Further up the beach are a variety of beach breaks. It is interesting to note that Australia's first 'boat people' — some 14 000 illegal Chinese immigrants — landed near here in 1857 in their quest for the gold which had been discovered in Victoria.

South of Robe is the Little Dip National Park, where an unsealed road to **Cape Lannes** takes you through sand dunes and beaches which offer plenty of opportunities for small, secluded waves.

North of Robe the Princes Highway runs parallel to the coastline with the Younghusband Peninsula (now a part of the Coorong National Park) and the Coorong waterway providing a buffer and denying direct access to the coastline.

The next surfing opportunites come at **Victor Harbor**, on the eastern side of the **Fleurieu Peninsu-** la, where some excellent waves can be found in the rugged coastline dotted with sandy beaches and coves which ring the softly undulating farmlands of the interior. The easternmost of these breaks are found around **Middleton** and **Port Elliot**, where there are some pleasant beaches but mostly small waves. This area is the mouth of the Murray River and, despite the rivermouth being regularly blocked by silt, severe tides and currents are a feature.

Better waves are found further south and west along the peninsula. Opposite the drive-in at Port Elliot take the turn-off to a break known as **Boomer**, which has a fierce nature and a bad accident record and has been compared with the famous Newport Wedge in California.

West of Newland Head are **Waitpinga** and **Parsons Beaches**, which require solid S swells or big SW swells but can produce quality beach breaks. From here out to the end of the peninsula, most of the swell action is blocked by Kangaroo Island to the south.

Cape Jervis is the southern tip of the Fleurieu Peninsula (and the departure point for the car ferry to Kangaroo Island) and to the east of the cape — in Gulf St Vincent — surfing opportunities are limited, depending on big SW swells to penetrate. **Rapid Bay** is the first spot to produce waves, mainly during winter. Further north, **Yankalilla** is another spot checked out by the locals when the swell lines start to work up the gulf. North of **Carrickalinga Head**, there is a left inside the cove (the nearest town is

173

Myponga) which can get good. Further north to the city of Adelaide there are a series of beaches — **Sellicks, Aldinga, Maslin** (Australia's first legal nude bathing beach), **Moanna**, **Triggs**, **Southport** and **Christies** — all of which get small waves at times, mainly beach breaks, and are close to the centre of Adelaide but tend to be bypassed by the keen surfers.

Top right *Country cruising.* **Above** *Victor Harbor seascape.*
Right *1987 Australian cadet champion Joshua Locke at Parsons Beach.* **Below** *Only two out and its a drop-in.*
Opposite *Good waves and even better fishing at Waitpinga*

174

MARK SUTTON

Kangaroo Island

Directly south of Adelaide and across the Investigator Strait is Kangaroo Island, Australia's third largest offshore island (only Tasmania and Melville Island are bigger). Access to the island is either by air (a half hour flight from Adelaide) or by the passenger/car ferries which operate regular services from Port Lincoln on the Eyre Peninsula, Adelaide and Cape Jervis on the Fleurieu Peninsula. There is no public transport on the island, though hire-cars and taxis are available from Kingscote. Keen surfers are advised to take a car; the island covers some 4500 square kilometres with 1500 kilometres of roads.

Kangaroo Island has a population of around 3800, most of whom live in three towns in the north-east corner of the island — Kingscote, American River and Penneshaw. These towns offer a range of accommodation, from motels to camping grounds, as well as providing most tourist facilities. Fishing and sightseeing tours are available. Heading east or west through South Australia a trip to Kangaroo Island is a good way of avoiding the mostly surfless Spencer Gulf. The island offers keen and well-heeled surfers a chance to escape the crowds and try some real Southern Ocean power.

The bulk of the surf spots are found on the extremely rugged southern and western coasts, which places them well away from the towns on the island. Ringed by steep cliffs, the island has claimed more than 40 ships since 1847. With access to most of the spots being difficult, crowds are rarely a problem; in fact the locals are often glad to have someone to surf with (and reduce the odds).

Kangaroo Island has a wide variety of breaks, from peaky beach breaks to classic points and grunty offshore reefs. These are mostly accessed from the South Coast Road, the most popular of which are in **D'Estrees Bay** (once the site of a whaling station), out towards **Point Tinline** and further out past Vivonne Bay Conservation Park to **Cape Kersaint**, where there is an excellent left-hander on the western side of the point which works in big S swells (to 3 metres) and N winds. To the east **Vivonne Bay** is the south coast's only protected port and home to a fleet of crayfish and game fishing boats, with four world record tuna catches achieved in these waters.

Further west there are numerous turn-offs to some classic reef breaks in and around Kelly Hill Conservation Park, where you'll find walking trails to the coast. **Cape Bouguer** and **Cape Younghusband** are worth a look both for surf and scenic setting. Further west to **Cape Du Couedic** and the lighthouse and bird sanctuary (at the tip of the cape) there is sometimes an excellent left, which grinds down the western side of the cape towards **Maupertius Bay** on large S to SW swells; best in E to NE winds.

The western tip of the island is all part of the Flinders Chase National Park and past Maupertius Bay the roads deteriorate quickly around **West Bay** and **Cape Borda**. This section of coast cops the full fury of the south-west swell and the roaring forties, with wild swells crashing into the high cliffs a common occurrence. North of here, near Cape Torrens, are the highest cliffs in South Australia.

At the eastern end of the island the rugged cliffs of Cape Willoughby catch some fierce swell action but have little to offer the serious surfer; however the cape gives protection to the popular stretch of coastline to its north.

175

THE YORKE PENINSULA

To the east of Spencer Gulf, the Yorke Peninsula juts leg-like out of the mainland (locals call it 'the only leg Australia has to stand on') in a south-westerly direction, catching Southern Ocean swells on either side of the peninsula north and east from Cape Spencer. The climate is harsh, the roads horrible, but there are some excellent waves to be had on this remote peninsula.

The coastline is characterised by towering, vertical limestone cliffs, waves crashing over rock ledges, reefs and boulders punctured by bays with deserted sandy beaches. To the south, Kangaroo Island blocks most of the swell action on the peninsula, except for the true SW swells which squeeze through between Kangaroo Island and Eyre Peninsula, particularly during winter. In these conditions, this place can be a well-equipped surfer's dream.

Access to Yorketown and the southern, toe-shaped section of the peninsula (where the waves are) is gained from the east coast road through Port Wakefield, Ardrossan, Port Vincent and Stansbury; or down the west coast through Port Broughton, Wallaroo, Moonta and Maitland. At the very toe of the peninsula is the Innes National Park, where most of

the best waves are found. The jumping off point to these breaks is Stenhouse Bay.

The first bay to the west has a left-hand break called **Chinamans**, named after the adjacent small island (called Chinamans Hat Island). This break is considered by many to be the best wave on the peninsula. Barrelling hard across a shallow and partly exposed rock shelf, Chinamans is a powerful and gnarly challenge that breaks boards and bodies whenever given the chance. Access is from the car park (right in front of the break), and getting in and out of the surf when the swell is big can be a traumatic experience. Works in big SW swells to 3 metres and NE to E winds.

Around **West Cape**, the westernmost point of the peninsula (and the place which catches the most direct swell), there are several breaks in close proximity. Off the cape itself there is a left and a right breaking over reef. South of West Cape is **Reef Head**, where the wreck of the *Ethel* lies beached and often the site of excellent waves.

North of West Cape is **Pondalowie Bay**, with an excellent right-hander off the northern point of the bay and peaky beach breaks down the beach. Further north, the deteriorating road — passable only in four-wheel drive vehicles — leads to **Royston Head**, **Browns Beach** and **Gym Beach**, which offer several reef and beach breaks for the adventurous.

There are several other breaks further north, around Point Margaret. These include the right-hand reef break at **Baby Lizard Beach**, south of Point Margaret, and **The Spit** — a long left — on the northern side of the point. North of Baby Lizard Beach car park there is a remote break known as **Trespassers** (access is on private property, so the only way in is around the cliff top).

Opposite, top left *East coaster Robbie Bain at Daley Heads.* **Below left** *George Wales inside nice textures at Chinamans.* **Above** *Clean Chinamans bowl.* **Below** *Rugged coast at Chinamans.* **Bottom** *Pondalowie Bay*

THE ANXIOUS COAST

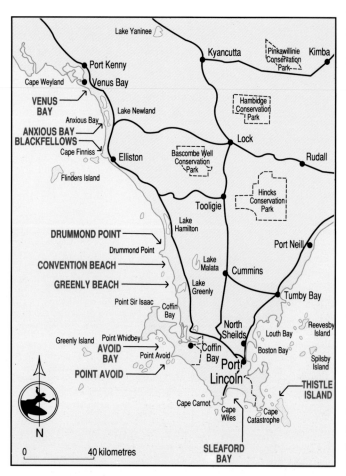

This section of the South Australian coastline, from Port Lincoln to Ceduna, is some 350 kilometres of rugged cliffs and vast bays spread along the coast either side of Anxious Bay. The waters here are abundant with a variety of marine life, from sea lions to bluefin tuna, prawns, crayfish and abalone. The area is also home to substantial numbers of the surfer's favourite fish: *Carcharodon carcharias*, the infamous white pointer shark (the local record is 1208 kg). There have been many attacks on this coast and surfing here is an anxiety-rich experience — you may well take up golf or tennis after this. There is a warning in the names of some of the places, like Anxious Bay, Coffin Bay, Avoid Bay and Cape Catastrophe, and if you have any real problem with surfing in the company of large ferocious sharks you should skip this part of Australia altogether.

Below *The rugged coastline near Elliston.*
Opposite, top left *Eyre Peninsula.* **Top right** *Blackfellows.*
Below right *Yorke Peninsula sunset*

MARK SUTTON

South of Port Lincoln the only real surf is found between Cape Carnott and Cape Catastrophe, with the best spots being **Fishery Bay** and **Sleaford Bay**. Fishery Bay was once the site of a whaling station and has left- and right-hand point breaks which work in SW swells and N winds. Sleaford Bay gets good beach breaks at times, especially at the western end of the bay in S swells and N to NW winds.

Like many other places on this coast, Cape Catastrophe was named by Matthew Flinders (who explored this coast in 1802) after a boating accident in which eight of his crewmen were drowned. Flinders named eight offshore islands in the Thorny Passage after these sailors.

Swell action on the east coast of Eyre Peninsula is mostly blocked by the Jussieu Peninsula and **Thistle Island**. Privately owned, Thistle Island catches plenty of swell and has several good reef breaks. There are cottages which can be rented on the island and flights are available from Port Lincoln.

Heading north-west from Port Lincoln along the Flinders Highway, it's some 49 kilometres to the township of Coffin Bay. Coffin Bay National Park takes up the hammerhead-shaped peninsula of land between Coffin Bay and Avoid Bay. **Coffin Bay** was named by Matthew Flinders after his friend Sir Isaac Coffin, though it might be an appropriate description of the history of the shipwrecks, drownings and shark attacks in the area. Coffin Bay National Park is around 29 000 hectares, with a 20 kilometre exposed section of coastline — between Point Sir Isaac and

Point Whidbey — which catches the full force of the Southern Ocean swells. Access is via a four-wheel drive only 'road' through the national park. At the end of the peninsula the road divides into several tracks leading to the coast in various places where rideable waves can be found, but the difficult access makes local knowledge invaluable in tracking down the best of them.

South of Coffin Bay is **Avoid Bay**, with many offshore islands and reefs blocking much of the swell. At the southern end of the bay is **Point Avoid**, where good reef breaks are found in front of the lookout in SW swells and NE winds.

179

North of Coffin Bay the swell action is blocked by Point Sir Isaac as far as Coles Point. Further north is **Greenly Beach** and, north to Drummond Point, the long stretch of **Convention Beach,** both of which at times have good peaky beach breaks in W to SW swells and NE to SE winds.

To the west of Mount Hope a series of gravel roads will take you to a variety of beach and reef breaks around the **Drummond Point** area. These breaks work best in W to SW swells to around 2 metres and SE to NE winds.

Sheringa Beach, some 10 kilometres off the Flinders Highway at Sheringa, offers some good reef and beach breaks, most of which work on smaller W to S swells and NE to SE winds. This long stretch of beach has many beach breaks to offer as well as offshore reefs, which involve difficult access and a long paddle. The beach breaks are discovered with a lot of adventuring down various tracks off the Flinders Highway.

North of Elliston is the vast expanse of **Anxious Bay.** At its southern end and north of Waldagrave Island is **Cape Finniss**, which for the unwary or inexperienced could be just that: the Finniss. The waves here are powerful and unforgiving.

Inside Cape Finniss is a power-packed left-hander called **Blackfellows**. Breaking over a shallow and sharp limestone bottom, Blackfellows is best in SW swells (to 2 metres) and E to SE winds. Over 2 metres the take-off is virtually impossible to get into; rather than get bigger, this wave seems to get thicker, making the take-off and following barrel an adrenalin-rich experience. If you don't make the take-off, you are likely to be in for a long paddle to shore followed by a short ride to the Elliston Bush Nursing Post for medical attention — this break can be fierce on boards and bodies.

Flinders Island

Around 35 kilometres offshore from Elliston, and only an hour's flying from Adelaide (ten minutes by air from Elliston), is Flinders Island with 14 swimming beaches and 40 kilometres of coastline. For the gutsy adventurer, there are several waves here and the size of the island (compared with the few surfers who surf here) almost guarantees you will find good, uncrowded waves, though surfing isolated waves anywhere on 'the anxious coast' is a risky, spooky experience; enough at times to want a crowd to paddle out and reduce the odds. The waves on Flinders Island are beach and point breaks as well as offshore reefs. The best wave on the island is the grinding right-hander known as **Kitchenview**, which barrels, in series of bowls, down a rugged rock-strewn boulder point on the southern side of the island. Accommodation is available in a recently renovated cottage and the original shearer's quarters which have also been updated. A boat and four-wheel drive vehicle are supplied as part of the package offered. (Phone [08] 262 3733 or [08] 344 9383 for information and bookings.)

Further offshore, south-west of Flinders Island (and also a part of the Investigator Group), are the Pearson Islands, which remain relatively unsurfed but have great potential and no crowds — if that's how you want to surf this coast. Remember that nearly all the shark footage for the *Jaws* films (and most other films involving huge white pointers) was filmed out of Port Lincoln — even the abalone divers here use cages!

Great waves despite the sharky waters

GRAHAM MONRO

At the far end of Anxious Bay is the resort township of **Venus Bay**, some 8 kilometres off the Flinders Highway (the turn-off is 10 kilometres south of Port Kenny) on a peninsula which forms one side of a lovely bay of the same name. To the north-west is Venus Bay Conservation Park, which has a variety of good waves at times from reef breaks at the base of the cliffs to good beach breaks scattered around the bay. Access, however, is difficult.

Some 63 kilometres north-west of Port Kenny (and around 100 kilometres south-east of Ceduna) is the picturesque coastal town of **Streaky Bay**, highly regarded for its surfing and fishing spots. The closest of these to town is **Back Beach**, in Corvisart Bay, which is reached from Wells Street. Right in front of the car park there is a left-hand reef which can turn on excellent small barrels, and either side of the car park are shifting beach breaks. Back Beach tends to be best in smaller S to SW swells to 2 metres and NE to SE winds.

Better waves are to be found to the south towards Sceale Bay. South from Streaky Bay (on the Sceale Bay Road) take the Westall Way turn-off some 10 kilometres south of Streaky and follow it out on the scenic loop around Point Westall. From the car park at the top of a steep, rocky coastline a short walk will get you down to **Granites**, a classic left-hand reef break some distance offshore across a deep channel (usually full of sharks).

On smaller days, Granites breaks as a peak with lefts and rights, but on big days the left walls across to the lagoon with a heavy, sucking and jacking take-off over an extremely shallow bottom. Then it winds off down the reef in a series of bowls and pitching sections. The Granites left will hold swells up to 4 metres, but is usually better around 2 to 2.5 metres when the take-off is less awesome and somewhat easier (possible) to make. Works best in S to SW swells and SE to E winds and is recommended for gutsy, experienced surfers only.

Close by are two further breaks, which are often surfed by visiting surfers in the belief they are surfing Granites. **Indicators** is outside Granites (about 800 metres up the point) and features a long-walled left-hander over a rocky bottom that works in similar conditions to Granites and holds swells to around 3 metres.

Further around the point is a break known as **Smooth Pool**, which can get very gnarly, breaking left powerfully along a boulder-strewn shoreline; works best in a SW swell and N to NE winds, but not surfed often and not recommended for anyone other than the most experienced. Further around is **Yanerbie**, at the northern end of Sceale Bay, where there are sometimes small rights in the corner.

Sceale Bay offers several beach breaks along its length, dependent on sandbank conditions. At the southern end of Sceale Bay, reached via Sceale Bay Road, is a couple of left-hand breaks along the northern face of Cape Blanche; one on the inside, one out at the point. Both are relatively protected from southerly winds and work best in SW swells and SE to NE winds. There is also a quality right-hand barrel known as **The Island,** which holds big S to SW swells and earns rave reviews from those adventurous enough to find and surf it; best in NE winds. To the south of The Island is another quality left-hander called **Squirrels**, which works in similar conditions to The Island but prefers smaller swells.

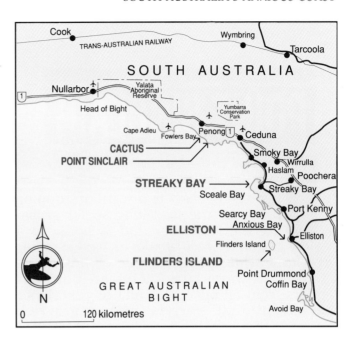

South of Cape Blanche is **Searcy Bay** and **Point Labatt**, a part of the Point Labatt Conservation Park and home to Australia's only colony of sea lions (*Neophoca cinerea*). The coastline around Point Labatt and an area extending one nautical mile seawards was declared an aquatic reserve in 1986 and designated as an aquatic sanctuary. No one is allowed into the area, so its surf potential remains limited.

Fur seals are common along this coastline

181

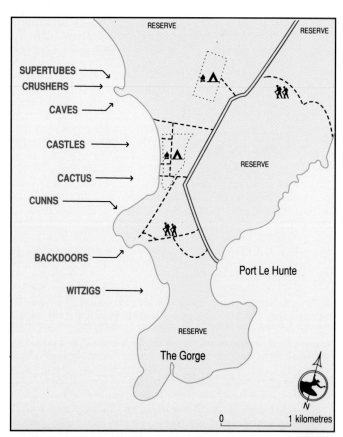

POINT SINCLAIR

This desert oasis is a regular stopping point for the travelling surfer crossing the Nullarbor and is home to a variety of quality reef breaks as well as some very large white pointers. One of Australia's best-known waves, the Cactus area attracts surfers from all over Australia to experience its exceptional barrels and shark-rich waters. Surfers who can say 'I surfed Cactus' enjoy the respect it brings from others, more from fear of the sharks than anything else.

Point Sinclair is some 21 kilometres south of the tiny town of Penong: take the turn-off at the school and follow the dirt road past the lakes right out to Point Sinclair. The whole point is private property, but there is an established camping area on the western side with showers and a small shop (which carries essentials and makes some of the best 'smoothies' you'll taste anywhere). Camping fees at the time of printing were $2 per night per person, with firewood supplied.

The area known as **Cactus** actually comprises eight quality breaks which range in shape and power and are found along the western coast of Point Sinclair. Starting from the south we have **Witzigs,** a powerful left-hander (named after Paul Witzig, who was one of the first to surf these waves in the 1960s and subsequently purchased some 550 hectares, taking in the whole of Point Sinclair). The wave breaks along an offshore bombora just north of

Above *Barrier dunes trap coastal lakes near Cactus.*
Below *Witzigs, a back beach near Cactus*

Granite Rocks. Just to the north (and right in front of the shop) there is a hard-breaking right known as **Backdoors**, which breaks hollow and hard with a double peak and heaps of power.

North-west of the shop and caretaker's residence there is a small bay with plenty of surfing options. At the southern end of the bay you'll find a left which breaks along the base of the cliffs called **Cunns**. Only works in swells between 1.5 and 2.5 metres and breaks over a shallow rock bottom.

Further inside is **Cactus** itself, an overrated wave which is actually a soft left-hander, although sometimes it does get good when it usually becomes crowded. Best in S to SW swells to 1.5 metres and E to NE winds; a wave for the less experienced surfers.

North we have **Outside Castles,** a grunty left with a fast, hollow take-off on an outside peak and a solid wall before the wave reforms into a thick, inside left. Holds big SW swells and is best in E to NE winds. There are lots of currents here, which makes getting out the back very difficult at times. All the shark attacks on surfers in this area have occurred here; there is even one local surfer who's been knocked off his board by sharks three or four times, but still surfs the break regularly. He's been nick-named Shark Bait by the locals.

Inside Castles is a reform on the inside of the reef. Peeling left this wave can be deceptive, often grinding off faster than you expected. The wave is only surfed on smaller days (under 1.5 metres) but can turn on some excellent small barrels.

Across a wide, shark-filled channel (but don't panic, these ones are only bronze whalers, a colony of some 100–200) we have a right-hander known as **Caves,** on its day the best wave on Point Sinclair. A perfect, hollow barrel, Caves pitches fast over a shallow and unforgiving shelf but tends to be blown out by the prevailing onshore breezes early in the day. The wave holds to about 3 metres and can turn on exceptional quality. Definitely only for experienced surfers and there is a heavy local crew here, who will not wear drop-ins: the rocks inside are too unforgiving. There is one particular local, known as Moose (you'll recognise him immediately — big, with a board

to match), who reportedly was in the first car to pull up here with boards on the roof in the 1960s. He's been surfing this wave ever since and is the local enforcer; if you're going to surf 'his' wave, it's strongly recommended that you don't drop in on him.

Sailboarders should note that Caves is perhaps not the best break to sail, as the locals have been known to discourage this activity with extreme prejudice by shooting holes in sails, for instance.

Further north, on the other side of a small headland, is a powerful left called **Crushers,** and a right-hander called **Supertubes.** Both spots have earned their names for obvious reasons.

The whole area works in a variety of tides, and W to SW swells. Offshore winds here are E to NE. There is excellent fishing and diving (if you're game), though it should be noted that this region has plenty of large white pointers and bronze whalers resident all year round.

Above *Cunns, windy but rideable.* **Below** *Inviting conditions at Cactus*

Visiting surfer Pierre Tostee samples some Western Australian juice

CHAPTER 5

WESTERN AUSTRALIA

The state of Western Australia has taken its place with the eastern states over the last decade and become known worldwide, not only for its corporate entrepreneurs but also for the quality of its surf breaks. Whether you travel north to the 'last frontier' breaks of the north-west, or south to the classic Margaret River district, Western Australia has thousands of kilometres of surfable coastline and many excellent waves.

PERTH AND ROTTNEST

The west coast within ready access of Perth's committed band of surfers is popular and competitive, though most of it is blocked from direct swell action by a string of offshore islands and reefs the largest of which is Rottnest.

The most immediately accessible breaks are those found along what appears to be one continuous beach stretching north from Perth for some 20 kilometres, from Cottesloe Beach to Sorrento. This is, in fact, many different beaches whose character, both on land and in the water, varies as we move north from the heavily developed beachfronts close to Perth. All these beaches get small peaky waves at times, although Perth's offshore islands, Rottnest and Garden Islands, tend to block most of the serious swell action.

The most consistent breaks for local surfers (apart from Rottnest Island) are at Cottesloe, Scarborough and Trigg Point. All require large SW to W swells and SE to NE winds, with the quality dependent on the condition of the sand which tends to track north along this stretch of coast. Several groynes have been built to stabilise this sand migration, and these have added new wave potential for the frustrated Perth locals. The best of these are at **Floreat**, Cottesloe and **Mullaloo**.

Clean water and strong waves straight off Perth's coast at Rottnest Island

PETER CRAWFORD

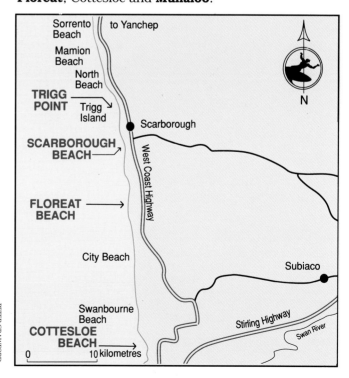

PETER SIMONS

Matt Manners at Trigg Point

When the swell is strong and from the south-west, it gets in behind Rottnest Island and Cottesloe can have several breaks: a big left at the end of the groyne called the **North Cott left**, a right-hand reef break on the south side of the groyne called **The Cove** and a couple of other reefs nearby. Further south along the beach are a variety of beach breaks which can be good but all suffer from the lack of consistency of other Perth beaches.

Scarborough is Perth's closest beach and can get reasonable swells when the general conditions are moderate to large, though the offshore reefs and Rottnest Island keep these days to a minimum.

Trigg Point is generally regarded as the best wave in this area, and often has ridiculous crowds of frustrated surfers, all competing for the waves.

The biggest wave in the west

JOHN CARR / AUSCHROMES

Situated near Hayden, 160 kilometres east of Perth, is a wonderful geological oddity: a permanent (and perfect) bowling 20 metre wave, frozen in solid rock millions of years ago. Formed in pre-Cambrian granite, which crystallised some 2700 million years ago, the rock has been eroded and undercut in the process of weathering, forming an overhang from which it earned its name. The process of erosion and chemical reaction has exposed pronounced vertical bandings on the face of the rock, which vary in colour from deep grey to rusty reds and accentuate its wave-like shape.

Wave Rock is part of the north face of a larger rock of eroded residuals known as Hyden Rock, which is some 3 kilometres east of Hyden township. The area has many unusual rock formations, including Hippo's Yawn, Eggshell Rock, King Rocks, Bates Cave and Whalehead Rock.

Rottnest Island

This small island off the Perth coastline is readily accessible by ferry and offers several excellent waves along its 15 kilometres of exposed coastline as it is open to the southern ocean swells. The island was named by a Dutch explorer, Willem de Vlamingh, who arrived here in 1696 and thought that the local quokka (a short-tailed scrub wallaby) were big rats, so he called the island Rottnest (Dutch for rat's nest). The island is now a nature reserve and the quokkas (*Setonix brachyurus*) are alive and well here (though virtually extinct on the mainland). In 1839 an Aboriginal penal settlement was established on Rottnest, where 'troublesome' blacks (who resisted their traditional lands being stolen by the European invaders) were brought from all over the state to be jailed. They were put to work on salt production from the saline lakes in the north-east of the island. The penal settlement was closed in 1850 and the island converted into a holiday resort for colonial governors, who built a mansion, now the Quokka Arms Hotel. Tourism now rules the island, with the governor's residence and the jail being converted for accommodation.

Facing south-east and the open ocean, Rottnest picks up all available swell and offers good waves along both sides of the south-western peninsula, with Strickland Bay probably the most consistent of a series of excellent breaks. This peninsula, with waves both sides, gives you a chance of finding a good wave no matter what direction the wind.

Starting from the eastern end of the island there are two reef breaks at Salmon Point, at the southern end of Porpoise Bay. On the eastern side of the point is a hollow left-hander called **Chicken Reef**, or Pocilporra, named for the sharp and jagged rock ledge over which the wave breaks; best in S to SW swells to 2 metres and N to NE winds, mid to high tides only. The **Salmon Point** reef is on the western side of the point and is a right-hander which works in similar swells and winds further to the east, when Chicken Reef can get blown out.

Rottnest's best waves can be found either side of the narrow peninsula west of the island's narrowest point. **Strickland Bay** is the best (and best known) of these breaks, with lefts and rights holding swells up to 3 and 4 metres. The right can be a perfect barrel, hollow and fast, but it's the Strickland left which is the most consistent break and holds larger swells. The take-off is deceptively easy, but the bottom tends to drop out as the wave jacks and walls before closing out over an inside shelf. Best in S to SW swells and E to NE winds.

Between Strickland Bay and the western tip of the island there are a couple of fierce right-hand reef breaks, called **Radar** and **Bullet Reefs**, which catch plenty of swell and can be ferociously good. There are also a couple of reef breaks at the western tip of the island, where they are exposed to the full might of swells from the south through to the north-west. Known as **West End** and **Cathedral Rock** (just north of West End), these waves would be two of the wildest and most exposed found anywhere in the country, although Cathedral Rock offers great protection from the summer south-westers.

Above and below *The left at Strickland Bay*

The major wave on the northern side of the island (and one of the best big wave locations anywhere on the west coast) is at a reef about a kilometre offshore from **Stark Bay**, where perfect left-hand barrels break at incredible sizes in SW to NW swells and SE to NE winds; mid to high tides only.

Ferries run from Fremantle (18 kilometres away) and Perth daily, from August until May, with intermittent services through the winter. There are also light aircraft services available from Perth Airport and Fremantle Heliport.

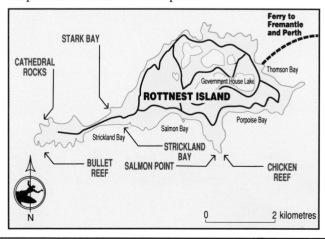

189

NORTH FROM PERTH

O n this vast stretch of wild coast, which receives the full brunt of swells from the Indian Ocean, are some of the best-kept secrets in Australian surfing.

Breaks such as Red Bluff and Kalbarri are now known and respected for their quality and power; they have made it on the lists of experienced surfers as some of the best waves in the country, with many

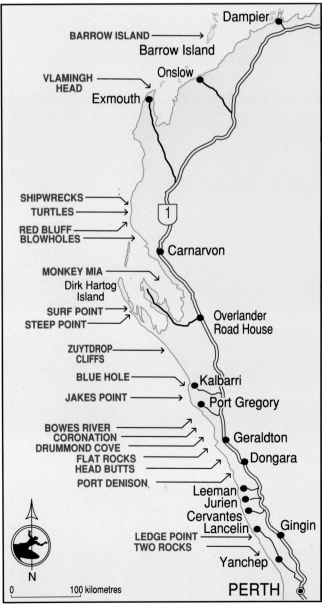

JACK McCOY

Red Bluff, an oasis for surfers on the north-west coast

inaccessible offshore reefs and islands — such as the Houtman Abrolhos, Barrow, Monte Bello and Cocos Islands — offering a number of little known breaks.

Heading north from Perth on Wanneroo or Lancelin Road, and some 3 kilometres south of **Yanchep**, turn off along a sandy track to the beach and follow it for about 1.5 kilometres until you come to a parking area, with a rocky reef outcrop visible at the southern end of the beach. This spot is a left-hand reef break which holds swell to around 2.5 metres (and can be excellent when the swell is clean), but it's usually pretty crowded. Good, hot dog wave, best in a S to W swell and NE to SE winds. This is about the closest of the quality waves north of Perth, which is reflected by the number of guys who surf here. Some beach breaks further south and north work in similar conditions, but the banks can be unstable and very fickle.

North of Yanchep is **Two Rocks**, which was — until the 1970s — just a quiet little fishing spot. Alan Bond changed all that with his Yanchep Sun City development (6 kilometres south of Two Rocks), which covers 7000 hectares along 16 kilometres of coastline including a marina, used as the base for his first two challenges for the America's Cup (*Southern Cross* and *Australia*).

North of Yanchep, along Lancelin Road, we cross the Moore River, with **Guilderton** on its northern side. The rivermouth is usually closed to the sea, but the long sandy beach offers peaky breaks at times although the offshore reefs tend to block out most of the direct swell action. Further north, at Seabird, we find another sleepy village with plenty of craypots and offshore reefs but not much in the way of waves.

South of Lancelin and some 5 kilometres in from the highway there is a boat anchorage with a break known as **Ledge Point,** which has good waves on large S to SW swells and SE to NE winds. Be prepared for a long paddle — perhaps 1–1.5 kilometres — to the breaks. There are a couple of closer reefs but they close out on most swells or have rock shelves at the wrong height in almost all tides.

Lancelin is another tourist/crayfishing port, which nowadays is also very popular with wind-surfers — especially the European speed sailors. Lancelin has potential for surf but, like most of the beaches in this area, breaks are almost non-existent, swell action being blocked by the offshore reefs. Some reefs produce waves, usually in a large S to SW swell with SE to NE winds. But you'll also need a boat to get you out to them. You could consider the options at a classic local pub, the Endeavour Tavern (overlooking the crayfish wharf), complete with huge adzed beams, sandstock bricks and good views. Don't camp on the town beaches — the ranger is very active — instead, use the camping area or find a secluded camp site. South of Lancelin there are some beach breaks; take the turn-off to the beach near the information board on the southern outskirts of town. Some offshore reefs are here as well; it is a good sailing spot. At **Surf Beach**, a wave breaks straight in front of the fishing wharf. If you fancy the outer reefs, try the 20 minute paddle out to the reef on the south side of the passage (to the south of the island). A long, hollow, right-hander which gets very good in SE to NE swells or large S to SW swells. Watch your feet though as tiger sharks and various other finned friends frequent this area and it's a long, long sprint to shore if one of these noahs takes a fancy to you.

North of Lancelin, the coast road deteriorates substantially and, at times, totally. So, unless you have a reliable four-wheel drive vehicle, you'll need to go back to the turn-off south of Guilderton and cut

Matt Branson, one of the west's best surfers, at Flat Rocks

across to the Brand Highway to Gingin, which is the route to all breaks north. Care should be taken if camping in the area between Lancelin and Wedge Island as it used as a naval bombing range.

As we head north on the Brand Highway towards Geraldton, widely known as the crayfish capital of the world, the coast is about 50 kilometres west of us with a series of small crayfish ports dotted along the coast; places like **Cervantes**, **Grey**, **Jurien Bay** and **Green Head**. All these are 'protected' by offshore reefs. Some of these reefs are accessible and surfable with a boat and local knowledge, but they are hardly premium waves for the travelling surfer.

The Brand Highway merges with the coastline at Dongara, around 80 kilometres south of Geraldton. At Dongara turn off the highway and follow the signs to **Port Denison** (yet another crayfish port), some 6–7 kilometres from the highway. On the southern side of the breakwall there is a long-walled left-hander breaking over a shallow reef bottom, which is best in S to W swells (to 2.5 metres), at mid tides, with NE to S winds. Further south there is variety of lefts and rights off the reefs on smaller days. Port Denison has camping grounds and the usual tourist facilities.

Between Geraldton and Dongara there are a variety of breaks accessible by rough four-wheel drive tracks, the most popular being **Headbutts** and **Flat Rocks**. Here you'll find reef running onto sand and peaks which break left and right. Flat Rocks picks up plenty of swell as there are few offshore reefs to block the swell, but it's best on small days — under 2 metres, when there are long walls (with hollow sections) to be had and a rock shelf at the end. Offshore winds here are SE to NE, and best swells are S to W.

In Geraldton and the surrounding areas there are some excellent waves to be had (and some pretty good crayfish). Around **Point Moore** there are extensive offshore reefs. The best of these is **Hells Gate**, a break in the reef used by the crayboats heading south (as an alternative to going right out and around the leader marks). It's a long paddle — the Gate is almost a kilometre offshore, but it picks up most available swell and turns on a hollow right-hander breaking over a shallow bottom. Works best on S to W swells (to 2.5 m) and NE to E winds. Closer to shore is a small left-hand reef break directly in front of the lighthouse.

Top *The roads north of Lancelin are not recommended for anything other than the best equipped four-wheel drive vehicles.* **Above** *Jason Buttenshaw at Flat Rocks*

North of Geraldton, turn off the North-West Coastal Highway into **Drummond Cove** for a small wave spot, again protected by offshore reefs. Works on S to W swell and NE to SE winds. Drummonds breaks over a reef bottom onto a sandy beach with rocky outcrops. This is a good wavesailing location, very popular with Geraldton sailors.

About 20 kilometres north of Geraldton and about 5 kilometres off the highway, **Coronation** is

The Pinnacles — Nambung National Park

Just south of the town of Cervantes is the eerie Pinnacles Desert, a part of the Nambung National Park. The spiky knobs of limestone which make this park one of the most spectacular landscapes in Australia were — perhaps 30 000 years ago — the root system of ancient plants and trees. As climates changed the vegetation was overwhelmed with sand, which converted the roots slowly to the limestone peaks exposed today.

another popular surfing and wavesailing spot. Best in S to W swell to 2 metres, and NE to E winds.

Bowes Rivermouth is a good, small wave spot just south of Horrocks, 25 kilometres west of Northampton. Here, you'll find left and rights over a sandy bottom, with reefy outcrops; best in S to SW swells and SE to NE winds.

As we head north from the Geraldton area and on to Carnarvon and further north to Exmouth, we are getting into real frontier country with vast tracts of virtually uncharted coastline. Access is limited, especially without a four-wheel drive, but there are some great waves.

The coastline around Horrocks has some good beach breaks in E winds and SW swell and the swell size tends to be bigger than around Geraldton. **Port Gregory** is a small natural harbour (and crayfishing port) 45 kilometres north-west of Northampton, where outside reefs protect a lagoon. There are pink salt lakes at the back of the township, along with Prince Leonard's Hutt Province.

Heading further north along the North-West Coastal Highway from Northampton, turn off at Ajana to **Kalbarri**, 66 kilometres off the highway. (Alternatively, there is a rough track along the coast, north from Port Gregory.) There are a number of quality breaks here, the most popular of which is **Jakes Point**, a long-walled, hollow left-hander which breaks off a shallow rock ledge just to the south of Kalbarri township. This is a thick, powerful wave (suited to only the most experienced surfer) which features a *hideous* take-off right next to an exposed rock shelf, followed by a long tube section before a workable wall wraps around the rocks to the beach. Jakes is best on a large S to SW swell and SE to E wind, but it's usually pretty crowded with the large local crew of surfers totally dominating the wave on good days (due to the tiny take-off area and their extensive local knowledge of the break). Well worth a

Above and below *Jakes Point, Kalbarri*

visit, but good manners in the surf are a must! (The consequences of dropping in here can be extreme.) Closer to town are a couple of other small wave breaks, working on SE to NE winds and small S to SW swell. The best of these is called **Blue Hole** and features a short peaky tube (both left and right) before the wave closes out onto a very shallow rock ledge. For beginners, the entrance of the Murchison River gets little reforms, breaking along the sandbanks which lie between the northern side of the river and the parking area to the south. The area also offers excellent fishing (rock, reef and beach) with good catches almost guaranteed. Good camping areas, plenty of facilities, petrol, food, etc. Further north of Kalbarri are the sheer and inaccessible Zuytdorp Cliffs, where you'll find good fishing but no surfable waves.

Located just south of Dirk Hartog Island and at the southern entrance to Shark Bay, **Steep Point** is

CLIVE SLATER

Todd Branson at Jakes Point, Kalbarri

mainland Australia's westernmost point. Access is via a horror four-wheel drive only 'track' that winds through barren rugged sandhills and rocky outcrops; turn off the North-West Coastal Highway at the Overlander Roadhouse into Hamelin, then along a series of tracks till eventually you (hopefully) arrive at Steep Point. This left-hander breaks over a coral bottom and requires a large SW to W swell to make it past the 'Niggerheads' which protrude into the face of the wave halfway along its length. Directly opposite Steep Point is **Surf Point**, a right-hander which works on SW to W swells and E to NE winds. A very spooky place to surf (as is Steep Point) with very strong tides and rips pouring through the narrow channel between the mainland and Dirk Hartog Island. Tiger and whaler sharks (and makos and other assorted varieties) *abound* here — they didn't call it Shark Bay for nothing!

All in all, not really worth the torture track in. Better to spend your time and money going to Monkey Mia (on the east coast of the Peron Peninsula) and check out the 'tame' dolphins. At least they won't try to eat you!

Around 50 kilometres north of Carnarvon are the famous blowholes which shoot water 20 metres into the air. Here you'll find beach and reefs which produce good, small, fun waves on S to SW swell and

SE to NE wind. A sailboarding location, camping area, good fishing and diving. Popular with fishermen, as are the cliffs further north.

Houtman Abrolhos Islands

These offshore islands are reputed to have good waves at times, but as they are so far offshore (80 kilometres west of Geraldton) and as you are not permitted to land, the only waves that get ridden are by the local cray fisherman, who operate out of these tiny, barren islands for 3 to 4 months every year. It is not advisable to sail in these waters, as the reefs are very extensive and dangerous, as Francisco Pelsaert's *Batavia* (among others) found out on 4 June 1629. So any surfers wishing to surf here had best try to score a deck job on a crayboat. With the current record prices crays are bringing, you had better be patient. Once again, plenty of potential but practically impossible to get to, let alone surf.

About 135 kilometres north of Carnarvon is **Red Bluff** (also known as Camp of the Moon), probably Australia's best known 'secret spot'. Here, the harsh desert environment is offset by abundant marine life (with dolphins, whales, manta rays and particularly large sharks) and excellent quality waves. Featured in numerous surfing magazines and movies, The Bluff has a well deserved reputation as one of Australia's best left-handers. Holding up to 4 to 5 metres, but usually best at 2 to 3 metres, The Bluff works on a S to SW swell and SE through to NE winds, breaking on all tides but usually best on mid tides. The Bluff features a steep, jacking take-off, followed by a long, hollow, bowling section before it backs off into the deep hole around the point called the 'shark pit' (don't ask). Breaking over an extremely shallow, urchin-infested coral and limestone bottom, The Bluff quickly sorts the men from the boys on the larger days with the fast falling lip axeing many a victim halfway through their bottom turn.

The camping area on the foreshores of the beach (just to the north of the point) is usually pretty crowded in the winter months, with travelling surfers, locals and until a recent crackdown by Carnarvon CES and social security office large numbers of Bob Hawke's surf team. A visit to The Bluff for any length of time requires extensive preparation as there is no food, water, petrol or shops, and no facilities other than toilets and garbage bins. A good first-aid kit is recommended as a 'meeting' with the bottom is inevitable here, and if not properly treated sea ulcers will severely limit your surfing. Further to the north is another break called **Turtles,** which is near the sandhills visible from Red Bluff and accessible by a rough dirt track. Turtles breaks over a coral bottom, peeling left and right, and works on S to W swells and SE to NE winds; a good alternative to The Bluff on small days as it picks up more swell, but usually closes out over about 2 metres. The left

Above *Sydney surfer Rod Kerr, at The Bluff.* **Below** *Fishing off the coast is invariably productive*

has a peaky take-off, with a hollow bowl section and workable walls. The right is shallower and usually faster.

Still further north is a break called **Shipwrecks,** although this is rarely surfed due to its position and the unfriendly reefs. The Bluff is definitely the best wave in the area. Worth a visit, but be prepared for basic living standards and crowds. Dogs are prohibited as The Bluff is on a private sheep station. Keep a sharp (and constant) eye out for man-eating sharks and surf within your capabilities as it's a long way to hospital.

From Carnarvon it's a long, hot 380 kilometre drive to Exmouth and **Vlaming Head** where you may find lefts though it's an inconsistent break as extremely large swells are needed. The wave breaks along a rocky point over a reef bottom, just below North West Cape Lighthouse and is best in large S to SW swells and SE to NE winds. Exmouth, the nearest town, is a support town for the extensive navy and airforce (both Australian and American) bases. Exmouth is arguably Australia's No. 1 nuclear target — anyway that's what it says on the beer coasters in Exmouth's Potshot Inn. This is a very expensive town to stay in, but offers some excellent gamefishing and nice beaches.

North of Onslow and 150 kilometres west of Dampier is **Barrow Island**, which is leased by an oil company for mining. Landing on the island is prohibited; there is no public transport, accommodation or camping allowed. The only way to surf here is to get a job with the mining company, but then you can only surf after work and leave must be taken off the island. Nevertheless the island has a number of good spots, offering a variety of quality left- and right-hand barrels. These waves work on S to W swells and SE to NE winds. The waves feature very shallow bottoms, the wave breaking over coral (with exposed niggerheads). The area also offers a vibrant marine life, including plenty of big tiger sharks. This is one of those spots you can only dream about as you've got very little chance of actually surfing it.

Top *Some of the waves on the north-west coast require a solid walk in.* **Right** *Mike McAuliffe finds some shade at The Bluff.* **Below** *The Bluff*

CLIVE SLATER

CLIVE SLATER

Left *Mike McAuliffe at Turtles.* **Above** *Brett Munro at The Bluff.* **Below** *Mitch Thorsen, one of the West's most successful surfers, finds some north coast isolation*

JEFF HORNBAKER

The Cocos Islands

Situated in the Indian Ocean 2768 kilometres north-west of Perth, the Cocos Islands comprise some 27 islands which were once privately owned by the Clunies Ross family. There are two main islands, Home Island which is where the Malay people live who were brought to the area as unskilled labour, and Direction Island which houses the Australian military and quarantine station. The arca has become a key military position and was taken over as an Australian territory in 1978. Special permission is now required to visit the Cocos, but surfer Jim Banks and intrepid photographer Peter Crawford were lucky enough to get in briefly in 1986 to record some great waves. The local school teacher, shop owner, and two grommets form the entire local surfing population.

Top *Jim Banks revels in the Cocos isolation.*
Right *Surfers go to extraordinary lengths to get onto the Cocos. Here, a group of keen surfers have disguised themselves as army personnel just to get into the island. Note the altitude. These guys are hoping the swell isn't over ten feet.*
Below *A wave very rarely ridden*

Paul Green comes off the bottom at Margaret River

SOUTH FROM PERTH

As we head south from Perth antici-pation builds for a stretch of coastline, from Cape Naturaliste to Cape Leeuwin, which produces some of the most consistent big waves found anywhere in the country.

Taking either Mandurah Road (along the coast and through Mandurah) or the South Western Highway to Bunbury, we find ourselves passing Geographe Bay, where the surf is very limited but the fishing and sailing excellent. **Mandurah** has some good waves at times. About 8 kilometres north of the town (at Peelhurst) try **Surf Beach** for some good quality beach breaks, but only when there is a solid swell. There are more breaks north of Mandurah at **Singleton** and south of the town at **Madora**, as well as breaks at **Blue Bay, Halls Head** and **Falcons.**

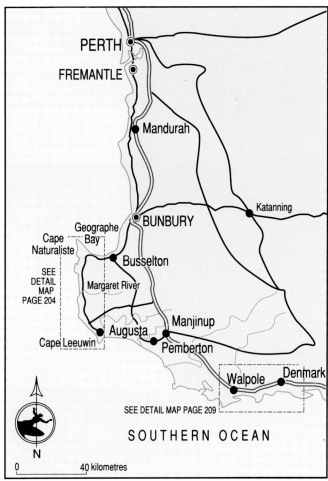

PETER SIMONS

Bunbury, a large industrial port and holiday centre (with a population of 23 000), has a surf beach which flanks the western shore south of the natural harbour. Not much surf (as the swell action from the south is blocked by Cape Naturaliste), but can be good for beginners at times. The tidal shallows of Leschenault Inlet produce quantities of blue manna (or blue swimmer crabs) — very tasty and well worth the distraction but, like most of this coastline (until we get to Cape Naturaliste), it hasn't much to offer the serious surfer.

Travelling south-west from Bunbury along the Bussell Highway, turn off at Capel to the **Capel Rivermouth,** which can produce quality waves on occasions but don't hold your breath waiting; its 'protected' location will keep those moments limited.

Further around the bay we come to Busselton and it's famous 2 kilometre wooden jetty, built in 1865 and extended nine times since. Cyclone 'Alby' destroyed the inner section of the jetty in 1978, but it's still possible to walk the entire length. The Vasse Estuary, behind Busselton, was named after a sailor lost from the French ship *Geographe* in 1801 and presumed drowned. (British settlers, 33 years later, were shown the grave of a white man who, Aborigines said, had spent his days gazing out to sea waiting for his ship to return!)

Following the bay around to the west along the Bussel Highway and then Caves Road, we come to Dunsborough. Just north-west of Dunsborough, along Cape Naturaliste Road, then on to either Meeup Beach Road or Eagle Bay Road takes you to Eagle Bay, Point Picquet and **Castle Rock** (where a cairn marks the site of Castle Rock company's whaling station, founded in 1845). This area sometimes gets waves but only rarely.

Heading north west from Dunsborough we enter the Leeuwin–Naturaliste National Park, which in various sections dominates the coastline from here to Cape Leeuwin. A long walk along the coast from Eagle Bay gets you to **Rocky Point.** A left-hander breaking over a reef off the low rocky point with a peaky take-off, the wave walls up and wraps around the corner into a small bay. This is a very popular

spot with surf skis and learners, a pretty place surrounded by bush, but it rarely lives up to its potential. Works best on large SW to W swells and SW to SE winds . There are a few small left-hand breaks between Rocky Point and the car park (in Eagle Bay), but they all close out over 2 metres and there are plenty of surf skiers here too. Nevertheless it's a popular area with fishermen and holiday makers, with a good bakery in Dunsborough (along with several surfing, sailboarding and accessories shops and factories).

Around to the west, and surrounded by private farming land, are two breaks, **The Farm** and **Barnyards,** which are accessible by a long walk along the beach either from Bunker Bay or Eagle Bay (turn off Cape Naturaliste Road). These breaks lack consistency due to their position (tucked in behind the cape), but sometimes — usually in the winter months — they get good quality beach breaks, mainly right-handers. These breaks all need huge SW to W swell (or smaller NW swells), and SW to SE winds. Good for small wave surfers, but definitely lacking the power and size (not to mention the consistency) of the south-west coast, just around past Cape Naturaliste.

The route up to the tip of Cape Naturaliste offers some spectacular views of this extremely rugged coastline. The full contrasts of the Cape — from the jagged cliffs and raging seas to the west, to the calmer water of Geographe Bay — can be fully appreciated by taking one of the many walking tracks. The cape has breaks on both sides, which offer waves in a wide variety of conditions. Perhaps the most accessible, and also the prettiest bay, is found at the break known as **The Quarries,** which is protected in the summer months from the prevailing south-west winds (known as 'The Fremantle Doctor'). This is an average left-hander, which holds swell to around 2 metres, breaking along the low rocky point and into a small bay over a reef bottom; needs a big SW swell to work.

Further out towards the tip of the cape are a few offshore reefs and bommies, which also need big

Below left *Pea Break.* **Below** *Injidup car park*

North Point

swells and are rarely surfed. But it's when we get around the corner of the cape that the action really begins. The first section of coast — between the lighthouse at Cape Naturaliste and Sugarloaf Rock — has two lefts, known as **Lighthouse** and **Other Side of the Moon,** and a good right, **Windmills.** All these waves need small, clean SW to W swell and light E winds.

To the south of Sugarloaf Rock near Kabbijgup Beach, along an extremely heavy four-wheel drive only track or a long walk along the beach from either Yallingup or Sugarloaf Rock, you'll find three left-handers known as **The Three Bears** — Baby Bear, Mama Bear and Papa Bear — with Mama Bear usually the best. These bears do their thing — intense, hard-breaking barrels — on small, smooth SW to W swells and NE to E winds. For experienced surfers only.

South of Kabbijgup Beach is a series of rugged cliff-lined beaches. Among them is a break known as **Shivery Rock,** a heavy-breaking wave with dredgy sandbars; access is very difficult. Further south along the coast you come to the small holiday town of **Yallingup**, which gets small average rights and lefts breaking over reef into the beach. This wave was surfed quite regularly in the early long board days and is suitable for assorted surf craft.

Better waves are to be found just to the south, around **Smiths Beach**. There is an average left-hander which breaks off the rocks at the southern end of the beach. A number of good waves can be had by walking north up the beach. The first is a hollow, powerful right-hander, which breaks in SE to E winds and SW to W swells to 2 metres. The second

break you come to is called **Supertubes**; a suckey, super-hollow right-hander. Supertubes holds swells up to 1.5 – 2 metres, with a steep take-off (over a shallow reef) followed by a very long, hollow section, living right up to its name when the conditions are right — SW to W swells and SE to E winds. Good manners and respect are required while surfing here as they are truly 'one surfer' waves. Further north along the beach are breaks known as **Stepping Stones** and **The Palisades**. The area has good camping, a scenic coastline and plenty of wildlife, as well as excellent fishing (rocks, beaches and diving). Accommodation is available in either Smiths Beach or Yallingup. Worth a look.

Further south from Yallingup along Caves Road take the Wyadup Road turn-off and follow it to Cape Clairault Road and **Injidup**. Around Cape Clairault there are several quality breaks. The first is called **Car Park** (because of its position) and has quality rights; works in SW to W swells and SE to NE winds. Similar conditions work for **Pea Break,** a classic right-hand reef break, peaking on the shallow reef bottom before throwing over into a long tube section. Holds to 2 metres, and gets very popular on smaller days.

Further around the bay to the south out near the end of the long sandy point is **Big Injidup,** a long left-hander which breaks along the rock-strewn shoreline. This wave needs a large SW to W swell and is protected in most sea breezes (offshore in SE winds). It's a 'soft' kind of wave but it can get good at times.

Along the coast to the south is another break called **Mufflers,** a good right-hander which needs SW to W swell and E to NE winds and tends to be at its best on smaller days.

Further south is a rugged coastal stretch with short sidetracks leading to headlands and cliff tops overlooking a turbulent ocean which has claimed more than twenty ships over the years in which records have been kept. There is a number of good breaks in this area, like **The Window,** and several good quality waves near **Moses Rock.** (Take the Moses Rock Road turn off from Caves Road.) Several left and right reef and beach breaks are found here in an extremely rugged — but spectacularly beautiful — section of coastline.

South on Caves Road towards Cowaramup Bay is a maze of tracks leading west to the coast through both private land and national park. Worth a look if you are adventurous — the camp sites are plentiful — but most of the tracks are unmarked and directions impossible to describe. But by turning down Biljedup Beach Road, Cullen Road or Juniper Road — and following your instincts along the rough tracks — you will possibly come across breaks like **The Gallows** and **The Guillotine** (if one doesn't 'hang you up', the other is sure to 'cut your head off' if you don't duck quickly enough). The Gallows breaks left off an outside bombie in a big jacking peak, before cleaning up over the inside reef. The Guillotine is found further south; a hollow, powerful left-hander, needing (like The Gallows) a clean SW to W swells to 2.5 metres and SE to NE winds. Breaks over a shallow reef and, like most of these extremely isolated reef breaks, it's a long way to the hospital. Neither of these waves were named for their gentle nature and they are recommended for experienced surfers only.

For more easily accessible waves on this part of the coast turn off Caves Road along Cowaramup Bay Road to Cowaramup Bay and Gracetown, a small holiday and retirement town. Unfortunately, this area gets very crowded. Probably the best of the breaks (but also the least consistent) is **North Point**; a heavy-duty, 'filthy', right-hand reef break. This wave is especially favoured by natural-footers in a state starved of good right-handers, but it is not for the faint-hearted whichever way they stand. Working best on the largest SW to W swells (when Margaret River is huge), North Point features a heavy, dredging take-off over the customary shallow reef, followed by a seemingly endless thick, hollow, bowl section. (Ian Cairns perfected the snap back here.) Best in NE to E winds and definitely only for experienced surfers. You can also find good quality waves (in similar conditions) across the bay at **South Point,** a long, wrapping left-hander, breaking along the inside of Cowaramup Point (after being cleaned up by the outside bommies). South Point has a jacking, peaky take-off, followed by a series of cut-back sections. This break gets good quality waves, especially when everything else is blown out by the sea breeze, and generally, it's worth the walk and paddle, though crowds can be a problem.

Between South Point and the car park are good, softer waves, both lefts and rights, called **Hassars**, which breaks over reef and is suitable for beginners. Best in SW to W swells and SE to NE winds. Around the back of Gracetown, to the south past The Tip turn-off, is a series of dirt roads and car parks which

South Point

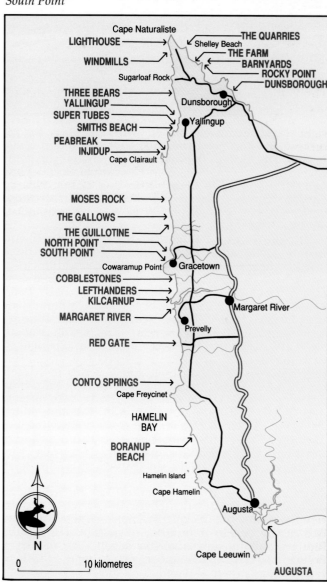

204

give access to a number of good surfing locations. The first is **Big Rock,** a heavy right-hander breaking over reef which works in SW to W swells and E to NE winds. Next down the coast is **Cobblestones,** a good right-hander which breaks in small clean swells to 2 metres over reef; best in E to NE winds.

Next is **Noises,** and even further along the beach, access by foot traffic only, is **Left-handers.** A good quality wave, Left-handers picks up plenty of swell and is best on small, SW to W swells and E to NE winds; an intense wave, with a hollow, suckey take-off, fast moving and powerful, but usually well populated too. Breaks over a shallow reef (one of many in the area), before closing out onto a rocky weed and urchin-covered shoreline. Well worth a look on smaller days; just be sure to count the numbers of surfers out before heading down there. It could surprise you.

Past Left-handers there are a few small swell spots, down towards **Cape Mentelle** on the northern side of the Margaret River. Like that north of Cowaramup, this coastline is extremely isolated, but the cliffs and shoreline aren't as hostile with sandy beaches and some good quality waves. Again tracks are unmarked and directions impossible to describe; a reliable four-wheel drive is usually essential to avoid getting stuck. Worth a look on smaller days, but take your fishing rod or diving gear as the quality waves on the coast are usually found elsewhere. On flat days there are many outstanding vineyards in the area, with wine tasting and cellar sales readily accessible at almost all of the established estates.

Margaret River is the focus of every surfer's vision of this coast, offering some of the best waves in Western Australia. From the township of Margaret River proceed along Wallcliffe Road, 10 kilometres to Prevelly. Here you will find (conditions permitting) a variety of good quality waves, among them Margaret

Above *The south coast has many quality breaks.*
Below *Mitch Thorsen at Left-handers.* **Bottom** *Left-handers*

River Main Break or The Point, Grunters, The Bommie, Suicides, The Box, Boat Ramp and The Rivermouth. The most famous of these breaks — and the one best known on the west coast — is **Margaret River Main Break** or **The Point,** predominantly a left-hander, although it can turn on quality hollow rights up to 2.5 metres (over this size the inevitability of being caught inside makes the left a wiser choice).

The classic **Margaret River left** holds quality waves up to 4 and 5 metres; a shifting peak with thick pitching lips and heart-in-mouth drops. The wave then goes through a dredging bowl section before backing off slightly and wrapping around the edge of the shallow rock bench, followed by a series of fuller cutback sections around past the 'Nigger Head' towards the small beach. Working best on SW to W swells and SE to NE winds and mid tides, the point is definitely for experienced surfers only with horror hold-downs and broken boards (and bodies) a regular occurrence. An added danger factor is preseented by the hardcore sailboarders who regularly rip the place apart whenever the wind and swell is up. Many surfers have found it very intimidating to have a sailboard bearing down at them, right at the most critical time. Luckily the wave sailors like it when there is plenty of wind, when it is usually too bumpy to surf.

Across the bay to the north from the take-off point is a notorious right-hander (reminiscent of Shark Island in Sydney) called **The Box,** which needs big swells and E to NE winds. A bottomless suck-out over extremely shallow rocks, The Box is rarely surfed; a place for the hardcore and/or crazy to dream about (what 'normal' surfers would describe as a nightmare). Surf it, if you are game, but be warned: it usually sucks dry on the take-off.

Between The Box and The Point is a small beach, and the entrance (usually closed) to Margaret River.

Sometimes getting good banks (due to heavy rip action), the rivermouth offers the beginner and small wave surfer an alternative to the reef breaks in the area. Holding swells to 2 metres, it is best on SW to W swells and SE to NE winds. About 200 metres south of The Point is another break called **Suicides**, which picks up the swell before The Point and acts as an indicator for the point crew. Suicides can produce good quality long rides, both lefts and rights, starting with a steep jacking take-off over an extremely shallow bottom (best surfed at mid to high tide), followed by long workable walls. The right-hander fades out into deep water but the left-hander closes out onto the shallow rock shelf. Holds big waves and is usually only surfed when The Point gets too crowded. Long paddles here plus strong currents and lengthy hold-downs are a constant encouragement for those surfers who smoke to give it away.

For the more adventurous surfer craving even more power and danger, a 300-metre paddle south from Suicides will get you to **The Bommie,** which only shows its real form on huge days. The car park on the point gives a perfect side view of these horror, gnarly, spitting left-handers. The right gets equally as good, but is harder to see from the car park. For an adrenalin rush and some real terror The Bommie easily rates a 10. Works on huge SW to W swells and SE to NE winds, on higher tides. A few surfers have taken on The Bommie having decided that the point was too crowded, only to find — after a trip over the falls and a savage pounding — that the point wasn't as crowded as first thought.

Further south are a series of offshore reefs, the best of them being a left-hander off the **Boat Ramp** at Gnarabup Beach. It's a long paddle and the break needs big swells and higher tides. Gets good quality

Margaret River

CLIVE SLATER

Tom Carroll makes his mark on a big Margarets wall

waves, but due to its distance offshore it's very difficult to judge the size. Again for the very experienced surfer only. Further south of Prevelly along a bumpy dirt track (through private property) past the boat ramp turn-off you will find, with a bit of effort, a number of right- and left-hand beach and reef breaks. The best of these is **Grunters**; a long, powerful, hollow right-hand reef break, which works on SW to W swells and is best in SE to NE winds. It is called Grunters because of its *awesome* power, shallow reef and thick, double-up take-offs, which makes the break suitable for the very experienced only.

Like Margarets, Grunters is a boon to local boardmakers, as both waves break similar numbers of boards. Surfers also get a severe mauling at the hands of the white water and the sandflies. Grunters holds swells up to 3 metres. As at all surfing spots, respect and courtesy should be shown to everybody, both locals and visiting surfers, as these waves are extremely powerful and can be lethal. (So can the guys you drop in on.)

Further south of Grunters there is a good small-wave break called **Gas Bay**; a hollow right-hand barrel which peels over sand-covered reef. Works on small swells up to 2 metres and best in SE to NE winds.

Still further south is **Boodjidup Beach.** (Access is limited to foot traffic only from Grunters, or you can walk in from Redgate Beach to the south.) Boodjidup produces good beach breaks in small swells and SE to NE winds; good left- and right-handers, on mid to high tides. Offshore reefs get pretty big but tend to close out on larger days.

Redgate Beach (access along Redgate Road off Caves Road) has small beach breaks. (It is also the site of the *Georgette* wrecking in 1876, where Grace Bussel gained fame for her rescue of the survivors — a monument commemorating the wreck can be seen at Isaacs Rock.) Redgate Beach works on small days, and is offshore in N to E winds. (The beach faces the same direction as Margaret River's mouth.) It's mainly a sand bottom, with some reefs in front of the car park near **Isaacs Rock**. Excellent fishing from rocks and beach and good skindiving too.

Further south along Caves Road just north of Lake Cave, turn off into the Leeuwin–Naturaliste National Park and follow the road for about 15 kilometres (being careful of the many blind corners) until you come to **Conto Springs** camping area, situated on the southern corner of a long sandy beach on the base of the rugged coastal range. The camping area has toilets, BBQs, picnic tables, grassy areas and reasonable rates. Fresh water is available from an underground stream which bubbles out in the southern corner of the beach. A left-hander breaks off the rocks (offshore in S to NE winds) and holds swells to 2.5 metres in S to SW winds. The wave starts with a wedgy take-off, followed by an intense long wall and a dredgy closeout towards the beach.

Past Cape Freycinet there is not much in the way of waves until you come to **Boranup Beach**. Access is gained via Caves Road to Boranup Drive, then on a series of rough tracks to North Point and Boranup Beach situated at the northern end of Hamelin Bay. A long sandy beach, with numerous gutters and shifting sandbanks, Boranup sometimes has good beach breaks, which work on large S to W swells (when Margarets is huge, Boranup is usually about half its size) and best in NE to E winds. There is excellent fishing from the rocks and in the many gutters to be found along this white sandy beach to Hamelin Island, a rugged island 200 to 300 metres offshore at the southern end of Hamelin Bay. Here, the remains of an old wooden jetty extends into the bay near the boat ramp and camping area. There are offshore reefs, bommies and rocks all the way to Cape Hamelin. Access to Knobby Head is along Cosy Corner Road, 3.5 kilometres off Caves Road; a good picnic spot with excellent diving, a rocky coastline and craggy cliffs, but nothing much in the way of surf. This stretch of coastline doesn't seem to pick up as much swell as around Margarets and further north.

Heading south towards Augusta, spectacular panoramic views of the coast can be had from Hillview lookout. Not much surf in Augusta and surrounding area, although on the right swell there are waves to be had at the entrance to the **Black-wood River** and Hardy Inlet (an extensive lake/river system, with excellent fishing and river cruises to Molloy Island and way upstream to Alexandra Bridge).

The rivermouth sometimes has good sandbars, which work on S to SE swells and NW to NE winds. Beach breaks can sometimes be had down the coast towards Windy Harbour and Point D'Entrecasteaux, but access is hindered by the rivermouth (there is no bridge across it); the only other way in is via a maze of rugged four-wheel drive-only tracks through dense bush, rivers and swamps, requiring local knowledge (to prevent getting hopelessly lost) and dry conditions, a rarity in this part of Australia.

Further down the coast from Augusta is Cape Leeuwin (the south-westernmost point of mainland Australia) and its lighthouse, constructed in 1896. This limestone structure stands 49 metres high, with a light which flashes 55 metres above the high tide mark. During the building of the lighthouse a spring was tapped to provide fresh water for the workers

and lighthouse keepers. The water from the spring was carried along a narrow wooden channel to a wooden water wheel. Its timber calcified by limestone sediments, the remains can still be seen today. Further to the east of Cape Leeuwin is a memorial to Matthew Flinders. Around Cape Leeuwin there's a scenic loop road, Skippy Rock Road, overlooking the Indian and Southern Oceans and Flinders Bay. The Dutch named the south-western region 'Land Van de Leeuwin' (Land of the Lioness) in 1627, in honour of the ship *Leeuwin*, which sailed in these waters in 1622. (Matthew Flinders didn't arrive until 1801.) Back 8 kilometres along Caves Road from Augusta you shouldn't miss Jewel Cave, which contains some beautiful underground formations. There are numerous caves in the SW region of enormous proportions, with massive pillars and myriads of delicate stalactites and stalagmites, as well as chambers, underground lakes and pools. Yallingup Cave, Mammoth Cave, Lake Cave and Jewel Cave are worth a look on flat days.

A few rules to remember

Please take note of the following points which apply to all national parks in Western Australia:

1. **Fires should be confined to use of portable stoves or BBQs provided. Open fires are dangerous and usually banned.**
2. **All vehicles must remain on approved tracks (as indicated by directional signs) and are required to be licensed.**
3. **All native plants and wildlife are protected and no firearms or domestic animals are permitted in the parks.**
4. **Don't destroy what you came to enjoy.**

Below left *Access out to the break at Margaret River means a swim at higher tides or a walk and a swim at low tide.*
Below *Hamelin Bay*

Coastline near Albany

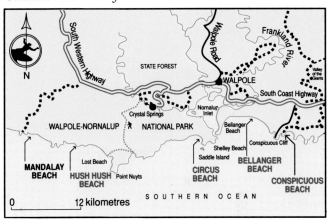

EAST TO THE NULLARBOR

Cape Leeuwin represents the place where the Indian Ocean meets the Southern Ocean and it signals a change in both the direction and character of the coast. This is one of the more inaccessible stretches of coastline. It's a coastline with some spectacular scenery, rugged granite and sandstone cliffs, sandy beaches and, if you're lucky, excellent waves as it stretches 1500 kilometres east to the South Australian border.

As we head south-east from Augusta there is little in the way of accessible surf until you get to **Windy Harbour**, reached via a sealed road from Northcliff. Snuggled up under the lee of the massive Point D'Entrecasteaux it's a wide open bay offering little protection for boats from the raging turmoil of the Southern Ocean. Like most spots down here it's a long way to go for limited possibilities of good waves, with the prevailing summer south-westerlies and huge seas and onshores in winter severely limiting the chances of catching it on.

The next surfable waves east of here are reached by turning off South Western Highway at Crystal Springs (where there is a store, petrol, ranger's office and camping ground); follow the directions for 8 kilometres down a narrow winding dirt track to **Mandalay Beach**. (Care should be taken as the track is extremely narrow with many blind corners.) Mandalay Beach is in a part of Walpole Nornalup National Park — as is most of the stretch of coastline right along to Irwin Inlet to the east. Mandalay Beach is a long, sandy beach ringed by steep headlands and cliffs, with Chatham Island just offshore. The heavy rip action here produces excellent southern ocean beach breaks, which are offshore in NE to NW winds and SE to SW swells to 2.5 metres.

Heading back along Mandalay Beach Road to the ranger's residence, turn off on Long Point Track from which you can get to **Hush Hush Beach** and **Lost Beach**, near Point Nuyts (the only declared wilderness area in the state). There are sometimes good beach breaks here; best in N to E winds, W through S swell to 2 metres, as well as good fishing from rocks and beaches. Further to the east, but virtually inaccessible, is **Circus Beach**. It is a popular fishing location with good beach breaks on a SW to S swell and NW to NE winds. Further around to the east is **Rocky Head**, a right-hand point break also most accessible by boat (as is **Saddle Island**, located just offshore). Needs large SW to SE swell and NW to N winds. Bellanger Beach can also get good beach breaks at times.

Further to the east on the South Coast Highway we pass Walpole and through the tinglewood and karri forests (worth a look, The Valley of the Giants contains some of the biggest trees in Australia, truly awesome, with tree trunks 20 metres in circumference). **Bellanger Beach** is accessible by turning off the highway onto Station Road. Perhaps a better bet would be **Conspicuous Beach**, just past Valley of the Giants Road and along Conspicuous Beach Road. Shifting sandbars and heavy rips sometimes produce quality beach breaks here, working up to 2.5 metres on N to E winds and sizeable SW to S swells, with plenty of power. Huge cliffs make this spot conspicuous; the power makes it memorable.

Off the easternmost point of Conspicuous Beach there are a couple of bommies, and good banks at times in the south-eastern corner. Going back along Conspicuous Beach Road a few kilometres, turn onto Ficifolia Road to **Peaceful Bay, Foul Bay** and **Rame Head**. (You will need a four-wheel drive to get to Rame Head.) Just past Peaceful Bay there is a good quality right-hand reef break, working on large S to SW swell and NW to N winds.

Further to the east is **Quarram Beach, Little Quarram Beach** and **Boat Harbour**. (Turn off South Coast Highway onto Boat Harbour Road.) Access is quite good to Boat Harbour, but getting to Quarram beaches can be pretty difficult with a long walk necessary. At the end there are some beach breaks but usually it's not really worth the effort.

There is also a number of other good beach breaks in **William Bay** (turn off the highway onto William Bay Road and National Park); this is a very scenic stretch of coast with Greens Pool and Madfish Bay (with its beautiful waterfall entering the ocean an ideal location for swimming and fishing). Just past Madfish Bay (access off either Procter Road or Lights Road) are **Lights Beach** and **Back Beach,** which get good beach breaks on SW to S swell to 2 metres with N to NE winds offshore.

The next spot, **Ocean Beach**, at the entrance to Wilson Inlet, is somewhat protected from SW swells and is usually quite small. Reputed to be one of the best surfing beaches in the state, it nonetheless requires a large SW to SE swell to fulfil its potential. Best when the Wilson Inlet is open to the sea (all too rarely), it gets long right-hand barrels but usually only has small beachbreaks in the western corner of the bay (Ratcliffe Bay). The most popular beach to the east of Ocean Beach is **Anvils**, where you'll find left and right peaks in N to NE winds and SW to S swell on higher tides. Breaks on shifting sandbars and is very popular with waveskiers!

From Denmark to Albany you can take either the South Coast Highway or the Lower Denmark Road; similar distances, 55 kilometres, but for access to some good beaches the one to take is the Lower Denmark Road. Some 6 or 7 kilometres along this road turn off on Tennessee South Road to **Lowlands Beach,** a small sandy beach surrounded by granite rocks where there are sometimes good beach breaks in the middle of the beach; best in N to W winds and S to SE swell to 2 metres. Plenty of rip action, and good fishing from the rocks.

Mutton Bird Beach picks up plenty of swell and gets long, hollow beach breaks; it involves a long walk along the beach and gets quite crowded, especially when Albany's few good surf spots are closing out. Works in N winds and S swells to around 2 metres.

The next surfable waves are at **Albany**, where you should turn off on Frenchmans Bay Road and then Sand Patch Road, which takes you to **Sand Patch** — a long sandy beach at the base of large cliffs. Sand Patch gets good beach breaks with numerous shifting banks and strong rips. Offshore in NE to N winds and holding to around 2 metres on SW to S swells. It's a steep scramble down to the beach after a rugged, narrow track in — more suitable for four-wheel drives.

Further to the east is **Cable Beach,** and **Salmon Holes**, a small bay on the southern side of the Flinders Peninsula. It can get OK small waves off a small reef in the corner of the beach, but it's really only suitable for the extremely keen (or desperate). Works in NW to N winds and small SE swells.

The Whaleworld Museum at Frenchmans Bay is worth a look. The museum is set up in the old whaling station, Australia's last (closed in 1978 after prolonged vigorous protests from Greenpeace, among others). It offers an interesting, although particularly gruesome, insight into the whaling industry, seeing the methods of the old whalers in their open boats and with hand-held harpoons.

There are a few small beaches in the Albany area offering limited surfing conditions (due to the protection from big seas by Flinders Peninsula and the islands in King George Sound). The most popular of these is **Middleton Beach**, which needs a large SE swell and NW winds to have any sort of wave to surf. Very popular with Albany learners. Middleton can get good beach breaks, both left and rights to around 1.5 metres, but only rarely.

Further to the east of Albany is **Nanarup Beach**, reached by first taking Lower King Road then Nanarup Road. Nanarup is open to south swells and is offshore in northerly winds.

From here you must go back to the South Coast Highway to gain access to any of the other spots between Albany and Esperance. The first of these worth checking is **Cheyne Beach** (turn off the highway to Cheyne Beach Road). It needs a SE to S swell but does get excellent right-hand barrels, offshore in W winds. Some good beach breaks can

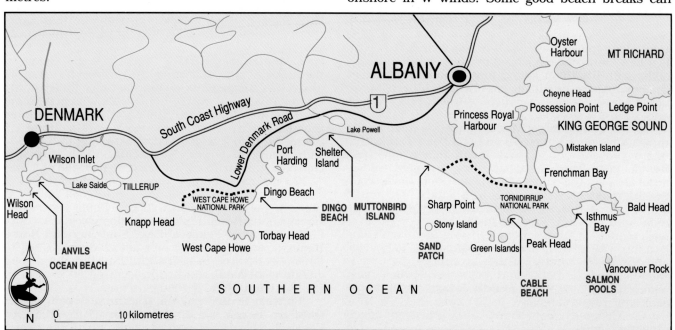

sometimes be found along **Hassell Beach**, but access is just that: a hassle! Back to Highway One and on towards Bremer Bay. Fishing is better than surfing in Bremer Bay owing to its protected position; sometimes good beach breaks are found at **Dillon Bay** , but it needs a large SE swell and N to NW winds.

Good waves can be had at **Gordon Inlet**, at the mouth of the Gairdner River on the right conditions (S swell, W wind) and, for the extremely lucky, **Point Ann** and **Point Charles** can get excellent waves. Point Ann is the more accessible of the two (turn off South Coast Highway to Devils Creek Road, and follow this to Point Ann Road) for quality right barrels off the point in large S swells with W to NW winds.

The next area of surf along this stretch of coast is near **Hopetoun**, 50 kilometres south of Ravensthorpe, where there are a number of good surfing locations with possibly the best one straight out in front of the Port Hotel and the Breakwater. A long paddle out through a deep shark pit usually keeps the crowd at **Crazies** to a minimum. The wave breaks over a shallow rocky bottom and gets excellent left-handers to 2.5 metres plus; best on a medium to heavy S swell and N to NW winds.

From Hopetoun (if your legs and arms are still intact) head along the Southern Ocean West Road to **Culham Inlet**. You'll find some nice sandbars along here which work on smaller S swells and N winds.

The next beach to the west of here is **Mylies Beach**, with some potential for good beach breaks especially in the south-west corner towards **Caves Point**; best in S swell and N winds. Next along, but requiring a four-wheel drive as the track deteriorates dramatically (with diff-chewing rocky sections and boggy sandy bits lying in wait to snare any normal car at the slightest provocation), is **West Beach**, which gets small beach breaks over a sand-covered reef bottom and works best on S swells and N winds.

From Hopetoun head along the Southern Ocean East Road to **Two Mile Beach**, and past Jerdacuttup Lakes to **Twelve Mile Beach**. Both can get average beach breaks on smaller S swells and N winds. From here you can either go back to Hopetoun, and the Highway, or to Powell Point and **Munglinup Beach**. The roads and tracks are all clearly signposted and work is currently being done to upgrade them. A few sections can still prove pretty tricky, but by sticking to the better ones (Springdale Road and Torradup Road) you will eventually get back to the Raventhorpe — Esperance Road (Highway One).

Although spectacular, these islands block a lot of swell to the beaches on the eastern side of **Esperance**, which are devoid of action in all but the biggest swells and even then they are practically guaranteed to be tiny. However, back around to the west you will find some good quality beach breaks, working on S to SW swells to 2 metres and N winds. These are (in order as you head west) **West Beach, Salmon Bay, Fourth Beach, Nine Mile Beach, Twilight Beach** and finally **Free Beach**, all of which feature a variety of lefts and rights on shifting banks, some sand over reef, with plenty of rip action as well.

Free Beach is definitely worth a look, especially on sunny days (being a nudist beach could have something to do with the numbers of surfers who regularly check the waves here). Heading back to the east is an island-strewn coastline with numerous bays and points, most of them being located in either Cape Le Grand National Park or Cape Arid National

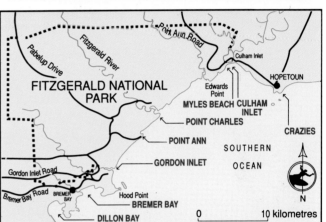

Top *The coastline near Hopetoun.* **Above** *Fitzgerald River*

Park. (You could probably find waves out off the islands, but a good boat would be necessary.) There is an all-weather road you can take to Israelite Bay with its small isolated settlement with the ruins of the old post office and homesteads. (A store provides limited supplies.)

There are, at times, good waves between **Point Dempster** and **Point Lorenzen** in SE to S swell and W to NW winds. From here you can either take the road back to Esperance (200 kilometres) or — if you're feeling adventurous and have a reliable four-wheel drive that you don't mind punishing — a track will take you all the way to Balladonia on the Eyre Highway (take plenty of petrol, and travel in the daytime only). Heading east towards the border there isn't much surf, and what there is , is inaccessible.

You might even see some waves near the **Eyre Sandpatch** or **Twilight Cove**, near the ruins of the Old Eyre telegraph station, but you will need to take your own parachute to get to them.

211

*Wally Jackson pulls neatly under a typical
Lighthouse Beach morning lip*

CHAPTER 6

TASMANIA

Tasmania includes some of Australia's last great wilderness areas, with vast sections of inaccessible coastline — particularly on the west coast — which receive the full brunt of southern swells and the Roaring Forties. The east coast has better access, climate and often, like the rest of the eastern mainland coastline, excellent waves. Most main-landers have no idea just how much good surf there is along the Tasmanian coastline, which is just the way the locals like it. The water temperature — particularly in winter — usually guaran-tees small crowds, though white pointers are a constant possibility.

Australia's smallest state and largest offshore island, Tasmania is actually more than 100 islands, scattered around the central island. To the north, the Furneaux Group are reminders of a time up until some 12 000 years ago when Tasmania was connected to the main-land by a land bridge. The rising waters that came with the end of the last Ice Age cut this bridge and isolated the local Aborigines, who, nonetheless, managed to survive their long isolation — until the arrival of Europeans in the nineteenth century.

THE NORTH COAST

Tasmania's north coast, stretching from the north-west tip east to Cape Portland, has limited surfing opportunities due to its protection from most swell action. However, in the right conditions there are several points and beaches along this coastline that get waves.

Just west of Devonport, there are several bays and beaches that catch swell when strong NW to NE winds push swells out of Bass Strait. The **Devonport rivermouth** is, on its day, a classic left with long walls and hollow sections, but the break is fickle and inconsistent with long flat spells between sessions. This break works on all tides and is best in N to NW winds. If you arrive in Tasmania on board the *Abel Tasman* you pass right by this break on the way up the Mersey River to Devonport. If you're lucky, it might even be working.

The best days along this coast usually occur in spring and early summer and it's easy to be a day late only to be told: 'You should have seen it yesterday!' The coastline here has beaches and rocky outcrops which look like perfect set-ups, but catching them with a decent swell is the hard part.

In the Launceston area, the most popular spot is a left-hand point break called **Tamashanta**, which, when it's working, draws locals from everywhere, resulting in instant crowds. 'Tama' is about an hour's drive from Launceston, with a kind of holiday town on its shores. In strong N to NW winds, the swell stands up and runs down the rocky point – best at high tides and swells from 1.5 metres to 2.5 metres.

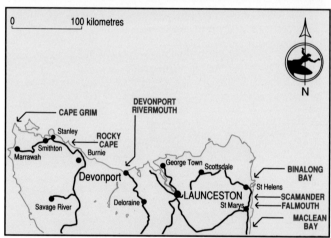

Top *Access to many of Tasmania's spots is via farming properties, so maintaining friendly relationships is important.*
Below *The lonely tip of north-west Tasmania*

THE EAST COAST

Called 'The Sunshine Coast' by local tourist promoters, Tassie's east coast has a more friendly climate (less rain and more sunshine) than the rest of the island and has many beautiful beaches. There are several points along this coastline which catch the E to SE swells and offer excellent surf.

To the north, St Helens is the jumping-off point to several breaks. Sitting at the head of Georges Bay, St Helens is a centre of tourist activity and offers a variety of accommodation. Several beaches and headlands around **Grants Lagoon**, **Binalong Bay** and **Perrins Beach** have beach and reef breaks which can offer excellent waves and no crowds. These breaks work in NE to SE swells and are best in NW to SW winds. Further north, waves are found in the Bay of Fires Coastal Reserve, but access is difficult.

South of St Helens, across the Georges Bay bridge and east through Stieglitz, are **Beerbarrel Beach** and **Maurouard Beach**, which catch plenty of

Top *St Helens fishing port*
Above *One of the east coast's many surfing treasures*

Wilderness waves in the south-west

Tasmania's rugged south-west coast is fringed by some of Australia's last true wilderness areas. Few roads cross the mountains from the east and access to these remote beaches is limited to light planes. For those lucky enough to get the chance to surf this coast, there are some of the emptiest waves to be found anywhere in Australia.

swell from the E to S and are protected from N to W winds. Further south is **Scamander**, situated on the north side of the Scamander River and **Falmouth**, both of which offer access to a variety of beach and reef breaks.

After an inland deviation to St Marys, the Tasman Highway takes us back to the coast and south towards Bicheno. Along this road many beaches are visible and if the conditions are right you can take your pick. Unfortunately, more often than not, these beaches — like most of the east coast — are dead flat. But the white sands, excellent fishing and seclusion almost make up for it. Just north of Bicheno a series of beaches and bays, a part of **Maclean Bay**, offer excellent waves at times, the best of which are usually **Red Bill Beach**, **Denison Reef**, **Golfcourse** and **Seymours**.

Bicheno is something of a crayfish haven and amateurs enjoy the easy access to these marine delights. South of Bicheno, a series of rocky promontories — accessible around **Red Bill Point** on foot at low tide — offer reef breaks in E to SE swells and are best in NW to SW winds.

South of Bicheno the highway heads inland towards Swansea, in Oyster Bay. Along the way the turn-off at Cranbrook takes you east to Coles Bay and the Freycinet Peninsula, now a national park.

Bull kelp, found around the Tasmanian coast.

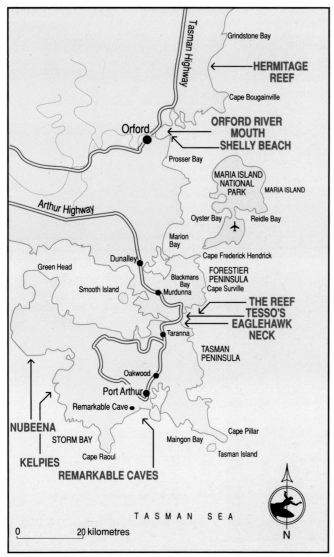

Road access to the peninsula is limited to the Coles Bay area and a boat is needed to reach the bays and reefs further east on the peninsula.

Excellent waves are occasionally found around Swansea, inside Oyster Bay, with a series of right-hand point breaks including **Swansea Point**, **Rubbish Tips** and **Buxton Point**. All these breaks need big E to SE swells and are best in W winds. South of Swansea the highway follows the coast to Little Swanport, with a long paddle out to an excellent left on the **Swanport sandbar** and a right off the point, which are best at mid tides. Many breaks can be found along the tracks which lead to the coast, including **Hermitage Reef** (take the marked turn-off just before you get to Triabunna and follow it 15 kilometres to the beach) and **Lisdillon**. These breaks tend to be best in big E swells and W winds.

South of Triabunna, **Orford rivermouth** offers long lefts in the right conditions (big E to NE swells

Another Tasman Peninsula wave goes unsurfed

Dave's Place, named after a local surfer who lost his life surfing here

A part of Pirates Bay, Eaglehawk Neck is formed by the junction of the Tasman and Forestier Peninsulas. During the time of convict occupation at Port Arthur this area had a fearful reputation for sharks, stories openly promoted by authorities to discourage attempts at escape from Port Arthur. The beaches here consistently offer a selection of peaky beach breaks.

and NW to SW winds). Although it's far from consistent, this break can be one of the best waves in the state. **Shelley Point** is south of town and has a right-hander off the point in moderate to heavy NE swells.

South of Orford the highway veers inland again (towards Hobart). At Sorell, the Arthur Highway heads south-east along the Tasman Peninsula (through Dunalley) towards the historic town of Port Arthur. The road passes right by Pirates Bay and **Eaglehawk Neck**, where there is often an excellent peaky beach break, which works in NE to SE swells to 3 metres. Eaglehawk Neck is an attractive beach with good fishing and craybakes at the local hotel.

Tessellated Pavements, or **Tessos,** is a suckey and demanding right-hander, which breaks over a kelp-covered rock shelf. It works in a heavy SE swell and almost any wind and is best at high tide.

Eaglehawk Reef, better known as **The Reef,** lies at the end of a short walk out from Tessos to the mouth of the bay, which brings you to a powerful, hollow left-hander which has a demanding take-off and peels fast across an extremely shallow bottom.

Works in NE swells from 1.5 metres to 2.5 metres and is best in light W winds and at high tides.

Further south, on the west side of the peninsula, good waves are often found at **Nubeena** in small to moderate S swells and NE winds. The best breaks are usually found at middle to southern end of the beach, under the cliffs. At the south end of the beach there is often a rebound peak with fast hollow rights. South of Nubeena and accessible through private farmland is a break known as **Kelpies**, a left-hand point break which features long walls and good hollow sections. Works in moderate to heavy SE swells and is best in SE winds.

South of the historic town of Port Arthur (site of the famous gaol) is a sealed road which leads to **Remarkable Caves**, one of the area's tourist attractions. Depending on tide and sandbanks, it's a walk or paddle through the caves to hollow, peaky waves, mostly right-handers; best on low to medium tides in a medium S to SW swell and NE to NW winds.

Classic conditions, Tasman Peninsula

SEAN DAVEY

SEAN DAVEY

SEAN DAVEY

Above *Mathew Fisher at Roaring Beach, Nubeena.*
Below *Artis Innes under the ledge of The Reef at Eaglehawk*

Below *Tessos, so named because of the reef directly off the Tessellated Pavement.*

SEAN DAVEY

SEAN DAVEY

No rush to beat the crowd here

SEAN DAVEY

BRUNY ISLAND

Bruny Island has become a popular haunt for Hobart surfers in search of bigger waves, though the ferry price has recently gone up to $15. In the south of the island just west of Mount Bruny is **Cloudy Bay**, also known as Middle Bay, where there are often quality lefts and rights over a sand bottom; best in SE to SW swells to 2 metres and N to NW winds. When the sandbanks are in good condition, Cloudy Bay is one of the best waves in Tasmania, with long rights and shorter lefts into the rip. At the western end of Cloudy Bay is a rivermouth break known as **Lagoons**, which turns on excellent lefts and rights when the sandbanks are good. This is a fickle wave and is best in heavy SW or moderate SE swells, W to NW winds and higher tides. The right tends to be the best wave at Lagoons, but breaks a long way off the beach requiring a long paddle.

At the southern end of Adventure Bay is a left-hand point break known as **Coal Point**, which breaks over rock and kelp. Coal Point can be a very challenging break, with a hair-raising take-off as the wave peaks over a rock shelf and peels fast, before flattening out into a workable wall. Works in heavy SE to NE swells and almost any wind, as the kelp keeps the surface reasonably smooth.

Other spots on Bruny Island, which can produce waves in the right conditions (but tend to be less consistent) include **The Neck** and **Lighthouse**, both of which produce peaky left and right beach breaks in E to SE swells and W to SW winds.

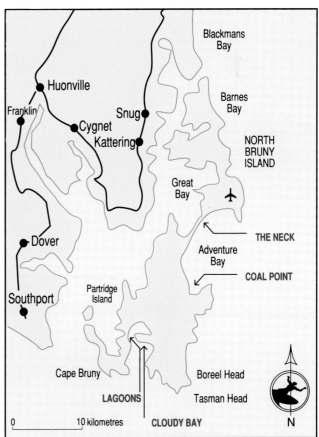

AROUND HOBART

Hobart's waves stretch along the southern face of the peninsula known as **South Arm**, from Clifton Beach in the east to Roaring Beach at the western tip of South Arm peninsula. Swells from SW to SE penetrate Storm Bay (between Bruny Island and the Tasman Peninsula) and make these breaks some of the best in Tasmania.

Clifton Beach, around 30 minutes by car south of Hobart, is the most popular South Arm beach and can turn on excellent waves (to about 2 metres) on medium to heavy SE to SW swells. At the south end of the beach there are consistent sandbanks which can be excellent in NW to SW winds. This is the site

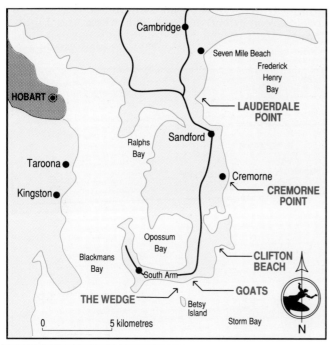

Clifton Beach on a small but remarkably clean day, considering the wind outside. Close to Hobart, Clifton Beach gets crowded at times, but on other days it's simply pick a peak.

222

One of Sean Davey's favourite Tasmanian haunts

of a proposed artificial reef, which the locals are hoping will bring even more consistent waves. **South Clifton** has a surf club, parking, toilet facilities and easy access to the beach. The beach breaks at Middle and **North Clifton** work on small to medium S to SE swells and are best in NE to W winds.

On the eastern side of the peninsula are several points which can turn on excellent right-hand point breaks in big S to SW swells; the best are found at **Cremorne**, **Mays** and **Lauderdale Points** and the western end of **Seven Mile Beach**. All these breaks are within 20-minutes drive from Hobart and work on huge S to SW swells, featuring rock and sand bottoms; best in W to SW winds and low or outgoing tides.

South-west of Clifton Beach, good waves are found at **Goats Beach**, a large beach with deep sand dunes which can have good peaky waves over a sand bottom; best in NE to NW winds. At South Goats there is often a peaky wave which rebounds off the cliffs in medium to heavy SW swells; best in W to NW winds at low tide.

East of North Goats over the bluff is a small beach break known as **Lumpeys**, reached by a 25-minute walk through private farming land. It works on smaller SE to SW swells and is best in NW to SW winds. South-west of Goats Beach is a popular spot known as **The Wedge**. Betsy Island, about 1 kilometre offshore, splits the swell into peaky left and rights in heavy SW to SE swells — best in N winds. Despite the access through private property, this beach is popular with Hobart surfers and can get very crowded. A further kilometre down the road is a break known as **Sandpits**, or **RSL** (so named because you turn off at the South Arm RSL), which offers beach breaks in medium to small swells and is best in NW winds.

East of Hobart, reached through Sorell, Lewisham and Dodges Ferry, is **Carlton**, where flat beaches and gentle waves offer excellent conditions for beginners. On some occasions the waves here can get really good, particularly at **Carlton River** where long-walled lefts are found in heavy SW to S swells and E to NE winds. This is also a popular location with wave sailors.

Top left *Wintery line-up at Mays Point.* **Right** *This is a crowded day, three people out at Mays Point.* **Top right** *Shane Able can't help but smile in this little beauty at The Wedge, one of Hobart's most consistent breaks.* **Below** *A pleasant surprise for these two surfers at Goats Beach*

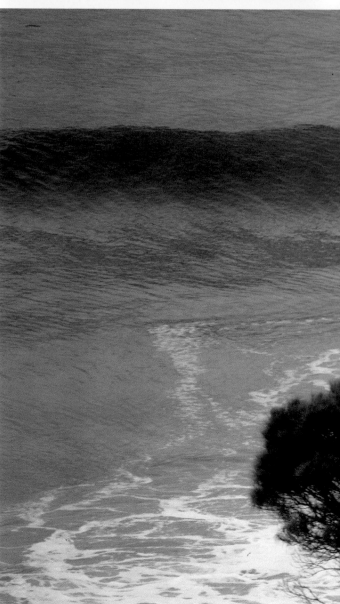

THE WEST COAST

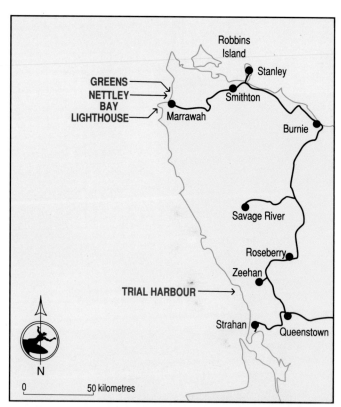

Most of Tasmania's west coast is wild and inaccessible, copping the full power of the roaring forties and the big SW swells, particularly in winter. Access is hindered by rugged mountains, fast-flowing rivers and dense rainforest.

West of the Zeehan Highway, Strahan is one of the few coastal areas you can reach. Further north (accessed through Zeehan) is **Trial Harbour**, a big, powerful and dangerous left (like most of the west coast) with difficult dirt track access and awesome ferocity. Trial Harbour is the premier big wave spot on the island and is only for those who like balls-to-the-wall experiences. Works in SW to W swells to 3 metres (best at 2 metres) and is best in E winds.

More popular and accessible are the breaks found around **Marrawah**, further north and reached

Maurice Cole experiencing some Tasmanian power, at Trial Harbour on the South Arm Peninsula

SEAN DAVEY

through Smithton. North and south from Marrawah are a series of beaches offering gnarly waves which can be excellent in SW to NW swells and SE to NE winds.

The nearest break to Marrawah is **Greens Beach**, where a kelp-covered reef off the car park produces long lefts and shorter rights. Greens tends to be more sheltered than most of this coast and, to the north, the beach stretches away for many kilometres. When the banks are right, all you have to do is walk down the beach and pick the break you fancy.

South of Greens Beach is **Nettley Bay**. At the southern end of the beach, lefts and rights with real power are found off the rocky headland. Off the rocks at the northern end of the beach is a right-hander which turns on big, fast barrels and has been been nicknamed 'Little Kirra'. Nettley Bay is on private property so courtesy is essential — make sure you shut the gates behind you.

Above *Dave Cover at Lighthouse Beach.*
Below left *Tasmania's west coast is exposed to the full might of the Roaring Forties.* **Below right** *Between sets, surfers get a rare view of the west coast's rugged beauty*

South of Marrawah a clearly marked turn-off will lead you to **Lighthouse**, at West Point. The bay inside the point is dotted with rocks which help sandbanks to form. A rip runs out next to the rocks and a good hollow left breaks into the channel. On the other side of the bank there is a fast right-hander. When the swell is big there is also a good left (over sand and rock) on the southern side of the point.

Further south are other, lesser known but equally good breaks — but you'll have to take the drive and try your luck. Several dirt tracks lead to beaches where you may find excellent waves, but this is rugged and wild country so carry your own camping gear. Marrawah has a pub but no caravan parks.

Glossary

PETER WILSON

backdoor An expression used to describe situations where a surfer is forced to pull into an already pitching barrel from behind the peak.

barrel The term used to describe the breaking motion of a perfect wave. Same as pipe (1960s) and tube (1970s).

bommie Abbreviation of bombora, a 'cloud break' or isolated, submerged offshore reef, where big waves break on large swells.

boogieboard Soft, flexible bellyboard, which can be used in flagged areas.

caught inside When a wave breaks outside a surfer paddling out; one of the worst situations to confront a surfer.

choppy A term used to describe a certain condition of water surface; usually in strong onshore winds.

closeout Not nice. Caused by formless bottom profile, which creates a wave breaking simultaneously across an unmakeable width.

Coolite Styrofoam trainee surfboard.

dredging As strong waves break in shallow water they draw water from ahead of them, sucking already shallow water up into the face of the wave. A dredging wave is the big brother of a 'suckey' wave.

MARTIN TULLEMANS

drop-in Surfing's most offensive behaviour, to paddle and then drop in on a wave someone else is already up and riding, on the inside.

eggroll Same as egg (1960s), kook (1970s) and rubberneck (1980s). There's a heavy pecking order in surfing: an eggroll is anyone who isn't as good as you.

fat-out A term used to describe a wave which has become less hollow and fuller, due to a deepening bottom.

filthy Same as hot, great, unreal, off its tits.

floater Has nothing to do with beer or pies. A floater is a new move, initiated by Cheyne Horan, where the surfer rides over the falling curtain of a breaking wave.

glassy When there is no wind, usually early in the morning when the ocean surface is silky smooth.

gnarly A dramatic term used to describe a wave with a real mean streak.

going-off Ripping! Unreal! Happening. When someone is ripping in perfect surf.

goofy-foot One of the oldest terms still current in surfing jargon, and one never revised; someone who stands on the surfboard with their right foot forward. Has nothing to do with being left- or right-handed.

grommet Same as gremmie (1960s). Young surfer-type person, intent on maximising beach and in-the-tube experiences. Trainee surf mongrel on the way to full 'surf nazi' status.

gun-style Boards designed for big to humungous surf. Generally longer, narrower and thinner.

hairy take-off Has nothing to do with Greek holidays, but when the wave jacks up and starts pitching faster than you can paddle in and get to your feet — and all you can see is red lights flashing — that's a hairy take-off.

hold-down Can refer to an amorous lover, but more often relates to the way certain waves hold you down when you're caught in the white water, either after a wipeout or being caught inside.

hoon Someone who tends to compensate for a lack of surfing ability with eye-catching performances in the car park.

human-lure The feeling a surfer experiences in sharky waters; not nice.

humungous When the surf is bigger than big, it's huge. When it's bigger than huge, it's humungous. Brown boardshorts material.

inside Refers to area inside breaking waves, as in being caught inside by a big set. Can also refer to the barrel, as in 'inside the barrel'.

jacking The process by which a wave gathers water and elevates as it moves suddenly from deep into shallow water.

ledges When an incoming swell meets underwater ledges of rock, usually reefs, the wave jacks up quickly and pitches forward in a powerful, thick lip.

left-hander A wave which breaks from right to left, looking at the beach.

lip The leading edge of a clean breaking wave.

local Anyone who's been there a day longer than you.

malibu Also called 'mals' and longboards; these boards are over 2.4 metres (8 feet) and similar to boards of the 1960s. Specially suited to older, physically impaired people or young mental retards.

max-out Has nothing to do with Headroom; over the limit, over the top, exaggerated expression as in 'the huge swell maxed out...' Also used to define upper limit of a particular wave, as in 'this wave maxes out at 2 metres'.

mushburger A shapeless wave, sometimes caused by unfavourable winds, though some spots just don't have a good bottom contour and the waves are always mushburgers.

natural foot A surfer who stands with left foot forward.

noah Rhyming slang, as in noah's ark = shark, the animal all surfers dread. Varieties include bronzies (bronze whalers), formula ones (hammerheads), terries (tiger sharks) and the surfer's favourite, the white pointer.

nor'-easter The prevailing summer winds along Australia's east coast.

off the richter Same as off its tits, off its face, awesome, outrageous, to the max. One of the most recent additions to surfing jargon — a term used by surfers to describe something very good. As in 'totally off the richter'.

offshore When the wind blows from the land out to sea; the best wind for quality waves.

onshore When the wind is from behind the waves.

outside When you're out in the water and someone yells 'Outside!', it usually means there's a big set approaching the break.

peak That part of the wave over the shallowest section of an undulating bottom.

pitching A term used to describe the way the top part of a wave elevates (jacks up) and throws forward, caused by the wave suddenly moving from deep into shallow water.

rail The edge of a surfboard.

re-form Often waves break on an outer sandbank or reef, before moving across deep water and then re-forming, usually as a shorebreak.

right-hander A wave which breaks from left to right.

PETER WILSON

slash A radical, carving cut-back, performed on the steep face of the wave.

sloppy With an onshore wind, waves collapse, shape is formless, and it's sloppy.

spaghetti arms A condition achieved by surfing for hours on end. In Australia when the classic point breaks are happening, you finish riding incredibly long waves and because there are so many good waves you can't stop and see them go to waste. So you surf for hours and all that paddling makes your arms and legs tired and heavy.

square An expression used to describe an extremely hollow wave, on which the bottom drops quickly as the top pitches, stretching the wave face vertically, creating 'corners' on the wave profile. Dangerous.

stand up The motion of a swell as it comes out of deep water and rises to break.

suckey Like dredging only slightly less awesome.

top-to-bottom Two possible meanings: 1. a very thick, hollow wave — a top-to-bottom barrel; 2. a state of optimum ski cover at Thredbo.

wedgy A term used to describe how a swell refracts or breaks up, then stands up over a shallow bottom in a compact, peaky fashion.

white The most feared species of shark, the great white is common in colder waters off southern Australia.

windwanker A term used by keen surfers to describe wave sailors whose egos are advanced beyond their skills.

wired To get a surf spot wired is to understand its individual nature, which swell, wind and tide conditions suit the break best.

woofy You can thank the antiquated Sydney sewage system for the introduction of this word to describe polluted water. Same as 'on the nose' or 'yuk' or 'surfing under-turd'.

Index